# Effective Educational Partnerships

# Effective Educational Partnerships

Experts, Advocates, and Scouts

Edited by Samuel Mitchell

PRAEGER

Westport, Connecticut
London

**Library of Congress Cataloging-in-Publication Data**

Effective educational partnerships : experts, advocates, and scouts / edited by
Samuel Mitchell.
    p.  cm
  Includes bibliographical references and index.
  ISBN 0-275-97048-5 (alk. paper)
    1. College-school cooperation. 2. Community and school.
  3. Interorganizational relations. I. Mitchell, Samuel, 1936–
  LB2331.53.E44 2002
  378.1'03—dc21        2001034629

British Library Cataloguing in Publication Data is available.

Library of Congress Catalog Card Number: 2001034629
ISBN: 0-275-97048-5

First published in 2002

Praeger Publishers, 88 Post Road West, Westport, CT 06881
An imprint of Greenwood Publishing Group, Inc.
www.praeger.com

Printed in the United States of America

The paper used in this book complies with the
Permanent Paper Standard issued by the National
Information Standards Organization (Z39.48-1984).

10 9 8 7 6 5 4 3 2 1

# Contents

# Prologue

Partnerships in this collection are initiatives by experts from higher education, efforts of activists in the community or attempts by scouts on the frontier to discover links for services to rural areas. Partnerships based on knowledge are a reason universities, higher education, and research institutes should be the primary link for schools. Business partnerships are more typical but they lose sight of educational objectives. Partnerships with business in the United States involve universities, but in Canada the social distance prevents universities from joining common efforts. University and school links are extended to include social services (Osguthorpe et al., 1995). Though higher education has many limits, partnerships draw on its resources and support for credibility (Mitchell, 1998).

Part I includes chapters on direct links between universities and schools, research laboratories that work with teacher and administrations in implementing changes, a network of supporting services for schools, and alternatives among individual resource personnel in assisting elementary teachers with science education. These partnerships link schools with people who have specialized knowledge. Chapter 3, involving a network for supporting services, foreshadows Parts II and III, because it deals with advocacy and exploration of new opportunities. Each chapter in Part I shows how different perspectives are an antidote to the limits of expertise.

Specific programs described in Part II are diverse and unrelated. Technology can be an investment; a school business becomes self-financing; university students provide a range of services; and musicians increase their role in schools with the help of a university department. Chapter 5 shows a technical project emerging from a university institute. The technological effort involves as much of a business perspective as does Chapter 6, which relates a school's creation of a way to recover and resell construction materials. Chapters 7 and 8 tell the stories of university students working with a host of community agencies and a university music department combining with an orchestra and schools.

Students and faculty from universities become advocates, but they use networking and other strategies similar to partnerships that are business-based. The aim of each project in Part II is to find partners or locations, where they can be cloned. The tendency to seek similar sites is influenced by catalysts who promote partnerships. Promoters develop strategies with precise rules, a sequence of steps, and a definite and accepted vision. These advocates justify their work through publicity, awards, grants, or new partners. These diverse projects need to be merged with missing activities into a reform movement.

New possibilities recognize ways to overcome long standing social differences. Boundary spanners or scouts seek these new approaches. Those seeking future prospects filter and represent the organizations to outsiders (Bradshaw, in press). Some scouts pursue their own individual interests in alliances, while others are forced to do so as a result of their social isolation (Mitchell, 2000b). New alliances are foreseen by those who see new ways to use existing resources, the classic role of entrepreneurs (Mitchell, 1990).

New opportunities for partnerships involve adventurers in rural areas whereas experts and advocates remain with similar partnerships in central areas. In rural places, people know each other, but their institutions are not coordinated. Some important representatives are outside the communities, those within them are divided from each other. Small towns and farms retain a concern for people, places, and religions. Outsiders can be ostracized or ignored if their ideas about partnerships do not fit, but others who make those within feel more important are accepted.

Racial differences within rural communities or across national boundaries are a challenge to partnerships. In Part III, the integration of social services is explored in small North Carolina towns; distance education is created for sparse settlements in New Foundland; efforts by individual teachers, social action committees, and coordination of three American states and two Canadian provinces results from catalysts from away; and community development and the integrated training of health professionals is evaluated in South Africa. Race, professional status, and gender are barriers that dreamers cannot overcome.

The contributors to this book are part of a safari to capture partnership realities. Experts capture specimens for a collection and analyze partnerships, but the advocates are after wilder game and are caught in the chase. The voice of advocates is blustery and repetitive—naming their organizations and praising them. The scouts are neither as passionate as advocates nor as focused as experts. The scouts explore new areas that scholarship cannot contain, and which advocates are yet to seize and promote. The scouts often travel in circles to explore new opportunities, where linear thinking is insufficient.

Combining these voices requires a different approach. My suggestions are to see the limits of experts and find common ground among the projects of advocates. The boundary spanner's exploration could be organized into a chart that others can follow. Since concern for partnerships is a fleeting affair for faculties of education, the final comments suggest new possibilities for these faculties to grow and multiply in the world of partnerships.

Many people helped to create this collection . The selection committee includes Bryan Hiebert and William Reeves from the University of Calgary and Bernard Baum from the University of Illinois. Charles Webber brought my proposal to many academics through his computer circle. Both William Reeves and Veronica Bohac-Clarke shared their reflections on these chapters. My graduate students listened to me during my struggles. My wife, Helen Mitchell, is the critical editor, who tries to teach current forms of writing. Praeger provided an advance contract to publish this work. The book is multifaceted because these diverse partners' advice is integrated.

# I

# Building on Expertise

We all know something. We are all ignorant of something. For this reason, we are always learning. . . . No one is ignorant of everything. No one knows everything (Friere and Macedo, 1987, p. 72).

The limitations of expertise are unrealized. Educators who are working within schools do not accept the contributions that parent volunteers make to education (Mitchell, 1998). Researchers are delighted when teachers imitate them, but they do not realize the limitations of a researcher's role. Researchers and other experts support innovations because of their interest whether or not teachers and the public support them. For experts, including teachers on stage, knowledge and skill are the criteria for selecting individuals for partnerships. Social skills and judgement are recognized only when they are invoked for support against those with more expertise.

In this collection, similar choices are made by experts in their innovations. Chapter 1 discusses a new link between universities and schools, the professional development school, which ignores the concerns of students, parents, and community members. The promoters act as if their three professional concerns are separable from their context: training future teachers, inservice for experienced staff, and research. Research involves a "natural" set of problems; natural for the immediate problems in schools. The issues affecting the distressed urban settings of the school are mentioned, but the author never pursues them.

Aside from partnership itself, the context for Chapter 2 is a series of school improvement efforts within schools. The complimentary nature of different perspectives is a reason for including teachers' ideas. The broader perspectives of others in the community are ignored. The importance of commitment and leadership is shown to be crucial for all innovations, but it is assumed that experiences within schools are sufficient to develop them. Leaders with varied and intense experience, such as in the arts, produce innovators (Mitchell, 2000).

A project studied in Chapter 3 is within a school based on technology and a new view of learning. Though this school division is named after the 16th-century scientist Galileo, it might be called the Reformation and Counter Reformation. It is not enough for teachers to think like a scientist or other experts in order to improve school performance. Researchers must help teachers develop judgment. Judgment depends on values and visions as much as theoretical knowledge and factual understanding.

In the Galileo case, attacks of the school project lead to a tactical retreat to a larger scale approach, a network of related school reforms. The opposition is confronted with an innovator on high ground. A further decision is to concentrate on working with teachers and schools who want the new vision of education. Successful projects are not enough to persuade the opposition.

Like other partnerships, the Galileo Network is fragile. Chapter 4 considers the general question of partnership endurance, but it is based on a study of individual resource professionals assisting elementary schools. This study asks: "What is the nature of partnerships?" Caught in a web of mathematical alternatives, the author of Chapter 4 ignores the context of the partnerships for science education. For example, the partners are sidetracked by protesting parents.

Partnerships may last only a few years. The lifespan of partnerships is two to three years. Individuals working in partnership discussed in Chapter 4 last two years. The case of a professional development school, Jackson, discontinues its relationship to its university after three years. In Chapter 2, schools attempting improvement through research found many schools do not start, and the average school in the research study lasts three years. As it approaches the cutting edge of its third year, the Galileo project moves away from one local scene to a larger political scene. The individual partnerships in Chapter 4 last an average of two years.

The context of schooling is important for the survival of any partnership. As the economist would say "all other things being equal" when they never are; the experts try each in their own way to abstract parts of a puzzle. The natural sciences, which pioneered this approach, find there are difficulties, when the context changes. Part II focuses on attempts to change. These changes reveal how complicated the original situation was. The partnership must develop supporting bonds to withstand future challenges.

# 1

# Paradoxes of Professional Development Schools

## Renee Campoy

In the spring of 1992 Jackson School became a partner with a university in a large midwestern metropolitan area. Jackson School–Midwest University Professional Development School (PDS) is initiated in order to provide an optimum learning environment for elementary students, a model site for the placement of education students and as a means to stimulate the development of new, quality programs and approaches to teaching and learning. Jackson Elementary, the school partner, is a small neighborhood elementary school in a low socioeconomic but stable residential area. Similar to other urban schools, its district faces declining school enrollments and an eroding tax base, and hosts many problems, including drugs.

The higher education partner for this school is Midwest University, a land grant institution and a major provider of teachers to the metropolitan community. The Midwest teacher education program graduates 300 to 350 new teachers each year and boasts a history of partnership work with various local school districts. The PDS is viewed by its planners as a means to solve many of the school's long-standing problems by providing an improved and enriching educational experience for elementary students, and, at the same time, it would improve the placements for its undergraduate program.

The university and school come to differ over this dual mandate. The central theme is how institutional differences between the university and the K–12 school produced cultural clashes with respect to rewards, educational missions, pedagogical views, and organizational evaluation of the changes. It does not meet the expectations of planners.

## PDS BACKGROUND

According to educational leaders, the Professional Development School is one of the most compelling and complex models of educational reform that has been attempted in this century (Book, 1996; Darling-Hammond, 1994; Goodlad, 1990; Nystrand, 1991; Wise & Leibbrand, 2000). The PDS reform model is compelling because PDS goals assert that educational change should take place simultaneously at the K–12 school and at the university in order for true educational reform to occur. The PDS addresses the preparation of new teachers, the professional development of experienced teachers, and improves the programs of K–12 schools at the same time and at the same place: the school site. By conducting reform at both levels of education, the PDS is to be more than the piecemeal reforms of the past.

The PDS proposes reform of both schools and teacher training programs by engaging specially selected public schools in a long-term partnership with a local college or university teacher training program. Such partnerships encourage the simultaneous reform of schools and teacher education programs with a synergy that helps institutions accomplish more than each alone could. The PDS offers a process whereby educational reform goals, agreed upon and implemented by both new and experienced teachers, are seamlessly supported at both levels. In a short time, the movement toward professional development schools changed the clinical education of some teachers and began to influence state policy. Many colleges and universities that conduct teacher training are embracing this partnership model.

Goodlad, in *Better Teachers for Our Nation's Schools* (1990), suggests that PDS and other school–university partnerships be the centerpiece of recommendations for improving teacher education. Darling-Hammond (1994) states, "A major aspect of the restructuring movement in education is the current effort to invent and establish professional development schools. . . ." (p. 1). Nystrand declares that PDSs "offer significant promise for restructuring university–school district relationships around a common agenda of modeling exemplary practice, preparing teachers, and conducting research" (1991, p. 24).

These three educational leaders advocate PDS as a way to connect the disparate parts of the educational process into a restructured and qualitatively different new whole. It is a holistic approach where the preparation of new teachers and the practices of experienced teachers are developed through congruent processes; unlike the schizophrenia of the current teacher education system where theory and practice of education are separate processes conducted at the university and the school site (Bullough, et al., 1997).

## MY PDS EXPERIENCES

Increasingly, qualitative methods are an area of research growing in importance as a means to document and understand complex educational events, such as partnership implementation. The experiences of the investigator are important in qualitative research as this individual becomes an integral part of the process by bringing "insights, ideas, and impressions that become part of the data of the study and inform the processes of data collection and analysis" (Whitt, 1991, p. 408). To that end, I include my experiences as a leader, participant, evaluator, and documenter of PDS partnerships.

My work in PDSs begins in 1992 with the implementation of the Jackson School–Midwest University PDS. My involvement in the partnership leads to a six year investigation and case study of that PDS. As part of my PDS duties, I am the primary evaluator and university liaison to the project. I collaborate in writing proposals to obtain funds for the partnership, organize meetings, conduct professional development, teach undergraduate courses, and created documents to legitimize the project. One of my roles does not include an official title, but it would be described by Lieberman (1992) as a "boundary spanner" and by Sirotnik (1988) as a "chief worrier." The duties of this role include worrying about daily activities, attempting to advance the development of the partnership, and endeavoring to smooth the functions and frictions between the partners.

I participate in the activities of the Professional Development School Collaborative (PDSC)—a PDS umbrella organization. The activities of the PDSC are initiated at the same time as the Jackson PDS. The PDSC is a regional, collaborative effort to promote and support the development of PDSs. Its members include public and private colleges and universities from the region that developed partnerships with elementary, middle, and high schools.

PDSC is funded by a private foundation, established by a prominent local city family with a highly successful international business. This foundation cannot be named because it became interested in promoting innovative educational reform efforts—particularly PDS. The foundation offices are in the city and foundation directors play an active role in the planning of PDSC activities. The foundation provides funds for both the individual activities of PDSs and for the collaborative operations of the PDSC.

The support functions of the PDSC are accomplished during monthly meetings at a central location during the academic year and at a two day retreat held each summer. At these meetings, PDS participants gather to plan partnership goals and determine ways to document and evaluate the progress of their partnerships. These meetings alleviate the isolation of individual PDSs by allowing members to share partnership problems and solutions.

My roles in the PDSC include program evaluator, liaison for my own PDS, and representative on the PDSC steering committee, the governing arm of the organization. Though not involved in the initial activities where the foundation provides funds, I write the annual reports for the foundation on behalf of Jackson PDS. Working with the PDSC allow me to observe and document the programs and activities of other PDSs, where I am able to note both common problems and the unique aspects of 20 different partnerships.

## DILEMMAS FOR A PDS

While the PDSs are often lauded as a significant reform initiative, other researchers criticize the PDS as being difficult and complex to implement (Howey, 1990; Scannell, 1996; Teitel, 1997, 1998). It may be the complexity of PDS implementation that leads to the high rates of reported partnership failures and to the documentation of modest educational outcomes. Teitel (1998) describes how during national conference sessions, a presenter may mention in passing a university drops a school and dissolves a partnership. Such partnership failures may occur for any number of reasons and most remain undocumented. The PDS literature reports only the most successful of partnerships, while findings from marginal and failed partnerships remain undocumented.

Researchers admit to conflict during the implementation of partnerships (Christenson et al., 1996; Huffman-Joley, 1996; Lieberman, 1992; Sanford & Mahar, 1996; Schverak, Coltharp, & Cooner, 1998; Teitel, 1996; Thiessen, 1996; Winitzky et al., 1992; Wiseman & Cooner, 1996). They offer lists of barriers that partnerships must overcome (Zimpher, 1994) and obstacles to partnership collaboration (Winitzky et al., 1992). Zimpher (1994) lists 13 critical issues documented after several years of PDS reform, including funding, governance, university policy, and collaboration. Zimpher admits surprise at this great number of documented partnership difficulties but for institutions that traditionally collaborate only superficially, it should not be so startling that the stress of tackling new organizational territory is overwhelming for PDS developers. PDS development creates the need to examine and fundamentally redefine the nature of collaboration between universities and K–12 schools.

In an effort to clarify PDS issues, I select three topics that present particular dilemmas to partnerships; they are unique to the PDS reform process. All educational reform initiatives experience problems with funding, governance, and collaboration. Issues specific to the PDS aspect of combining the functions of two institutions need particular attention, as those are most likely to threaten the PDS as a viable reform. These dilemmas include: (1) the need to develop new policy and reward systems to support university faculty and teacher participation in PDS partnerships; (2) the problem of differing pedagogical views between school teachers and university faculty that has frustrated program development; and (3) the issue of designing evaluation processes so the educational effectiveness of PDSs can be determined.

## UNIVERSITY POLICY AND REWARD SYSTEMS

The problem of supporting university faculty in PDS work proves to be one of the most difficult dilemmas facing the PDS reform initiative and the issue is one that echoes against future missions by schools of education. This is a problem that was unanticipated by the national group of universities supporting PDS, the Holmes Group. In their 1995 report *Tomorrow's Schools of Education*, PDS is identified as the cornerstone of teacher education reform but the report does not discuss the competing factions in higher education that makes this reform so difficult to accomplish.

PDS researchers report reward systems as presenting difficulties for partnerships (Button, Ponticell, & Johnson, 1996; Sandholtz & Merseth, 1992; Winitzky et al., 1992). Others report that junior faculty members who are drawn to PDS work fear risking their careers because clinical work is not valued when they seek promotion and tenure (Bullough et al., 1997; Clark, 1997). Typically, junior faculty are advised that the surest means to promotion and tenure is through steady publication, and yet the labor-intensive nature of PDS clinical work limits faculty time to devote for publications.

For the university faculty at the Jackson PDS, the prospect of rewards and promotion influences faculty decisions to work in the Jackson PDS, but it is not the only consideration. The Jackson PDS is initially a favored project of the Dean of the College of Education at Midwest University. In the beginning, university faculty feel compelled to comply with the Dean's ambition to implement a PDS site, as the university is a member of the Holmes Group. While in the beginning faculty are not knowledgeable about PDSs, they anticipate professional benefits.

One PDS faculty member, interviewed during early partnership development, lists five specific ways that working in a PDS would benefit her, including:

> It gives me experience in the school that I don't have access to in many other ways and this gives me credibility in the eyes of my university students; I enjoy working with teachers and sharing the ideas that I have about education; it makes me feel that I'm using what I know; and, it provides a research project for me to work on.

Another faculty member describes anticipating the opportunity that the PDS would provide as a setting for her transactional instructional style, which means teaching according to student needs. She explains how the content of her course and the curriculum of the school could be integrated to produce a setting for undergraduate students to begin the process of reflective inquiry. She notes that students would more readily value the use of children's literature in instruction when they develop and teach literature-based lessons with real students. She explains a dynamic instructional setting, like a school, is needed to allow students to integrate the observations of the classroom with the discussion, assignments, and objectives presented in her methods courses.

Jackson PDS faculty note that working collaboratively with teachers at the site where their students participate in field experiences is an attractive aspect of PDS. It is only later, when the PDS faculty discover how much time and effort is necessary to teach in the PDS compared to teaching campus courses, that faculty began to question this decision. Faculty soon realize that labor intensive PDS courses are given the same weight as campus courses and they begin to question whether the traditional university reward system would adequately compensate their PDS work.

PDS leaders, such as Zimpher (1994), argue that the reward policies of schools and universities are not accommodating PDS goals and these policies require modification in both organizations. The reward structures of the school and the university create partnership problems when university faculty and teachers are differentially compensated for their PDS work. Schools compensate teachers for work with K–12 students, not for work with university students, while university faculty are better compensated for research and publication, not clinical work. The PDS creates the need for a broader educational mission for both groups of educators—the teachers' role is expanded to include teacher education and the university faculty's expanded role into K–12 education. Policy changes are needed by both organizations to fill the gap created by the expanded roles PDS work creates for teachers and university faculty.

In the case of the Jackson PDS, many calculating senior university faculty members choose not to engage in PDS work. Others attempt a short stint in the PDS, but when they discover the time and work that is involved, they withdraw. As for other institutions, even when the University of Utah creates specially designated clinical positions for PDS work, the clinical faculty report a sense of abandonment by tenure-line faculty. The clinical positions ghettoize the clinical faculty within the department, where they are viewed as second-class citizens with low pay, heavy teaching loads, and lesser prestige (Bullough et al., 1997).

As for the Jackson PDS, no matter how much university administration encouraged faculty to engage in PDS work and expressed verbal support for these efforts, faculty could not be certain this work will be viewed by university tenure and promotion committees as anything more than service. Because a record of extensive work in service would not qualify a faculty member for promotion and tenure at a research university, most junior faculty spent only a year or two in the PDS, withdrawing to allow more time for writing and publishing. This left PDS with a revolving door of university faculty, that hinder the development of trust and confidence in the university's role in the partnership.

In the larger picture of the dilemma, the PDS initiative is caught between competing forces that have produced the professional schizophrenia of modern teacher education (Bullough, 1982). This schizophrenia is caused by forces in the university that value and reward the publication of research and theoretical work for a limited scholarly audience, and those forces that value clinical work aimed at solving educational problems for the host of teachers in schools. In the modern school of education, university faculty members typically align themselves into three major groupings: content-driven researchers, who associate their research with a discipline area such as psychology, philosophy, or history; field-focused researchers, who conduct research in the methods of teaching; and clinicians, who concentrate on teaching and supervision of students rather than conducting research (Bullough et al., 1997).

These groups form a hierarchy of prestige and reward in accordance with the traditional university value system, which rewards thought over practice. Schools of education struggle within the medieval university structure to find respect for their work equal to that of the traditional content discipline areas of science, languages, and mathematics. Moreover, clinical faculty who work with education students in public schools engage in few of the purely scholastic activities of their university.

The Holmes Group (1986, 1990, 1995), anticipating the need for a new breed of university faculty, advocates the creation of clinical faculty.

These so-called "boundary spanners" would be important for embodying both the school and university perspectives, and for conducting the primary work of PDSs (Lieberman, 1992). Their mission was different from that of other university faculty who are responsible for generating and disseminating new knowledge; this new faculty would work to improve schooling and the educational system.

What the Holmes Group fails to consider is how these boundary spanners would be recognized by research-driven faculty. Since the faculty who are focused on research have the status and power within the university, they can determine the evaluation of the new PDS faculty. Although there exists a national trend to recognize nontraditional research and clinical work as legitimate pursuits for teacher education faculty (Glassick, Huber, & Maeroff, 1997), it remains to be seen how such change will be judged by the larger university community.

The problem of supporting PDS university faculty runs deeper than changing university policies to accommodate PDS faculty. By exposing the schizophrenic nature of modern teacher education, the PDS begs answers to basic questions about how higher education institutions choose to define themselves. For if universities do determine to change policy to reward PDS faculty, the work of teacher educators would have to change. The existing division between the service mission of schools of education and the research mission of the larger university community would increase. Increasing this division would risk alienating and further decreasing the prestige of teacher education with respect to the university community. Many university teacher educators value their association with liberal arts tradition in teacher education and the university. They oppose new policy to support PDSs that threatened to undermine that association.

## DIFFERING PEDAGOGICAL VIEWS

The second dilemma facing PDSs results from the differing views of pedagogy held by schools and universities. The Holmes Group (1986, 1990, 1995) calls for significant change in the pedagogy of schools and universities, a shift from traditional, didactic, or transmission approaches that view learning as replication of the teacher's knowledge to constructivist or transactional approaches that see learning as the development of students' conceptual understanding. These approaches utilize very different instructional methods and offer different interpretations of the teacher's role in the classroom.

Traditionally, school and university education programs differ in their educational approaches. Because of their experience in research and theory development, many university faculty members working in PDSs ascribe to a transactional approach to instruction, while in public schools, the transmission approach dominates. According to the literature, conflict surrounding pedagogy plagues PDSs and this conflict frustrates the development of collaborative programs (Book, 1996; Christenson et al., 1996; Pasch & Pugach, 1990; Teitel, 1996; Winitzky et al., 1992).

In many schools, there is a small number of teachers who employ progressive or transactional practices, and university faculty depend on these few classes for their student placements. In the PDS, which is a total school reform approach, all the classrooms in the school are used for student placements. This compels university faculty to utilize the classrooms of teachers who model traditional classroom practices. Conflict around differing pedagogical approaches results when university students observe and work in teacher-directed classrooms. Teachers and university faculty plan innovative projects, but teaching still occurs in a set manner. University faculty want their students to observe teachers who subscribed to a transactional style of instruction, where students create or construct knowledge. A lack of agreement about the instructional methods practiced, observed, and emulated by university students during field experiences leads to a significant educational dilemma.

The Holmes Group and university teacher educators assume teachers would quickly adopt transactional instruction, but this was a naive expectation. Classroom methods are deeply rooted in teachers' structure of values and conceptualization of learning (Clark & Peterson, 1986; Zeichner & Gore, 1990), and researchers report that attempts to change these methods are unsuccessful (Kagan, 1992; Richardson, 1996; Richardson-Koebler, 1988). Competing factors in the culture of the school present considerable obstacles to teacher change.

In the Jackson PDS, one teacher educator expresses the following concerns about the differences between teachers and teacher educators:

> What I have learned is that elementary and university people see education from different perspectives and that's a misconception of outsiders who don't understand the workings of PDS. Elementary teachers are not as concerned with a full scope of a K–6 theoretical program as much as they are with immediate results. This is because they want to see an immediate pay off in terms of achievement. Short term, mechanical teaching gets you quick results. My courses push the idea of a developmental program that works over a period of time for conceptual understanding that will pay off in the long run, but it is difficult for teachers to take that risk since they are under a lot of pressure from administration to get quick achievement results.

This teacher educator recognizes that teachers are often under constraints from the school and community, apart from PDS goals, that make instructional change difficult. At the Jackson PDS, when the state mandates a new achievement test, teachers are pressured to increase standarized test scores. The previous year's achievement scores are under the state average, and since these scores are published in the local newspapers, administrators are frenetic to produce higher scores.

Not only are the Jackson school teachers reluctant to use the new instructional methods because of accountability constraints, they question the value of the methods advocated by university faculty and suggest these methods would not work with children who demonstrate low motivation, lagging achievement, and who came from poor home environments. In an effort to address this difficulty, school and university administrators at the Jackson PDS decides to solve the problem through professional development. They feel that since the teachers are not conversant with the methods the university faculty advocated, they could not be blamed if they did not practice these in their classrooms.

There was an underlying assumption that when the teachers are knowledgable about the new methods, they would readily change their instruction. The university faculty attempts to verify the benefits of their methods by providing professional development sessions, by demonstrating lessons in the classroom, and by team-teaching with the teachers. After several years of professional development, when Jackson teachers are questioned about the benefits of working in the PDS, they report that they were improving their instructional practices. When university faculty are asked about the PDS, they report that they view the traditional pedagogy of the teachers as a problem and they question the benefit of placing their students at the school.

One explanation for the discrepancy between the progress the teachers feel they are making in improving their classroom methods and the lack of progress the university faculty cite involves instructional perspective. The teachers may be improving their methods by adding new activities and improving existing skills, but they are making these improvements in a teacher-directed style of instruction. While the teachers report improvements, the university faculty are not impressed by their attempts. The university faculty want the teachers to abandon their transmission style of instruction in order to adopt their own transactional style of teaching—something the teachers are incapable or unwilling to accomplish.

Professional development research indicates teachers change their practices if they act as their own experts, network with other teachers, make a choice about participating and planning processes, and school boards provide adequate time and funds for professional development (Darling-Hammond & McLaughlin, 1995; Glickman, Hayes, & Hensley,

1992; Lieberman, 1995; Sparks, 1995). University faculty provide many of the elements from this list, yet Jackson School teachers resist changing their methods. The lack of professional progress creates a defensive atmosphere between the partners, which made collaboration difficult. It leaves the university faculty puzzled about how to proceed with professional development and uncertain about continuing the partnership with the school.

Other partnerships in the PDSC express similar conflicts to those of the Jackson School–Midwest University PDS. When teacher educators collaborate to share information about their partnership experiences, they report the same problem. A magnet school, designed from its inception with its university partners to support a specific pedagogical perspective, reports teachers utilize traditional methods. The teachers hired to work in the new school are interviewed to determine their match with a constructivist pedagogy, yet teacher educators complain that only a few teachers represent this perspective in the classroom. When asked, teacher educators explain that they are required to hire district teachers for the new school and the teachers who wanted positions in the new school misrepresent themselves during the interview process.

The PDS literature reports similar concerns regarding pedagogical conflict. At Ohio State University, one teacher educator, who taught in the elementary classroom of a PDS, expresses dismay at the simple, routine subjects taught and low academic expectations of the teachers (Christenson et al., 1996). Winitsky and colleagues (1992) describes confrontations over pedagogical differences when university students attempted transactional lessons in traditional classrooms. Teachers object to the nontraditional methods, interrupt lessons, and contradict the instruction of the preservice teachers. During these confrontations, university students conform to the classroom teacher's expectations, showing why teacher educators did not want their students placed with traditional teachers. Teacher educators' fears about the school's influence are realistic, according to Richardson-Koehler (1988). After a month in a placement, according to their research, 80 percent of the student teachers' practices are from their cooperating teacher, not their university methods course instructors.

Teacher educators agree that it is difficult to prepare prospective teachers with a theoretical understanding of teaching and that extensive field experiences are required to do so (Renzaglia et al., 1997). To provide a placement site where theory is demonstrated, supported, and encouraged by practicing teachers is a PDS goal, yet efforts to achieve this basic goal prove frustrating for teacher educators (Hill, 2000). The complexity of the situation is unanticipated by many; Winitzky and colleagues (1992) believe that veteran practitioners cannot model and coach novice teachers in instruction which they have not experienced and the university cannot impose a pedagogy on them; teachers must be persuaded to change, and the responsibility for change is theirs. The values of collaboration, programmatic democracy, community, require the Holmes Group to be open to teachers' views.

Winitzky et al. (1992) develop the reasons for this dilemma. Teachers and teacher educators know there are reasons for holding different views about teaching. Changing these views for an entire school faculty is not likely when pedagogical change occurs slowly in a personal and individualized manner. In the meantime, what options do teacher educators have for the placement of their students? Shall they send their students into classrooms where they will learn to replicate traditional practices, leading to another generation of the same educational system? How long should teacher educators wait for a school site to reflect PDS pedagogical goals?

In summary, the current state of PDS partnerships leaves both teachers and teacher educators stalled and frustrated by PDS goals that are worthy but in many cases unattainable. These goals are unattainable because the present research on teacher change processes is ambiguous about how to support teachers to make pedagogical transformations. Our best understanding is that staff development is successful when the new instructional practices match the teacher's existing belief system and underlying assumptions about teaching and learning. Traditional professional development methods are not effective, and research indicates professional development should be confrontational in approach in order to make lasting change in teachers' methods of instruction (Kagan, 1992; Renzaglia et al., 1997; Richardson, 1996; Richardson-Koehler, 1988).

## EVALUATION PROCESSES

PDS leaders admit to a lack of evaluation information regarding the educational effectiveness of PDSs (Abdal-Haqq, 1996; Clark, 1997; Scannell, 1996). To some extent, it is the PDS itself that creates evaluation difficulties, with its ambitious educational goals (Book, 1996). PDS goals are not only ambitious but interwoven, as PDSs endeavor to improve teacher education, the education of students in public schools, and the practices of experienced teachers, as well as conduct educational research at the school site (Book, 1996).

Most PDSs discover that this is an overwhelming agenda and focus on one or two PDS goals (Clark, 1997). The choice of most researchers is to base their studies on preservice and in-service teacher outcomes (Abdal-Haqq, 1996). Given the difficulty of PDS evaluation, PDS leaders are still adamant that, if the reform effort is to be sustained and supported by policymakers, legislators, and educators, convincing evidence of the PDS's effectiveness must be documented (Scannell, 1996).

Cohen and Kible (1993) explain that projects like PDSs are described by program evaluators as "misbehaved" because they are so difficult to evaluate. "Well-behaved" projects stick to their design, are carefully controlled to minimize outside influences, and are short-lived (Cohen & Kible, 1993). PDSs are design nightmares because participants may be uncertain about specific goals they wish to pursue when they first begin their partnership work.

The goals of PDS partnerships are complex and involve areas of education with which participants may be unfamiliar. Teachers may be unfamiliar with current teacher education practices and teacher educators may have outdated notions about the programs of K–12 schools. This is true of the participants of the Jackson PDS, where as familiarity about mutual programs grows and participants acquired a more complex understanding of what they needed to accomplish, partnership goals changed to reflect realities.

PDSs are "noisy" projects where it is difficult to isolate PDS effects in the jumble of other causes of change in the partner schools (Cohen & Kible, 1993). At the same time the Jackson school is a PDS, it becomes an Accelerated School and in accordance with the Accelerated School development process, participants design a strategic plan for identifying long- and short-term goals for school improvement. Along with that, the state initiates a new state-wide standardized achievement test. As a result, teachers are under considerable pressure to improve test scores. The school district aligns instruction to state curriculum objectives and undertakes other state reforms.

These multiple efforts make it difficult to filter out PDS curriculum efforts from those mandated by the district. The PDS is a long-term, not a short-term, project—anticipating years of collaboration and evaluation of efforts (Cohen & Kible, 1993). These factors make it difficult to resolve the question of an improved educational program because the participants are uncertain about the goals they want to achieve and they are unable to attribute program improvement to PDS efforts, when they occur.

Fullan and Stiegelbauer (1991) provide another explanation for the difficulty of conducting PDS evaluation. They explain the problems that PDSs attempt to resolve are complex, difficult, and in a category they describe as "unsolvable." These unsolvable problems are so complicated and the number of intervening variables so large that it is impossible for any one individual to comprehend the total picture.

If one individual can assess the full nature and solve the problem, the problem-solver finds difficulty in helping others to reach the same conclusions or to act on the knowledge that another person finds.

According to Fullan and Stiegelbauer (1991), it is difficult to understand the full nature of complex problems because differing perspectives on the same information leads to different assessments about how to reach solutions.

For PDS planners, this would mean an entirely different style of problem solving. Fullan and Stiegelbauer (1991) suggest processes should be designed to allow participants to use, express, and discover multiple solutions to their own problems. Then, as these solutions are attempted and evaluated, participants will learn to appreciate a slow, incremental approach to problem solving. PDS planners need to commit to long-term problem resolutions, rather than the quick-fix solutions more typical of school planning.

In another view, Scannell (1996) suggests that PDS planners collect both formative and summative evaluation data. The formative evaluation is designed to monitor the process of partnership development, where interviews, focus groups, participant observation, and other ethnographic techniques are utilized to determine the participants' perspectives on such issues as the degree of shared governance, the level of satisfaction with partnership activities, and self-perceptions of change. Data for summative evaluation should be collected in order to focus on educational outcomes such as student achievement scores, absenteeism rates, dropout rates, placement rates for teacher education graduates, and scores on certification exams.

Scannell (1996) advises PDS developers to conduct both types of evaluation because different data are needed to convince different constituents of the PDS's effectiveness. Legislators would expect school scores to improve after PDS while parents anticipate new opportunities for their children. Scannell argues the support of a variety of constituents is necessary to safeguard the opportunity for PDS to develop into a viable model of educational reform.

Alternatively, the reform ambiguity may be confronted by having the partnership participants conduct the evaluation (Sirotnik, 1988). This partnership inquiry should be ongoing—relating to what and how the partnership develops—and should be formative. He lists guidelines for the types of data to be collected, including letters of agreement and other formal documents: minutes of meetings; budgets; reports; monographs; articles; newsletters, and calendars of events; project-related events such as teacher workshops and task forces; and, finally, public forums. Sirotnik (1998) suggests that documentation should cumulate into yearly reports designed to develop the project by promoting reflection on current partnership progress from problem identification to goal setting.

The method suggested by Sirotnik resembles the evaluation methods used by Jackson PDS and other related schools, members of PDSC. The support efforts of PDSC are critical to the development of Jackson PDS, because the PDSC provides time for partnership organization and communication when, during the early years, the partners do not provide this time for themselves. The PDSC compels PDS members to meet on a regular basis as a requirement to receive grants from the private foundation that funded the collaborative's work.

During PDSC meetings, facilitators present processes for developing and evaluating partnership program goals. The PDSC retains consultants to assist partnerships in developing evaluation processes in order that program benefits be documented. The first evaluation methods attempted are much like the ones described by Sirotnik, where the process of partnership development is documented so that progress could be reflected and evaluated by participants. Later, the collaborative attempted more elaborate methods that included teams of PDSC evaluators visiting peer partnerships to determine the extent to which the partnership is able to reach its stated program goals.

PDSC participants report experiencing many problems with these evaluation methods, including the difficulty of overcoming fear and defensiveness when peer teams visit to collect data. Many PDSs are defensive about their modest partnership efforts and are reluctant to reveal their lack of progress. Finding time to collect evaluation data proves difficult when the time demands of PDS work in teaching students and future teachers are overwhelming. The teachers complain they had little time and energy for evaluation efforts.

PDS work expands the roles of both teachers and teacher educators, but their institutions did not reduce their previous workloads. The PDS partners are pressed to collect the evidence to prove that the experiment is beneficial. Many participants do not value or understand the need for a time-consuming evaluation process. The school culture promotes an "action" mentality and hard-working PDS teachers become resentful of the university's effort to document, reflect, and discuss the process of partnership development (Robinson & Darling-Hammond, 1994). Such acts of organizational introspection are unfamiliar and seem abstract, impractical, and a waste of the teachers' time—another example of the university's ivory-tower theorizing. Differences over the need for program evaluation expose additional incongruities in the perspectives of teachers and of the university faculty, revealing further evidence of organizational differences and presenting additional cultural obstacles to overcome.

So while educational leaders remain insistent that the survival of the PDS model depends on developing effective evaluation procedures, this is a difficult task to accomplish. PDSs are inherently difficult to evaluate due to the complexity of their mission. PDS developers seldom provide the necessary resources of time and technical assistance. The

Jackson PDS investigates a number of evaluation formats only through the assistance of the PDSC. Lastly, the cultural norms of schools inhibit change and evaluation.

In summary, the aim of evaluating PDSs is questionable. NCATE offers some assistance as quality standards are being developed and field tested to identify "the essential attributes of a PDS associated with fulfilling the PDS mission" (Levine, 1998, p. 9). The draft Standards comprise five critical attributes: Learning Community, Collaboration, Accountability and Quality Assurance, Organization, Roles and Structures, and Equity.

After the Standards have been field tested and finalized, they will be presented to the NCATE Standards Committee to consider how they might be used as a part of the NCATE accreditation process. The development of these Standards and the possibility that they will be used in NCATE accreditation, demonstrates the growing influence of the PDS and increases the urgency for developing evaluation processes that will demonstrate PDS effectiveness. One unidentified partnership utilizes the NCATE Standards for partnership evaluation and they recommend, similar to other PDS literature, that PDS developers seek partners with compatible practices and explore ways to reward educators engaged in partnership work (Shelley and Washburn, 2000).

The PDS is the latest attempt by teacher educators to solve some of the unsatisfactory aspects of its association with higher education, and to reconcile the theory and practice debate within institutions. Because this is a sensitive area in American education, the PDS becomes something of a lightning rod within the national debate. It should be recalled that PDS promises to reconcile the theory and practice question by producing a new synergy of higher education and K–12 schools, but the institutional structures for this synergy are not developed. The litany of unanswered questions threatens the PDS initiative.

Institutions are fiercely resistant to change, and universities are particularly unyielding. Without institutionalized change to accommodate the PDS, it risks being drowned in a churn of ignorance about the real decisions that teacher educators need to make concerning the value and identity of their work. To this end, teacher educators will have to formulate a new synergy for their work by reconceptualizing educational institutions, and determine how they will redefine their mission in terms of theory and practice combinations. Only then will PDS be able to make its promised contribution to the educational reform effort.

## EDITOR'S NOTE

The conflicts over evaluation processes should be related to survival of Jackson PDS. The parties disagree so fundamentally that continuation is questionable. Professional arguments over documentation and reflection on PDS occur because change is emanating from teacher educators, which causes teacher resentment. The university should change as much as the schools, if PDS or many other educational reforms are to be successful. The university includes far more than teacher education. Teaching has to be more valued than scholarship at the university if reforms of schools are to be achieved. The system interlinks.

In the Jackson case, change appears to be based on good will and mutual understanding. There was never a written agreement or contract in this school or the related umbrella group. The lack of formal planning means neither mutual problems nor benefits for students are central to this partnership. Having teachers alone reflect on their teaching will never lead to a mutual goal. Teachers can criticize university faculty teaching in the university as a means of mutual improvement. Teachers are dealing with evaluation of student learning, which is every bit as complex as documenting the effectiveness of PDS. Changes in student evaluation to portfolio and other approaches may make teachers interested in transactional learning, particularly when such evaluations are practiced in the workplace and the university.

Teachers and university faculty need to confront the problems change efforts involve. Neither reflects on their own beliefs nor the necessity to alter their individual behaviors. Rather than a concern for educating future teachers and students in schools, institutional inertia seems to guide the conflict between professional warriors. Those in the sparing institutions are thinking of themselves as independent of students, parents, and community. The social problems of schools in St. Louis is mentioned but the concerns are ignored by the author. PDSs try to be very separate as they attempt to bring universities and schools together. A broader view, which involves multiple parties, is developed in Chapters 2 and 3.

Perhaps the Jackson PDS survives accidentally like many other partnerships—for about five years (R. Campoy, personal communication, September 2000). Evidence for this more typical pattern is shown in Chapters 2 and 4. Jackson still considers itself a PDS, but it is a partnership without a partner, since the university is not involved. The PDSC umbrella group, including the foundation, continues to meet.

Nationally, it is difficult to determine how effective PDS partnerships are. In 1997, there were 84 PDS partnerships, involving 96 colleges and 344 schools (American Association of Colleges for Teacher Education, 1997). There are several trials of this innovation in other countries, including Canada (Alberta Teachers' Association, 1999). Like many leagues for school reform, it is questionable what membership or the claim to be a PDS school means.

Difficult as it may be, it is important for the PDS to establish greater legitimacy. Chapter 12 (in this volume) shows doctors involved in community health can only provide global support for their efforts, rather than isolating separate effects. The total PDS approach should involve both school teachers and university faculty and include rewards for both their efforts. "Synergy" will not happen by accident. PDS must be a part of other efforts for reform, not competing with them. The oyster of PDS should be in the community. The broader vision requires an act of will, something the naysayers in the language of unanswerable questions cannot understand.

# 2

# School Districts and a Research Organization

Patricia A. Lauer, Stephanie B. Wilkerson,
Bryan Goodwin, and Helen S. Apthorp

*After several hours of driving on narrow, twisting country highways, the research consultant arrives at the school district office in the remote, rural town. She was anxious to report her latest analysis of data derived from her research project with the school. But when she arrives in the crowded meeting room, she senses from the stillness that something is wrong—something has happened since she last visited the isolated district several weeks earlier. Within minutes of sitting down at the meeting table, her suspicions are confirmed. The district's "second-in-command" stands up and explains that in light of the superintendent's recent resignation—the latest in a long string of such departures—he is rethinking the partnership with the researcher's organization. In fact, he felt it is best that they discontinue the partnership, two years into what was to be a four-year study. He does not see where the work is going and cannot identify a reason to continue.*

*The consultant looks at the research report she has painstakingly crafted for the district. It now seems as if all the effort she put into analyzing the data and writing the report—not to mention the past two years of working and countless trips to the district—might be wasted.*

This scenario, based on an amalgam of our experiences in working with schools and districts, illustrates the complexity and unpredictability of partnering with such organizations. Partnerships with schools can be difficult to establish and maintain because they are influenced by many factors from individual interests to changes in leadership.

In the current political climate, educators are bombarded with pressures to change and often turn to partnerships with outside agents to undertake those changes. At the same time, outside agencies, such as research organizations, are realizing that to influence change in education, they need to work directly with schools and teachers. Such collaborations might seem like a simple arrangement—a mere matter of coming to an agreement about a scope of work, shaking hands on it, and getting down to business. In practice, however, creating successful partnerships can be a challenging task.

A number of writers (e.g., Berliner, 1997; McCullum, 2000) identify key principles for creating effective partnerships, including the need for mutual goals, effective communication, trusting relationships, adaptive leadership, and assessment of progress. In our experiences with school districts, additional factors affect the stability and effectiveness of partnerships. These factors involve the unique political pressures, work cultures, and motivations found within schools and districts, which collectively influence whether partnerships with schools roll smoothly down the tracks or result in a collaborative train wreck. Partnerships created by Mid-continent Research for Education and Learning (McREL) are designed to facilitate school improvement through collaborative action research.

## BACKGROUND

McREL is one of 10 regional education laboratories (RELs) funded by the U.S. Department of Education through the Office of Educational Research and Improvement (OERI). The purpose of the RELs is "to promote knowledge-based school improvement to help all students meet high standards" by conducting and disseminating research on education in the nation's K–12 schools (Spencer & Stonehill, 1999, p. iii). To carry out this mission, RELs are expected to work with state and local educators in using research to foster education reform.

In keeping with this expectation, McREL launches an initiative in 1997 to create collaborative research partnerships with school districts in the seven states it serves. The purpose of these partnerships is to engage in collaborative action research projects that promote education reform. The projects' goals are (1) to build the capacity of district and school staff to use data and action research methods to identify areas in need of improvement and (2) to design and implement interventions to address those needs.

McREL selects seven partner sites, one from each state in the region McREL serves, to represent various geographic locations (i.e., urban, suburban, and rural) and student populations (i.e., African American, Native American, Anglo, and Hispanic). In keeping with McREL's federal mission to serve disadvantaged populations, most of these sites are in low-income communities. Each of the partners is assigned a pseudonym using the names of the first seven American presidents.

After identifying partners, a design team consisting of McREL researchers, district staff (e.g., administrators, curriculum coordinators, school psychologists), principals, and teachers is created. Together, the design team selects a research problem, develops a research project, collects and analyzes data, and reports the results to district staff. The focus of each project varies according to local needs as well as McREL researchers' areas of expertise. For example, one team examines the alignment of the district's curriculum, instruction, and assessment; another assesses school climate in the district; and yet another studies the extent to which teachers are using learner-centered practices.

McREL's principle role in these partnerships is to facilitate the research projects and help district partners implement changes in policies, programs, or practices. Throughout the partnerships, the researchers guide district staff in designing research questions and data collection methods, provide technical assistance in various areas, and help local staff make decisions based on research findings. Local educators provide input into all aspects of the research process, carry out data collection, and make relevant recommendations for change to district and school officials.

## METHODS

As the work of the research partnerships progressed, McREL researchers develop case studies and reports, using informal interviews, focus groups, and observations of team meetings. These reports document background information about the partner sites, the process of planning the research project, collaborative research activities, technical assistance provided to the districts, effects of changes implemented by the districts, and evidence of district capacity building (Lauer, Apthorp, Vangsnes, Schieve, & Van Buhler, 1999). It is important to note that the focus of these documents is school improvement, not building partnerships.

As this work unfolds, a wide variance in the stability of our partnerships emerges. Of the seven partnerships, only four are maintained for three years as initially planned—Jackson, Jefferson, Madison, and Monroe. The Adams partnership does not proceed beyond early negotiation stages, the Quincy partnership ends before data collection could begin, and McREL's partnership with Washington ends after one year of research. These varying degrees of success in the partnerships prompts a reexamination of efforts to form partnerships and why some collaborations are more successful than others.

McREL's first analysis leads us to conclude there are several types of education partnerships—from simple exchanges of services to the creation of new entities where there is a mutual exchange of benefits (Barnett, Hall, Berg, & Camarena, 1999). According to this analysis, partnerships are dynamic—what may begin as a simple arrangement can evolve into a much more complex relationship. The issues and concerns that partners need to consider will vary depending on the type and purpose of the partnership. Why are some partnerships more successful than others? Why do some evolve into more integrated, sustained efforts? Our findings are based on a content analysis of the case studies, notes from meetings at partner sites, and a report that described influences on early partnerships (McREL, 1999).

## FINDINGS

After documenting and analyzing the development and outcomes of the partnerships, five factors are identified that influenced the sustainability and effectiveness of these partnerships:

1. The political and cultural contexts of school districts influence multiple facets of the partnerships, including the collaboration process, the work focus, and the length of the partnership.
2. Partners' motivation to engage in the partnership increases when they see their efforts make a difference, when they feel ownership of the project work, and when the focus of the effort aligns with their interests.
3. Establishing clear goals keeps the partnerships on course, sustains commitment, and expedites the work.
4. Partnerships are strengthened by partners' different yet complementary resources and skills.
5. Committed leadership at various levels within both organizations are critical to maintaining the partnerships and facilitating the work.

There is some overlap between these five factors and the factors influence one another. For example, strong *leadership* can help to ensure that sufficient *resources* are committed to the project. Each individual factor is a separate issue.

## UNDERSTANDING SCHOOL POLITICS AND CULTURE

A fish most likely pays little attention to the water in which it swims until it finds itself on the shore. So, too, organizations may pay little attention to their own surroundings—or the political and cultural contexts in which they operate until they attempt to form a partnership with another organization. The partnership forces them to operate, at least in part, within another organization's political and culture surroundings and leaves them feeling like a fish out of water.

To avoid such discomfort and possible missteps, organizations partnering with school districts need to be aware of both the political pressures acting on the districts and the cultures in which they exist. At the same time, partnering organizations should be aware of their own organizational cultures, which they may take for granted. The different political and cultural contexts of the school districts and of McREL influence our partnerships.

A growing number of districts are operating under systems of high-stakes accountability. In nearly every state in the nation, input-based accreditation systems are giving way to results-oriented accountability (Fuhrman, 1999). Instead of monitoring schools' compliance process regulations (e.g., number of school days), states are beginning to focus more on student outcomes (e.g., scores on state-wide assessments) and attaching high stakes to these results. As a consequence, educators are placing more focus on student performance. In many districts, this concern can be all consuming.

It is only natural that before entering into a partnership, participants ask themselves, "What's in it for me?" In today's political context, the most compelling response from districts and schools may be that the collaboration will help them address accountability concerns. Indeed, in our partnership with Jackson, the research project (examining how closely the district's curriculum is aligned to its district-wide assessment) serves to help the district address state requirements.

By analyzing whether students are being given the opportunity to learn what is included in the district assessment, district staff hope to learn what curriculum changes are needed to improve student test scores. Thus, the project is closely aligned with district officials' most pressing concerns and is not viewed as an "add-on." It is likely no coincidence that officials support this project financially and that it is sustained and productive. It is in step with the new realities of schooling under a system of standards-based accountability.

In contrast, if outside organizations do not take into account the political contexts of districts, partnership progress can be stymied. In Madison, some district officials are concerned with standards-based curriculum changes, while others are focused more on the achievement gap between Anglo and minority students. The design team choose to focus on the latter because the group with minority interests is more vocal. The standards-based group has more power in the district, and eventually changes the direction of the work. In this case, our partnership does not reach fruition because it does not reflect the priorities of the most influential people in the district.

The culture of schools affects what they do as much as power. Cultural differences involve the way adults in schools approach their work and work together and approach partnerships with outside organizations. These unique aspects of school cultures are much more than just an academic consideration; they often impact the success of partnerships. Schools differ from one's own organizational culture. A key cultural gap that exists between McREL and its partners is that school staff are inclined to feel that researchers lack experience in the "real world" of K–12 classrooms. This gap is bridged through the use of our field service liaisons and local consultants, who act as boundary spanners. According to Baker (1994), these "linking or bridging positions" are critical to the success of collaborations such as ours (p. 29). McREL's field service providers and consultants are able to build relationships with district partners due to the close connection RELs have with field-based issues and concerns in education, a connection that is not usually present between researchers and the world of practice (Huberman, 1999).

Aside from the belief in practicality, teachers in schools are extreme individualists. A stroll through the hallways of a typical school reveals an important characteristic of school culture—teachers typically work inside separate classrooms, behind closed doors, cut off from one another. They may interact in the faculty lounge, but their conversations are rarely of a professional nature. In his sociological study of schools, Lortie (1975) observes that teachers "work largely alone" (p. 76). Although they may share ideas, the sharing is usually limited to picking up a few "tricks of the trade," as opposed to larger theories of instruction (p. 77). More recent writers, including Johnson (1990) and Hargreaves (1994), make similar observations about today's schools—they are fragmented organizations where little professional collaboration occurs.

Due to this isolation and fragmentation, partner organizations find themselves struggling to work with people who have little experience, or desire, to work with one another. Our efforts are hampered by local staff members' lack of experience in working collaboratively. In some of our sites, teachers are divided into camps and there is mistrust and unresolved conflicts among staff members. In other districts, gulfs exist between teachers who teach at different schools. For example, teachers from the various towns in Jefferson are unable to come together to create a unified research project. Instead, teachers from each town pursue their own projects independent of one another, which disperses the design team's energies. During the second year of the project, McREL contracts with a local consultant who is familiar with teachers in all three towns. Through networking, the consultant helps us pull the team together to focus on a shared project.

The political and cultural contexts of school districts influence multiple aspects of each partnership, particularly the collaboration process, but also the focus of work and how long the partnership is maintained. Without a deep understanding of the political pressures confronting schools or districts, partner organizations may fail to design collaborative work aligned with the school or district's most pressing needs. Similarly, if partners are unaware of the fragmented work culture in many K–12 communities, they may incorrectly assume that the school or district they are working with is a unified group.

## CHANGING MOTIVATIONS TO GOALS

Without a doubt, partners often have different motivations for entering into a relationship. It is important to note, however, that *motivations* are not the same thing as *goals*. Teachers enter into a partnership hoping to gain skills that will help "reach" their students; district administrators may endorse the collaboration in hopes of improving district reading scores; and researchers view the relationship as a means of collecting data on the impact of a reading intervention program. In the end, though, all parties in the partnership must agree on the same goals—in this case, to implement and study a reading intervention program.

McREL has its reasons for creating the partnerships, to fulfill our federal obligation to improve educational practices through research. However, because the partnership activities are conceived collaboratively among design team members, from the outset we experience tension between our need to meet contractual obligations for dissemination and the necessity of addressing district concerns. The district staff is hardly united in their reasons for creating the partnership, as Quincy illustrates:

> Observations and interviews indicated a need and willingness to learn and to change, to work with McREL, and to support such an effort. However, among teachers, there was an interest in more staff development and less concern with turnover rates than among principals. The design team was having difficulty in reaching consensus about the focus of the research. (Lauer et al., 1999, p. 58)

School culture influences teachers' motivations to participate in the partnership. As Lortie (1975) observes, teachers tend to be autonomous, especially those protected by tenure. Although some teachers flourish under this independence, using their independence to avoid cooperation with administrators (Deal & Peterson,1999). The implications for organizations planning to partner with schools is clear: stakeholder buy-in is crucial. Although many of the teachers in our partnerships are eager to provide input and take part in the work, in some cases members are assigned to the design team group by their supervisors and did not want to be there. Through passive resistance, they became what Deal and Peterson call "deadwood" (p. 122), not participating in the work.

Teacher autonomy and the resistance associated with it is a source of frustration when partnering with schools or districts. Partners need to address this resistance head-on by aligning partnership efforts with their own motivations. Partners should be aware that teachers traditionally are not rewarded monetarily for their efforts; many are motivated by emotional rewards, such as knowing that they have reached students (Lortie, 1975). This means that teachers' primary allegiance is to the classroom, where they derive most of their job satisfaction. They tend to resent being pulled away from their students (Johnson, 1990). Although principals and other school leaders may be interested in broad school improvement issues, teachers often are not. They may resent devoting time and energy to the efforts unless it is clear how those efforts help them to "reach" students.

A critical aspect of addressing teachers' motivations is the link to the classroom. All too often, action research projects in school districts tend to focus on adult activities and issues external to instruction (Calhoun & Glickman, 1993). In our experiences, our partners are motivated to engage in the collaborative research project when it has a clear potential to affect teachers in their daily practices. Although some of the goals are broad and the work is at the district level (e.g., alignment among standards, assessment, and curriculum), we emphasize the potential impacts at the classroom level. Without connecting the goals of the partnership to teaching and learning, teachers are liable to become disengaged from the work.

During the first year of our partnership with Jefferson, district design team members conduct individual action research projects on the relationship of various school and classroom practices to student learning, such as strategies to improve student writing. Our results are connected to the classroom, and teachers show a high level of enthusiasm:

> Action research projects gave teachers opportunities to systematically define a problem, collect data to describe the problem and inform possible solutions, talk with colleagues about their practices, and collaborate with colleagues by sharing skills and resources (e.g., data organization and presentation). (Lauer et al., 1999, p. 28)

In contrast, the questions that the Madison design team members originally want to investigate are broader and the connection to student learning is not obvious, for example, how to find a common district focus for reform efforts and how to accommodate diverse views in designing an improvement strategy. It is only after we encourage the design team to look at teachers' classroom practices that members begin to show a greater buy-in for research partnership.

Another influence on educator motivation is the stress and demands of the job causes teachers to "burn out," and thus they lack energy to engage in partnership efforts in a meaningful way. The major symptom of burnout among educators, according to Evans (1996), is a feeling of inconsequentiality, that nothing they do really matters. Such attitudes can make it difficult to engage educators in partnership activities. When they see evidence that their efforts make a difference, their motivation to sustain the partnership increases. This sense of efficacy, whether in affecting policy or procedures, enhancing professional skills, or increasing student achievement, is an important motivator for remaining committed to a partnership.

For example, in Jackson, educators are able immediately to use results of the research project—a study examining the extent to which the district's curriculum is aligned to its tests. As a result, researchers are able to build buy-in early on among staff members. On the other hand, Madison's project on the assessment of teachers' classroom practices does not produce immediate visible changes in instruction. After eighteen months, Madison educators begin to question the value of the research partnership.

The partners' motivations to engage in the work are not static; they can fluctuate over time in response to changes in the collaborative work. For example, in Washington the design team, comprised mainly of district and building administrators, set out to examine the district's use of data in decision making. One key aspect of this research, is it allows the district to gain access to certain kinds of data which are previously unavailable. Once these data are collected, district officials become noticeably less interested in the partnership. Their immediate need is met, and their motivation to partner diminishes.

Similarly, in Jefferson, when the research project changes from conducting individual studies to designing a single project related to district goals, some teachers become less active. The partnership no longer appeals to their interests, and therefore their motivation to contribute time and effort to the work diminishes. In Jackson, we are able to change the focus of the research project to make the work relevant and meaningful for teachers. Specifically, the project's focus shifted from district-wide curriculum alignment to day-to-day classroom practices, and interactions between teachers and students (Lauer et al., 1999).

Allowing partners to feel a sense of ownership of the work is key to sustaining the partnership. For example, the Monroe design team members demonstrate a strong sense of ownership and independence from McREL during the research process. As the project progresses, district staff members begin to recognize the importance of the data they are gathering, so they decide to meet on their own to get the design team's second research project underway.

The Monroe team requests data and tools from the project be made available to them after the work of the partnership is completed (Lauer et al., 1999). In this case, design team members seize the opportunity to provide input, which leads them to a sense of ownership for the work. Because members believe their work is meaningful, they engage in carrying it out. The opportunity to provide input into something important gives teachers the motivation to partner. The partners will have different motivations for engaging in collaborative work. Based on our experiences in partnering with school districts, all of these various motivations must be adressed. It is important for partners to express their reasons for engaging in the partnership, and for each partner continually to be aware of motivations and to address them throughout the course of the collaboration.


## ESTABLISHING CLEAR GOALS

Organizations partner because they realize they cannot reach their goals by themselves. As Sparks (2000) comments: "the most critical attribute of strong educational partnerships is a compelling, stretching purpose that motivates and directs the work of the partners" (p. 3). Although McREL establishes its own overarching purpose for research partnerships, each individual partnership needs to establish its own goals. Although goal setting is a simple task, the design teams often find it difficult to stake out enough common ground to identify mutual goals.

In those cases where the teams could not delineate goals and plans early on, the partnerships floundered. In Quincy, district officials are interested in examining the factors that contribute to students in one high-poverty elementary school posting higher levels of achievement than other similar schools. They want to know what the principal at the school "was doing right and what the other principals were doing wrong" (McREL, 1999, p. 8). During private discussions with school staff members, research on leadership at the higher performing school is unwittingly undermining leadership at other schools.

As a result, some members of the partnership thought that the project should examine the factors contributing to effective leadership in the high-performing school. Other members of the team, namely district leaders, did not want to examine the district's role in supporting or hampering school leadership. Without clear agreement about the scope and focus, the research project could not move forward (McREL, 1999). Eventually, the entire project is abandoned.

On the other hand, when there is a clear vision about the goals of the district and research group, design team members are more committed to the partnership, which, in turn, expedites the progress of the partnership (McREL, 1999). Jackson design team members quickly arrive at a focus for the research project, and their project progressed. The most successful partnerships are those with a clearly identified problem that requires a solution or intervention. People are motivated by a sense of direction and purpose, especially when they believe with McREL's help they could realize their goals. We often work with design teams to see the "overall picture" and how the pieces fit together, as Madison illustrates:

> The district was implementing many reforms but without a common theme or direction. The district, through the efforts of the Design team, was unified in the adoption of a learner-centered framework for their reform efforts. (Lauer et al., 1999, p. 39)

An important caveat is in order here. A partnership's stated goals may not be the same as what partners perceive to be the partnership's goals. When there is a difference between stated and perceived goals, problems occur (Baker, 1994). In one of the districts, a member of the design team perceives one goal of the partnership is to collect data in relation to another district project. Since this purpose is not articulated, the way in which data are collected for the partnership project does not allow them to be used for the other project. As a result, this member is angry and disillusioned with the work of the partnership and communicates that to the rest of the design team.

Partners must avoid the tendency to take on more than they can achieve. Many of our partners establish goals that are unreasonable for the time allotted. Moreover, the teams fail to develop indicators by which to measure progress. In these cases, the lack of reasonable goals and indicators begins to affect the partnerships as they enter their third year of work. The result is an inability of the partnerships to document their successes and, for some individuals, frustration with the project. In Madison, the failure to set goals and indicators beyond the first year creates frustration in the second and third years about the purpose of the partnership and what it has achieved.

Drafting clear goals affects how quickly a partnership becomes established and begins its work. Goals are necessary to provide markers for success so that those involved in the partnership point to progress. Without a mutual understanding of the purpose and work of the partnership, frustration jeopardizes effectiveness. People lose interest and their sense of commitment. Worse, participants become disappointed with the partnering organization, which affects future relationships. When partners are explicit about partnership goals and they revisit the goals at meetings, their commitment is sustained. As a result, the partnership is likely to stay on course.

## RESOURCES AND CAPABILITIES

McREL provides the lion's share of resources for the partnership efforts, including financial resources as well as varying levels of technical assistance, such as workshops on learner-centered instructional practices or assistance in aligning curricula with state assessments. This second type of resource, McREL's ability to provide technical assistance, motivates many district members to engage in the partnership. Partners state that working with McREL staff gives administrators and teachers more opportunities for growth and professional development. In the study of Monroe it is stated:

> The district appeared to view the partnership as a support for their restructuring efforts. Decisions were made to involve McREL in outreach visits to the schools and to include McREL in the inservices. The Superintendent also became increasingly involved in Design team meetings and encouraged McREL staff to bring . . . training to all faculty and administrators. (Lauer et al., 1999, p. 51)

Districts contribute to the partnerships primarily by providing staff time. For example, the Jackson school board allocates funds to support the project, and, in turn, requests quarterly progress reports. This official commitment to the project facilitates its progress and signals its importance to school staff. The design team submits results from the collaborative research effort to school board members, which prompts changes in the district's curriculum.

In contrast, Quincy is a struggling district and resources are scarce from the outset. Schools are understaffed, making it difficult for teachers to participate in the partnership. Teachers leave their classrooms unattended in order to attend design team meetings, since substitute teachers are not available. This partnership flounders and ends once threats of losing state accreditation diverts the district's attention away from the project (McREL, 1999).

Financial commitment by both partners is essential to sustaining the partnerships. As one superintendent states bluntly, "There is no real partnership unless each organization brings its checkbook." Unless both partners are financially committed to the partnership, they can easily withdraw from the collaboration without losing anything:

> An important element that emerged from the meeting was the value of the team-building activities. Although the local participants knew each other as employees of the same school district, they had not interacted as team members, nor had they interacted with the McREL participants. The team building thus established how the members would work together in designing and conducting the action research. Members were passionate in expressing the need for ground rules, and safety of expression was a particular concern. (Monroe, meeting notes, November 13, 1997)

One way around this problem is to use an existing group as the main partner group. In one of our partnerships, the district designates an already existing curriculum team as the design team. The use of this district infrastructure for collaboration facilitates their research project, which develops sooner than projects at the other sites. Another district uses its school improvement teams to facilitate the partnership's work.

In their studies of school-wide action research, Calhoun and Glickman (1993) find that school faculties' understanding of the research process is essential to the success of research projects. We found this is true in districts where data collection is synonymous with evaluation in the minds of staff. A low level of research and school improvement capacity among staff in Madison contributes to their inability to identify a research question. The concerns they initially express could not be easily categorized nor translated into questions for which data could be collected. On the other hand, in Jackson, staff members are familiar with data collection, since they are in a state and district where stringent data collection procedures are already in place. It is easier to generate enthusiasm for collecting data and using it to guide school improvement activities.

To outside observers, it might seem that our partnerships are not very collaborative because McREL completes most of the technical aspects of the research. Although we often provide technical guidance and research expertise, school staff have an important role in providing "real-world" insights into the problems at hand. New ways of thinking about issues and problems are developed. John-Steiner and colleagues (1998), in a study of collaborative inquiry by teachers and university researchers, find complementary experiences and training could be assets in joint efforts.

The McREL researcher uses the design team's input to construct a final version of the survey. In the third year of the Monroe partnership, the design team conducts a study of instructional practices in relation to teachers' classroom structures, multiage or single grade. The district members of the design team study and develop questions for a teacher survey. After data collection is completed, the McREL researcher analyzes the results and delivers a statistical report to the design team for interpretation. The design team uses the results to draft recommendations for teacher staff development, which are distributed to certified staff and school board members.

The district designs the focus and content of the study and interprets the results in light of local conditions. McREL provides the research expertise for instrument development and data analysis. Both partners learn about the relationships between classroom structure and instructional practices. Both contribute resources that are different but complementary. Human resources are as important for partnerships as finances. Partners' skills in collaboration and understanding of research influence partnership progress. The contributions of resources to an education partnership do not need to be the same in amount or kind. As John-Steiner and colleagues (1998) note, combining resources and capacities is the essential effort for creative outcomes.

## COMMITTED LEADERSHIP

Complimentary partnerships are dependent on leadership, but leaders are constantly changing, which affects the initiation and maintenance of education partnerships. Growing political pressures and turf battles among school board members are largely blamed for the rapid turnover among district superintendents as well as numerous vacancies among top positions in school districts (Heim, 1999). Similarly, many districts are seeing an acute shortage of building-level leaders (Learner, 2000). High-stakes accountability systems are increasingly putting principals in the "hot seat," making fewer educators willing to take jobs that they view as having relatively low pay but high stress.

Leadership issues repeatedly influence our work with the districts. After initiating a partnership with Adams, a large urban district, the superintendent resigns unexpectedly. This leads to a long transition period while the school board searches for a suitable replacement. During this period, it is impossible to move the partnership forward with interim leaders, since they want to wait and see what the new superintendent will do. Eventually, after a long period of limbo, the district hires a new superintendent, who decides to end the relationship.

According to Sagor (1997), sustaining a process of action research for education change requires the support of school leaders to send signals to staff that such work is valued. The ongoing presence of committed district leaders provides access to needed resources and staff and lends legitimacy to the research projects (McREL, 1999). In Jackson, the superintendent monitors the design team's progress and requires principals to participate in data collection. This level of interest increases the visibility of the project and encourages participation by school staff. In contrast, the sporadic involvement of Jefferson district leaders in the research project hampers its progress.

Partnerships require the support of informal leaders. District champions on the design teams are important, while Osguthorpe and Patterson (1998) note, such informal leaders are vital to the collaboration as formal leaders. Current literature on organizational leadership argues that organizations should abandon the "myth of the hero-leader" (Senge, 1999, p. 11) or the lone "gunslinger" who rides into town and saves the day. Change occurs when leadership responsibilities are shared among many people. Not only does this sort of broad leadership facilitate staff buy-in, it also ensures that change initiatives are less likely to falter when formal leaders depart or "the gunslinger leaves town" (McREL, 2000, p. 11).

Our collaborative initiatives weather changes in leadership when there is support among a school system's informal leader. In Monroe, both the superintendent and assistant superintendent leave during the course of our work. Ordinarily this might end the partnership, but a principal and another leader, the district's psychologist, champions the work of the design team:

> She [the psychologist] seems to be very eager (and even hungry) for a research atmosphere in the district. At the same time, she exhibits sincere concern for the needs of the students and wants research that will make a difference to them. (Monroe meeting notes, January 16, 1998)

Subsequently, this specialist is instrumental in facilitating most of the design team activities. In another site, a veteran elementary teacher embraces the notion of inquiry into practice. Her attitude and enthusiasm helps generate and sustain the research activities of the partnership.

Our own leadership group changes. After three years, only one of the original McREL researchers remains involved with the collaborative research initiative. New researchers are hired, trained, and assigned to districts as needed. In one site, the departure of the McREL staff member working with the district coincide with the district's own changes in leadership. The new district leader on the team uses this as an opportunity to change the direction of the project by casting doubt on the work we have accomplished. In cases where our work is already aligned with district needs and partner motivations and guided by clear goals and logic models, new researchers are able to take over where their predecessors left off with relatively few disruptions. Once again, broad-based leadership sustains the project if individuals leave.

## CONCLUSIONS

The five findings capture the complexity of school systems by collectively addressing the entire system from individual motivations to external political pressures. It is important to consider each of these issues in a partnership because failing to consider any one element leads to failure. A partnership can be guided by committed, broad-based leadership, yet if the focus of the work fails to address the motivations of everyone involved in the effort, it will have minimal impact. For renewed partnerships, five recommendations are made.

1. *Know your partners.* Organizations partnering with school districts need to understand the political pressures confronting school organizations so they design collaborative work that helps schools address critical issues. If they do not, school leaders will view the partnership as a distraction and will be more likely to abandon the work or offer few resources in support of the partnership. Similarly, partners need to be aware of the unique work culture within schools because this influences the extent to which people in the school organization engage in partnership activities and collaboration.

2. *Address the role partners' motivations play in the partnership and connect the work to the classroom.* Aligning partnership efforts with individual motivations is critical to facilitating and sustaining partnerships. This increases partners' engagement, buy-in, and sense of efficacy. In other words, the partners value the partnership when they see how their efforts make a difference, especially when those differences link to the classroom. Educators need to know that their investment in a partnership will directly or indirectly affect daily practices and student learning. It is important to understand and address partners' initial and continuing motivations for engaging in the partnership.

3. *Establish long-term goals with short-term indicators of progress.* Sustaining partnerships depends on the establishment of clear goals that are perceived in the same way by both organizations. For our partnerships, participants' vision of the collaboration enhanced their motivations to begin working. To continue that effort, partners needed to realize they are making progress and that results eventually would impact student learning. Establish goals early, assess participants' understanding of the goals, and continually

revisit the goals. Realistic indicators should be chosen and then used to celebrate progress and to make mid-course adjustments.

4. *Use the complementary resources and capacities of each partner and build the ability of each partner to collaborate.* Partnerships need resources to function, and partners need appropriate capacities and skills to make the best use of these resources. Partnerships do not hinge on whether the partners contribute an equal amount of resources. What matters is the commitment to the collaboration. Because collaboration is a capacity essential to most partnerships, it is important to devote time to examining partners' collaborative skills and to providing appropriate training if necessary.

5. *Identify and foster leaders.* Obviously, committed leadership is critical to securing resources for the partnership, maintaining collaboration, and facilitating the work. The key message here is that leadership of the project needs to lie with more than one or two individuals whose departure could imperil the partnership. Instead, leadership should be considered broadly as a group of people who share responsibility for guiding and carrying out the work.

Following these recommendations is no guarantee that such research partnerships will succeed. One of our key messages is unanticipated events are quite likely to occur when partnering with school districts. In other words, partners should expect the unexpected. Our recommendations are a way to ensure that partnerships weather unforeseen events. The following scenario offers a positive amalgam of our experiences in the face of adverse circumstances.

*The researcher dreads what she might encounter when she arrives in the district office at the end of yet another long drive—this time over snowy mountain roads. A week earlier, she learns the superintendent resigns after a contentious battle with the school board, leaving the district in a state of turmoil. She is bracing herself for, at best, a long period of limbo in which it would be difficult to advance the work of the partnership toward its established goals, and, at worst, loss of administrative commitment and teacher buy-in, resulting in the eventual demise of the partnership. To make matters worse, the snow falling on the mountain roads delays her arrival, and she is running about 30 minutes late.*

*When she enters the meeting room, she is surprised to see that the team has started the meeting—a working session to analyze student performance data without her. An influential principal now seemed to be leading the meeting. The acting superintendent, the district's curriculum developer, is also seated at the table.*

*As soon as the consultant sits down, the curriculum developer explains that several teachers who were working on the project have been talking about it after a recent district meeting "to see what all the buzz was about." After learning more about the project from design team members, he, too, is excited about the project because it promises to yield information that could be valuable for their accreditation review by the state.*

*At that point, one teacher explains, apologetically, that over the past few weeks, they began taking it upon themselves to conduct their own analysis of the data and to draft a report for the school board. In addition, some other teachers say they want to work on the project as well. Was that okay? The consultant laughed. Yes, that was okay, she said. It is more than okay. It is great.*

## EDITOR'S NOTE

This chapter is full of valuable insights and will repay rereading. Issues of leadership, developing goals, and formulating strategies will be repeated in a number of chapters in Part II. There is one critical difference between this chapter and later ones. The partners are restricted to researchers and teachers. This lack of diversity is ironic when the value of different perspectives is being discussed as a source of creative collaborations. Partnerships need to involve more than one group, whether it is concerned about its grants or focused on classrooms.

The individualism of researchers and teachers is an impediment to larger organization and broader sense of purpose. As later chapters show, involving artists, businesspeople, or rural community leaders are ways of avoiding parochialism. Educators are caught in their own traps. Few think community leaders will propose changes for teachers and academics. No one in this case seems to think about community support as a way of enhancing continuity when administrators move along among bureaucracies.

Individualism and practicality as values need to be augmented by a broader sense of vision than those directly involved in the teaching or research task are unlikely to possess. The political reality of the individual school or school districts is transcended when a league of schools is developed. John Goodlad ironically develops leagues for research, but the league becomes more important than the research (Mitchell, 1990). New leadership can unexpectedly emerge from such ventures.

For developing new leadership or the partnership itself, the authors identify the critical question involved in converting partnership motivations to partnership goals. A shared purpose is required. A common language is necessary and future steps must be identified. Evaluations are important in supporting the tentative steps made by those in fragile partnerships. Professional measurement or surveys are not the aim. Bringing their checkbooks is a measure of commitment. Partnerships can develop from either the resources of people or money, but the most effective ones require both.

A common vision is necessary for a concerted strategy to be created. The result in this case is a basic guarantee of the ingredients for partnerships, which is proven by teachers evaluating research themselves. Other authors will show networks develop from business resource alliances or pairing of student teachers in a music partnership for schools. Specific steps develop from a general understanding of politics and negotiation necessary to partner with schools, which is the essential contribution of this chapter.

# 3

# From Project within a School to Provincial Network

## Michele Jacobsen and Brenda Gladstone

*So, what you're telling me is, you go into a school and work alongside teachers in their classes for varying lengths of time. At some point they walk through a doorway with you. Once they walk through that doorway, they see their teaching differently, they even see the world differently and they never want to go back. So it is like a transformation*

*—Martin Kratz, Bennett Jones*

As a member of a prominent Canadian law firm, Mr. Kratz illustrates the understanding that can develop between outside partners and the Galileo Network. Corporate, government, and community partners join together in the Galileo Educational Network Association (GENA). GENA is an independent, charitable organization consisting of leading educators, a business manager, and a high profile Board of Directors.

After an initial project, GENA's expert teachers help school staffs create an integration of learning, technology, and professional development. The network provides on-line examples of innovative student and teacher learning and sustains face-to-face initiatives via its website: http://www.galileo.org. GENA asks willing teachers to discover their concerns, relate technology to their commitments, and extend their passion for enriched education. If they make a three-year commitment, GENA provides schools and teachers with sustained mentorship in classrooms, augmented by on-line collaboration.

In the province of Alberta in Western Canada, GENA forms strategic alliances to build a reform initiative. An initial school project becomes a network to integrate information and technology across school districts (Jacobsen & Gladstone, 1999). This network is grounded in current educational research, and its members contribute to knowledge by publishing and disseminating their results. GENA provides opportunities for educators and school division leaders to plan, together with business, universities, community, and government, toward strategic goals. From these four sectors, individuals who are interested in learning and who link with many other people find ways to implement GENA's vision. GENA's partners hold teachers accountable; they expect improved student achievements as much as educators do.

## PILOT PROGRAM—FROM TALK ABOUT A NEW SCHOOL

Before its approval in 1993, parents and teachers were discussing how a major investment in a new school building could change the education of students at the Rocky View School Division in Bragg Creek, Alberta, Canada. An assistant principal, Brant Parker, and two parents, Fred and Heather Gallagher, initiated the Galileo concept as a basis of funding. The partnership coordinato for the district, Brenda Gladstone, together with other staff, helped develop the initial idea. Along with linking with the early scientist Galileo, a business idea of bringing people to work and study in the new setting, and then return to their own organization was the model.

Fred Gallagher interested his father, Jack Gallagher, a grandparent of a student in the new school, in the Galileo approach. In 1997, a generous donation by the Gallagher Education Foundation allowed a visionary group to design a professional development center in Banded Peak School in Bragg Creek. Jack Gallagher's earlier goal was to develop Canada's North, which he did as the founder of Dome Petroleum. His later commitment to teachers' professional development inspired others who came to support the Galileo Centre.

Jack's commitment continued as his health faded. He called members of the Galileo team early Saturday mornings to ask about their progress and to share his ideas. Once, he placed a phone call while he is waiting for an ambulance to take him to the hospital. Although Jack Gallagher is in great pain, he still wanted to ensure that school personnel are meeting his expectations. After Jack's death in 1998, the Gallagher family continues to support the Galileo Network through personal involvement and the Gallagher Educational Foundation.

From the beginning, Jack Gallagher insists that a Galileo team travel to visit centers of educational excellence. These visits are to augment the original model, which is drawn from Harvard Business school. The Harvard plan brings successful businesspeople together to work and study, and then returns them to their own companies with new knowledge, experiences, and approaches. Similarly, the Galileo pilot is to remove constraints imposed by traditional practices so innovative teachers advance their practices, thereby transforming education from within.

The Galileo ideals derive from an image published in the age of Galileo. The title page of Bacon's *Novum Organum* portrays a ship sailing through the Pillars of Hercules. In the 16th century, these pillars symbolize the limits of possible human exploration. The four new pillars defining the work of the Galileo Centre are: 1) student learning, 2) professional development, 3) effective use of technology, and 4) classroom-based research. Foremost, the Galileo Centre aims to impact on student learning. A variety of projects try to explore aspects of mandated curricula in creative and exciting ways.

The commitment to improving teaching practice beyond the walls of Banded Peak School is a feature of the second pillar, professional development. The Galileo Centre gives teachers from school divisions across the province an opportunity to spend one year in a collaborative teaching and learning experience at Banded Peak School. The project teachers spend part of their time teaching students, investing the remainder with experts and colleagues. They provided in-service training, acquired new skills, and conducted classroom-based research. Afterward, project teachers return to their home school districts as leaders, share their expertise with other educators, and become linked with similar teachers in the province.

The Galileo pilot focuses on exploiting the educational potential of technology in schools, pillar three. Although "effective use of technology" is only one of four pillars, this project is misunderstood to focus solely on high technology. Educators from within and beyond the Rocky View School Division refer to Banded Peak School as "that high technology school." The student–computer ratio is below more advantaged schools, but the stereotype persists.

The fourth pillar of the Galileo Centre, classroom-based research, complements and extends the other three pillars. In partnership with the University of Calgary, the Galileo project tries to bridge the gap between educational theory and teaching practice through developing new knowledge about teaching and learning. School-based advocates, who relate technology to educational reform, stress research on the enhanced abilities of students and teachers to collaborate on projects.

Classroom-based research projects make a valuable contribution to advancing understanding about significant issues in teaching, learning, and professional development. A Galileo Doctoral Fellowship is established to sustain cooperation between teachers at Banded Peak School and the University of Calgary, and the Centre funds a doctoral student committed to its research program. In 1997/1998, the first Galileo Fellow, Michele Jacobsen, pursued a three-part role that included professional development, classroom-based research, and liaison with the University of Calgary (Jacobsen, 1998). The second Galileo Fellow, Trevor Owen, commuted from Ontario to pursue an electronic mentorship project. The third Galileo Fellowship recipient, Rosina Smith, investigates the integration of technology into academic core subjects.

## THE TEACHERS' ROLE IN THE PROJECT

The original role for visiting teachers neither expands teachers' research leadership in research nor extends professional development beyond the school. Teachers around Alberta are reluctant to leave their homes for one-year periods to live in Bragg Creek. The expectation that individual classroom teachers return to their home division after a one-year immersion experience and become effective change agents is unrealistic. Classroom teachers conform to bureaucratic and institutionalized expectations. The "checks and balances" inherent in school divisions do *not* promote and support innovation among peers or teachers elsewhere.

Teachers by training are neither researchers, writers, nor advocates. In order to increase corporate support, the Galileo project needs to document the substantive differences in student performance. Teaching is an isolated activity, and does not provide teachers time to pursue professional development, action research, or publications. During 1997/1998, teachers in the project are criticized for having "free time" that others in the school are not given. Teachers resent people who are free from the restrictions they feel. The Galileo committee provides time away from classes for other teachers in the school. Aside from free time, the other teachers need opportunities to collaborate on projects, to participate in conversations about pedagogy, to join in action research, and to write. An unintended effect is to create another type of professional isolation for project teachers who have so many opportunities— no one else in the school has "time" for them.

Effective project teachers depend on their own resources rather than the project. Those in the Galileo project come to believe there must be time for other teachers to take part in a dialogue. The Galileo committee decides other teachers need capable and experienced mentors. The project teacher is reconceptualized as a facilitating teacher for the project's third year. Facilitating teachers provide learning and teaching experience for project teachers, support staff who explore the four pillars in their own practice, share methodologies, research, and ideas from the school and beyond, plan research, and align measures to the Galileo Plan.

The facilitating teacher role is more effective than the project teacher approach, but is an expensive approach to maintain. To involve teachers equally is not enough; the staff in the school are polarized about the project. The Galileo Centre is told by corporate, community, and educational partners to expand into other schools and other school divisions in order to achieve its broader objectives that will avoid the confrontation issue.

## A TRIP TO RHODE ISLAND

In November 1997, a Galileo team visited Brown University to meet with the educational reformer Ted Sizer and members of the Annenberg Foundation. The team included the Dean of Education at the University of Calgary, Ian Winchester; the first Gallagher Galileo doctoral fellow, Michele Jacobsen; the principal of Banded Peak School, Brant Parker; and a classroom teacher, Pat Clifford. The team visited school sites and met teachers and leaders who are committed to change. Visiting with these reformers is exciting because they are involved in similar efforts for decades. Sizer, Amy Gerstein of the Coalition of Essential Schools, and Mark Starr, Managing Director of the Annenberg Institute of School Reform, share their insights about educational reform, and show a keen interest in the idea of a professional development initiative with a province-wide agenda. Besides their past experience, these educational reformers relate their most recent initiatives and projects.

The team emerges with five key findings pertinent to a province-wide educational reform initiative in Alberta:

1. There is an increasingly international movement for school reform led by the Coalition of Essential Schools and the Annenberg Institute of School Reform. This movement receives significant private and public support. It has three major strands: capacity building, accountability, and public engagement.
2. Significant educational reform comes from powerful ideas, not preset models.
3. Breakthroughs in school reform occur in small schools, where there is a clear vision for change. These schools bring their vision to life through on-site autonomy and freedom from bureaucratic structures.
4. Successful reform initiatives are bold from the outset.
5. Single schools attempting bold initiatives become targets; they need support and advocacy.

These five key findings revolutionize thinking. We seek a province-wide organization supported by a range of allies and housed at the University of Calgary.

The first key finding suggests we develop a parallel to international movement for school reform led by the Coalition of Essential Schools. This coalition receives significant government, private and public support in the United States. *Capacity building* is enhanced by professional development and the coaching of critical friends. *Accountability* includes performance-based outcomes, peer contributions to administrative reviews, and an examination of existing good practices in public. *Public engagement* of parents, businesspeople, and other community members are asked the fundamental questions about the school they would like to send someone they love. This question is meaningful whether or not these partners have children in school.

Public engagement means facilitating a dialogue about the purposes of public education, which brings together a wide range of people for educational reform and provides support for the schools that have a vision for change. It means enlisting powerful benefactors and community leaders for advocacy, support, and change. Key business leaders and the provincial education ministry are to generate involvement from outside schools. Key business leaders open doors for others to contribute to a project. When the Galileo Centre pilot approaches the end of its third year of seed funding from the province, it becomes difficult to secure more funding and support. Potential partners see the results of student learning, but they want to expand beyond the pilot to other school districts so that growth can attract other sponsors.

The second key finding from the Sizer group is realizing that reform comes from the powerful ideas they hold together, but apply differently. The Coalition of Essential Schools lists nine Common Principles that underlie their commitment to school reform, but insists on the importance of the diverse local contexts. Ideas do not belong to individuals or to a small number of people, but arise from an interconnected community committed to the common good. Shared ideas provide informed conversation and debate among friends. GENA is based on responsiveness, relationship building, and community engagement. GENA comes to include 5 school divisions; 10 schools, partners, and researchers in 3 universities; and a range of corporate, government, and private sponsors. GENA's action plan is collaborative, responds to different localities, and results in a different course for each Galileo site.

The third key finding stresses breakthroughs in school reform occur most often in small schools with a clear vision. Small schools bring their vision to life through on-site autonomy and freedom from bureaucratic structures (Meier, 1995; Sizer, 1992). People work in support of ideas in which they believe, and when their voices are heard. Reform of this nature is egalitarian and democratic. Hierarchically organized, bureaucratic school systems, while voicing support for innovation, discourage innovation (Schoor, 1998). While bureaucracy may crush a project in one school, it is more difficult to silence an independent organization with many sites and a common purpose.

In order to achieve a province-wide agenda, the professional development initiative becomes legally separate from any one school division, and achieves complete autonomy in its decision making in order to respond to diverse requests. The core group at the Galileo Centre in the one school are constrained in making decisions and raising funds. Refusing to allow one more team member to travel to Rhode Island is one of the many decisions imposed on the school-based team by bosses in one school system. The imposition of decisions from above leads to the formation of an independent network.

That successful school reform initiatives are bold from the outset is the fourth key finding, which arises from reflecting on the trip. Initiatives that begin with small steps are swamped at the start. The initial idea of a center within a school is new for the province of Alberta. Boldness brings wider recognition and restrictions from the original school division. GENA is a broader venture, which create greater profits in terms of ideas, people involved, and supports for the unfettered network.

The new Galileo Educational Network is a result of its many strategic alliances with government, corporate, private, and public industries. The high profile partners support and advocate the work of GENA. GENA is not overly reliant on any one of its partners or strategic alliances, and it is autonomous, responsive, and flexible in its decision making. No one partner dictates or drives the GENA initiative, but it responds to input from each of its partners. The Network reacts to creative and innovative ideas, proposals, and requests.

The fifth key finding from the trio's meeting with the Annenberg group enables them to name their problem in attempting reform within a single school site. The project within a school is a "target." Banded Peak's principal, Brant Parker, takes the brunt of criticism from administrators of the school division and teachers and parents in the school. He has to defend and protect the innovative teachers. The school division supports the Centre's mandate in principle, the teachers in the school claim they endorse it, and parents favor the project. The position of these three groups changes as principles become practice.

In 1997, when new images of practice emerged, many teachers in the school reacted. As reforms begin in a few classrooms, the integration efforts draw visitors to the school. The project and its appeal to outsiders create tensions within the school and school division. The tension between innovative teachers and the more conventional "others" leads to sabotage of the Galileo Centre and attacks are directed against individuals leading the pilot. To build support, the Coalition of Essential Schools establishes centers, often aligned with universities, to support innovative schools.

The push to a similar center mounts because "contrapreneurs" undermine the reform initiative (Morgan & Murgatroyd, 1994). The School Galileo Committee meets weekly in the school and agrees on strategy to meet its stated goals. The Committee invents ways for other teachers to participate. Unaware of the extent to which they are becoming targets, the Galileo advocates believe that evidence of a best practice will sway critics both in the school and the school division. As Pfeffer and Sutton (2000) lament from their experience in business environments, "you would think that . . . best practices would spread like wildfire in the entire organization. They don't (p. 9)." New practices from project classrooms do not spread throughout the school because contrapreneurs interpret them differently.

Evidence of tension and suspicion in the school begins to appear. School administrators hear complaints about the "negative culture" in the school. The two lead teachers in the Galileo pilot are insulted. The previously mentioned cadre of contrapreneurs complains to colleagues in other schools. Condemning stories and negative anecdotes spread throughout the division and filter back to the Galileo committee.

In 1998, a major event occurred in a graduate course held in the original school. Those who enroll agree at the outset to keep conversations confidential so that the seminar is a safe place to ask questions and express concerns. More than 20 staff members join the course in order to reflect on teaching practices. Based on suggestions by Meier (1995) and Sizer (1992), teachers engage in sustained conversations about shared readings. They reflect on Palmer's book *The Courage to Teach* (1998) and discuss what his vision means for the day-to-day classroom.

During one seminar, a teacher volunteers the opinion that the use of timed "Math Mad Minutes" with young children is counter to the Galileo vision, and interferes with understanding mathematics as a discipline. Within 24 hours, this teacher's position is distorted into "those who use Math Minutes are awful teachers." The Galileo committee receive comments from individuals about "their practice being just as good as 'the others.'" One individual claims they "had never witnessed or observed an example of bad teaching practice." This incident personalizes teaching practice and names individuals. In the seminar, teaching practices are discussed, not individuals. The contrapreneurs are successful, the course folds, and individuals guard their views about teaching or educational reform.

As a result of the tension in the school and rumors about the project, the parent community becomes deeply divided. Stories from the community come back to the Galileo committee about teachers who attempt to coopt parents into thinking that innovative teaching practices are too experimental. Parents are told children need to practice 100-word spelling lists and Mad Math exercises to meet curriculum requirements. Some parents tell school administration that the "curriculum wouldn't be covered." Other parents circumvent school administration and ask to see the superintendent of schools. Still others write to the Minister of Education about their fears. The response from the school division is authoritative damage control. Any issue, complaint, or concern that hints at discontent from teachers or parents is a problem to be solved, rather than an opportunity to generate understanding of reform efforts.

## GENA

The Galileo committee learns that schools and educators who are seeking breakthroughs need a supportive network to provide credibility and protection for their reform efforts, to mediate conflicts, to ease transitions, to provide professional support, and to build capacity for change. Allies should include political and financial friends to ensure both support and accountability to the community. The Galileo Centre is defunct. A new legal and philosophical alliance emerges. Modeled on the centers of the Coalition of Essential Schools, a provincial educational reform initiative seeks professional development through technology integration.

When the initial project faces internal resistance, the Galileo Committee is sought after by those outside the division. School boards throughout the province want to be involved. The provincial education minister visits the school, and compliments the team on their accomplishments. Researchers from Rice University, in Texas, tour the Galileo classrooms, and are impressed by the students' learning. Papers about new practices from the school are presented at provincial, national, and international conferences (Clifford et al., 1998; Gladstone & Jacobsen, 1999; Jacobsen, Johnson, & Ellis, 1998; Jacobsen, Stockton, & Fritsch, 1998). The business community seeks faster outreach to other schools and school divisions.

In January 1999, an external evaluation is commissioned by the Rocky View School Division superintendent of schools to evaluate the effect of the Galileo Centre. The report describes the Centre as "a supportive environment for new ideas, an enabling atmosphere for risk-taking with new approaches, a connection centre for collaboration and shared questioning of daily practices, a home for enthusiastic conversations among teachers, students, parents and partners" (MacIntyre et al., 1999, p. 2). The evaluators conclude that the "Galileo Centre is having a positive impact on student learning by fostering its four purposes . . .

students are effectively learning and using the concepts of project-based inquiry, integrating technology, and multiple forms of reporting and assessment" (p. 11).

With respect to transforming teachers, the report states, "The evaluation team is clearly convinced that teachers who spend a school year immersed in the vigour of this growth environment become better teachers in the future" (MacIntyre et al., 1999, p. 11). The recommendations call for expansion beyond one school. The report says the Galileo project is successful in acquiring funds and could acquire more funds in the future. Though support from the school system is needed, the system risks "criticism of inequity" if it provides additional funding (p. 12). An independent organization is essential.

The new initiative requires a new name, separate legal status, and a changed image. This new approach will liaison with the Rocky View School Division, but would be separate from it. At the April 1999 Galileo Advisory Council meeting, members support a proposal to create a new and independent entity for a provincial not-for-profit initiative if outside support is secured. Crucial help comes from the Minister of Education, Gary C. Mar.

## ALLIANCE WITH ALBERTA LEARNING

In November 1998, Mr. Mar visited the Galileo Centre at Banded Peak School. In April 1999, Mar's executive assistant, Kelley Charlebois, met the teachers and students. Mar and Charlebois asks the Galileo advocates: "What do you need to have this initiative grow?" The Galileo advocates request and receive $200,000 a year for 3 years from the Alberta government to develop the Galileo Educational Network. The funds support an independent and autonomous organization, capable of working within a number of school divisions and schools concurrently to achieve a province-wide impact on educational reform. Studies of parent organizations killing their disruptive prodigies are chilling (Christensen, 1997). From their own experience, the Galileo advocates focus on *the essential conditions for change*. A core number of leaders will go into schools to work alongside of teachers as mentors and coaches in order to create new ways of teaching and learning.

Both Kelley Charlebois and Gary Mar relate their excitement for the Galileo initiative is based on technology, the training program by teachers, and the zeal of those involved. Though Mr. Mar changes ministries, he shares the new Galileo approach with people around the province, with his colleagues in government, his fellow Education Ministers across the country, and with audiences on his overseas missions to China, Japan, and other countries. This minister's advocacy and support creates the initial strategic alliance. Dr. Lyle Oberg, the Minister of the newly formed Ministry of Learning, continues to provide support and advocacy for the GENA (Gladstone, 2000). In Fall 1999, he announced further funding for GENA and demonstrates his commitment by attending the official opening of GENA in November 1999. Dr. Peter Darby, the new Chair of the School Technology Task Group in Alberta Learning, joins the alliance's board of directors. Dr. Darby helps link GENA with other provincial initiatives.

## INDIVIDUAL ALLIES

As a result of the negative and acrimonious reaction to the initial project, later teachers and schools are only accepted if they are open to new ideas and supportive of GENA. Efforts to convince the unconvinced are not profitable; the Galileo Alliance will "water the flowers, not the rocks." Alberta Learning funds GENA for three years, but measurable results are required in every year. A three-year commitment is sought from schools who are willing to work collectively and collegially toward changed practices.

Similarly, GENA wants committed supporters who are willing to enter into strategic alliances and flexible relationships. GENA is attempting to infuse the thinking drawn from different business and industry models into the work of GENA's teachers. There is a shift from large organization partnerships between whole school divisions and corporations to the one-on-one personal relationships that GENA seeks from its partners. GENA designs each relationship individually according to the partner organization's unique circumstances. With some organizations, including the Universities of Calgary and Lethbridge, or the Pacific Institute of Mathematical Sciences, GENA receives expert advice. Other partners, such as Cavendish Investments, provide donations. Financial or in-kind donations are offered by IKON and the Alberta Science and Research Association. IBM offers donations, knowledge, and expertise. AxiaNetMedia and Galileo's lead staff are co-developing an on-line professional development model for teachers. This new communication model extends our ability to work within a number of additional school divisions across Alberta. GENA has strategic alliances with Alberta Learning, the Faculty of Education at the University of Calgary, the Institute for Professional Development at the University of Alberta, Shaw Communications, Rocky View School Division, Foothills School Division, the Calgary Board of Education, Bennett Jones, IBM Canada Limited, IKON Office Solutions, the Pacific Institute of Mathematical Sciences (PIMS), Stellarton Energy Corporation, Chinook's Edge School Division, Golden Hills Regional School Division, Cavendish Investments, the University of Lethbridge, the Gallagher Education Fund of the Calgary Foundation, and AxiaNetMedia. GENA receives the Industry Canada—CanConnect Award for business–education partnerships, which is part of the "National Partners in Education Awards" sponsored by Royal Band, Daimler Chrysler Canada, Human Resources Canada, and Industry Canada.

For any of these partners, there is no set approach to joint planning and goal setting, instead each agreement is unique. Individual relationships enhance commitment to educational reform, which strengthens advocacy efforts. The issues of joint planning and goal setting for a successful educational partnership should be a means to an end (Canadian Chamber of Commerce, 1992; O'Connor & Allen, 1996). Each of the strategic alliances with GENA is important as long as there is a direct and measurable impact on GENA core mission and goals. Commitment is to an understanding of the mutual benefits from the alliance or relationship. Some relationships change over time and, if an alliance or partner is no longer making a contribution to GENA's mission, the relationship ends.

All business partnership agreements have a clause to determine how they will get out of the relationship when it no longer suits their needs. GENA does not look for a "mate for life" when forming alliances with other organizations (Robertson, 1998). GENA's vision for strategic alliances is built upon a "play" or "sandbox" model—children do not stay in the sandbox once the fun (the mutual benefit), is over simply because they originally agreed to work on the same sand castle. Educational partnerships are based on mutual benefits and learning.

## BUILDING EFFECTIVE LINKS

To establish GENA's various links, group members need to learn about each other, find common ground, delve into their reasons for participating, and discover mutual benefits in the relationships. Several of the original allies choose to shift their support. Several new partnerships are developed, and some are concluded.

A profit from partnering with a high technology company is enhancing the credibility for educational innovations. Companies in technology help us look beyond education for ideas, practices, and advice. The Alberta Science and Research Authority (ASRA) publishes a report (1998) outlining an aggressive strategy to position Alberta as a leader in information and communication technology (ICT). The strategies ASRA outlines involve strengthening the province's participation in the global ICT marketplace through education, developing the ICT infrastructure for research and development, and creating ICT businesses.

Alberta can establish a national pattern to enhance the preparation of students to enter ICT-related fields. GENA's proposal to pursue these educational implications is accepted by ASRA after a competitive review.

## THE CORE

Outside support is matched by the dedication of Network staff. During its first year as an independent network, the program relies on the dedication of three individuals: two teachers, Pat Clifford and Sharon Friesen, and a general manager, Brenda Gladstone. In August 1999, GENA registers as a Charitable Society under the Societies Act of Alberta. The five people with signing authority members are the three dedicated staff members and two lawyers. Without the two lawyers, the registration process would be longer.

At the first meeting of GENA in September, a board of directors is elected. Though board members are dedicated, daily work falls to the staff members. Pat and Sharon are seconded from Rocky View School Division so they are paid their teaching salaries during these beginning months. Brenda works full-time without compensation until the end of October. The core activists are constantly discussing, brainstorming, and inventing new solutions; implementing ideas in schools; and involving new allies.

This group is upset by the Board's insistence that a president be responsible for the entire operation. The three advocates want to operate as a collaborative. They believe the unique combination of skills and attributes among them leads to better decisions. Pat Clifford becomes president, and there is a playful debate about the titles and roles of the other two people. They do not want a hierarchical, traditional organization.

The combination of Pat and Sharon's educational expertise, and Brenda's practical acumen, business contacts, and attention to detail makes GENA possible. Pat, Sharon, and Brenda agree to work for less money in order to get the first budget approved by the Board of Directors. Though Pat is president, Sharon is vice-president and Brenda is general manager, together they live and work as if each one, not just the president, is accountable for the success of GENA.

The individual roles that each plays throughout that first year are multifaceted. Pat Clifford provides visionary leadership and on-site coaching for teachers and administrators in three schools several days each week. Pat also searches for strategic alliances; writes grant applications, concept papers, planning documents, and business plans; negotiates with school and division administrators; conducts research;

and makes public presentations. Sharon Friesen leads others through her perception of GENA's goals, on-site coaching in three schools, building of strategic alliances, development of mathematics initiatives (SumTalk for Students and SumTalk for Teachers), and creation of GENA's website.

Complementing the teachers is Brenda Gladstone. Her responsibilities range from selecting and grooming the board of directors, being answerable to both the president and the chairman of the board, taking the lead in fundraising and partnership development, and establishing financial systems for accountability. She controls and monitors the budget, establishes office procedures, manages daily operations, and maintains contact with government agencies, businesses, and the school divisions. She also writes and signs contracts, plans public relations, updates the website, and drafts business plans.

In the second year of operations, 2000/2001, the Galileo Educational Network is expanded to 10 schools across five school divisions. The staff increases to eight full-time members and many part-time teachers. Among the five new staff is an administrative assistant, a certified network engineer who was formerly a teacher, and three more expert educators, who are seconded from the Calgary Board of Education and Foothills School Division. Each of the five expert educators works on-site in the schools several days per week. Pat Clifford and Sharon Friesen schedule one day per week of professional development and mentorship for the GENA staff. The Network warrants each school will receive 80 days of coaching in each school, which equals 880 days of professional development.

## FOUNDATIONS FOR THE FUTURE

In 1999, GENA began operations with in-kind donations only. The University of Calgary donates office space and basic furniture, and the Faculty of Education covers the salaries of two employees until GENA could pay them. Furniture and equipment are donated, some of it from the home of Galileo employees. In October 1999, the first deposit from Alberta Learning is made, which means the general manager collects a salary.

One year later, GENA's operating budget is over $1 million. Approximately 20 percent of this budget is provided by the Alberta Learning grant. A similar 20 percent of its budget is from the grant from Alberta Science and Innovation. Support comes from a variety of private, corporate, and institutional organizations, which reflects the strategy of not being overreliant on any one partner. A fundamental goal is to protect the autonomy and independence of the organization.

The core members realize that they have to find more enduring revenue sources so that they will be able to plan GENA's future. The first person they co-opt onto the board of directors is Robert (Bob) Steele, president and CEO of Stellarton Resources, now Stellarton Energy Corporation. He is an advocate, supporter, and network creator for GENA. His connections in the corporate world open doors to the Galileo staff, and he helps place reform on the agendas of several new partners. Bob Steele contributes to strategic planning and goal setting.

For both outside corporate supporters and professionals in schools, the dominant image is one of "critical friends" who support, criticize, and suggest new directions (Sizer, 1996). Bob Steele is joined by other critical friends, such as Annette LaGrange, Dean of the Faculty of Education at the University of Calgary; Earl Hickok, president of Tecskor, Inc.; Dr. Norman E. Wagner, former president of the University of Calgary; Ursula Mergny, a former school division superintendent of finance; and Dr. Bert Einsiedel, of the Institute for Professional Development at the University of Alberta. Bob Steele, Chair of GENA's board of directors, says the biggest challenge is a "lack of synchronization or connection with where the world is going" (personal communication, June 2000). Jack Gallagher's enthusiasm and interests are reincarnated in this group.

GENA is a very small, personal organization focusing on relationships. A key theme of their work with teachers, students, and school boards is building relationships for a common goal. The prime directive for their work with business, government, and community partners is personal relationships for mutual benefits. Just as there is no template approach to working with individual teachers and different school divisions, there is no set approach to seeking out and connecting with potential partners and alliances. GENA looks for individuals like Bob Steele, whose corporation encourages every employee to volunteer with an organization of their choice. In his firm, there are no mandated volunteers, but there is a strong corporate culture that stresses participation in the community.

Aside from business executives, GENA pursues cutting-edge experts in technology, such as Jan Vandenbos, an IT architect in Seattle. To establish a technical network for Banded Peak School, Jan becomes involved in the initial Galileo Centre. In the ever changing world of technology, Jan moves among many employers. Although he now lives and works in the United States, Jan Vandenbos continues with GENA.

People like Jan are similar to those who earn the Gallagher–Galileo Fellowship. This grant enables an *exceptional new scholar* to work for one year to consolidate research training, develop and initiate original research in information and communication technology, and contribute to the activities of the Galileo Educational Network. The ongoing relationships built with new scholars supports and extends the work of GENA.

The process of building relationships to secure financial support and find new people is shown by the unusual partnership with a law firm. Vance Milligan of the law firm of Bennett Jones is to incorporate the Galileo project under the Charities Act, but becomes a continuing partner. Since Vance is a senior partner with a large multinational legal firm, he cannot give much of his own time, but what time he does give is always donated. In the first meeting, he says "My time is cheap, but Gerald's time is expensive." He introduces GENA's core group to Gerald Grenon, who drafts the application for charitable status. In turn, Gerald comes to serve on GENA's board of directors after he moves to Donahue, Ernst & Young. There are two legal firms that advocate for GENA. Both Vance and Gerald continue to offer advice as well as bringing in others from their firms.

In the professions, businesses, universities, and schools, there are many advocates for GENA who provide ready testimonials about the importance of the project for their personal satisfaction and its importance for their children and grandchildren. These like-minded people support new models of thinking, energetic school staff, and new expectations for the teaching of mathematics and technology. GENA brings together a group who creates diverse ways of thinking—many voices with a common purpose.

## MEASURING BENEFITS

In response to questions like, "How will you know that you or your organization has made a difference?" most of the partners respond that they may never know. The overall impact of the Galileo Educational Network will be measured, but it would be impossible to ascribe particular outcomes or benefits from any one organization's support. The network of strategic alliances that support GENA are collectively working toward the common good (Sizer, 1992).

Ideas do not belong to individuals or to a small number of people, but arise from an interconnected community. This community shares ideas and provides informed conversation (Sizer, 1992). The value added by education is a new way of thinking that partners use in interpreting GENA. Looking at the educational process or play, Michele Jacobsen, the first Galileo Fellowship recipient, conducts a two-year evaluation of GENA's work in schools, disseminating the results among academic audiences. Her study is part of a comprehensive key performance indicators research shown in Table 3.1, which

**TABLE 3.1**
**Key Indicators for Evaluating the Galileo Network**

1. Increased student achievement of participating students as documented by the following:
   a. Alberta student achievement results for Grades 3, 6, 9, and departmental exams for Grade 12
   b. new Alberta ICT assessment tasks for Grades 3, 6, 9, and 11
   c. North Central Regional Educational Laboratory (NCREL) indicators of engaged learning and high technology performance
   d. student portfolios
   e. student self-assessments.
2. Participating teachers and administrators perceive improved implementation of ICT program.
3. Documented prototypes of collaborative on-line and face-to-face learning communities, a number of different models that show effective teaching and learning in technologically enhanced and innovative environments.
4. Established support from business, government, and education stakeholders.
5. GENA advising government on policy issues.
6. Number of schools and school divisions requesting GENAs on-site mentoring program.
7. Number of individual schools and school divisions requesting GENAs on-site mentoring program.
8. Teachers are granted accreditation for their participation in Galileo Network programs—evidence of post-degree continuous learning.
9. Contributions to the body of research on effective ICT implementation in K–12 educational institutions and in post-secondary institutions.
10. Research and prepared models for ICT leadership and professional development.

reflect the concerns of the Network. Table 3.1 is a summary of GENA's development.

GENA defines goals that will challenge them for the next three years. The network of innovative schools with proven examples of effective infusion of the new technology curriculum and engaging examples of student projects are available on-line. GENA seeks entrepreneurial educators to help transform education. After one year of operation, GENA develops some set ways of doing things, which it must examine! If GENA wants to continue to innovate, advocate, and develop as a reform initiative, the Network has to be very careful in hiring, looking for people different from themselves. New alliances are sought with different kinds of partners. The individual approach to partners, schools, and staff continues.

## THE NETWORK'S WORK

The goals and procedures implemented in each school are jointly created and are unique to each situation. As a result of joint planning in 1999/2000, one school listed six categories of expectations for the working relationship and outcomes of this commitment to GENA. The school's first expectation relates to *network access.* Their goal is for students to access a computer and network whenever they want, from any place in the school, and the response time for support from GENA would be fast and reliable.

Their second expectation is to achieve a *high degree of collaboration* among teachers, students, school, and home. The school wants to develop relationships that influence parents to invest in the school's vision. They select teaching staff members who learn from and with one another. The nature of this school's collaboration is based upon interdependence, a community of learners, and strong personal connections.

This school's third expectation relates to *student achievement.* School staff concentrate on increased depth, and set a new benchmark to ensure that students reach their potential. Staff members foster a passionate engagement with learning, and provide opportunities for students to share and produce knowledge. Students do projects that add to the community, which *focuses on citizenship*, the school's fourth expectation. The school develops an emphasis on social justice and empowerment of students to make a difference in the community. A related concern is acceptance of diversity among cultures.

This school's fifth expectation is to *improve teaching and learning.* The school staff critique practice, focus on teamwork, work openly, share knowledge with others, and develop leadership. These practices change the *organizational structure,* the school's sixth expectation. This school's plan is to increase enrollment by infusing technology in the classroom from preschool to Grade 6. School staff build a new computer network, wiring, and classroom configuration, and plan for building renovations to maximize the space for learning possibilities. They plan long blocks of uninterrupted time, and multigrading or other mechanisms to keep children together for more than one year.

Aside from its intensive coaching and mentoring with 10 individual schools, GENA is involved with higher education. GENA is a part of undergraduate and graduate programs at the University of Calgary. GENA is coordinating post-degree continuous learning opportunities for teachers involved in on-site coaching programs for graduate credit with the Universities of Lethbridge and Calgary. GENA staff collaborate with a series of universities' research projects, including a nationally funded evaluation project with the Institute for Professional Development at the University of Alberta. An encouraging finding of this national study is that teachers implement different teaching and learning strategies and integrate new technologies, which the teachers admit they would not do without support of the Galileo teachers.

The role of the Galileo Educational Network is to advocate for educational innovators. In order to promote GENA, extend its mission, and enhance its impact, there are new activities emerging: summer institute, video and CD-ROM, newsletter, continuing press stories, school events and demonstrations, new partnerships, and an expectation for each partner to both promote and advocate for GENA. A high profile partnership is developing in China that creates a virtual classroom for a middle school In Haikou, the capital city of Hainan Province (Galileo Educational Network Association, 2001). These additional activities are a part of the GENA strategy to promote the project. Promotion is essential to GENA's success because its existence depends upon maintaining demand for its services in schools, and continuing a supportive network of organizations, corporate and private supporters, universities, and others. Promotion requires supporting results.

## EDITOR'S NOTE

Educational change is like a religious movement. In the massive reforms of Chicago and Kentucky, political leaders died while working for reforms in education (Mitchell, 1996); Jack Gallagher is the martyr for the Galileo network. The core group of staff are as dedicated to their mission as any disciples. The faith of the believers is a reason why "there is no point in watering the rocks." Justification is through the results of research and the networks of partners, not by faith alone. The research on GENA is done by believers in the project.

It is perhaps surprising to find religious parallels in a project involving technology. GENA seeks an inspirational model from general American reforms while ignoring significant technological reforms, such as those affiliated with the Triangle Coalition for Science and Technology Education (Fowler, 1991: Williams et al., 1992). The trip to Rhode Island occurs when opponents at home are intensifying their attacks. The Coalition of Effective Schools suggests a path for independence while building on the support offered by its existing corporate and professional partners. The description of five expectations for one school reveals that technology is only related to a plan for attracting more students. Otherwise, GENA is repackaging educational objectives.

The partners and technology are alike in providing a means for reforming education. The quality of relationships leads to an individual conception of school projects. The individual relationships are the process that makes GENA a way of life for those who have seen the light. This is a striking contrast to the educational innovations discussed in the previous chapters. Perhaps for the founders, professional development schools had a similar function. When teachers and administrators in Chapter 2 adopt the researcher's perspective, they have only one part of GENA's broader focus. Business and professionals outside of education add valuable insights and create alliances that make a partnership more attractive. The next chapter looks at the options among partnerships and shows how individual professionals contribute to education in different kinds of relationships.

4

# Why Do Some Partnerships Endure with Individual Professionals?

Deborah Bainer Jenkins

During the past two decades, school reform advocates discussed educational partnerships as a promising vehicle to provide resources, improve teaching, and enhance student learning. Collaboration among educators at all levels with state and local policymakers, business and industry representatives, parents, and the community at large, is essential for significant change in education. In the early 1980s, the federal government of the United States recognized the need for schools to draw on the resources of the business community. As a result, partnerships spread across the country at an astonishing rate. By 1989, the Department of Education estimated that over 140,000 partnerships between schools and businesses existed nationwide (Rigden, 1991).

The momentum to establish partnerships continues, as illustrated by the 1996 National Science Foundation (NSF) theme, *Dynamic Partnerships: Seeding and Sustaining Education Reform*, and NSF's interest in funding collaborative partnerships are viewed as the means to achieve lasting reform in education (L.S. Willimas, personal communication, December 13, 1995). National organizations, such as the Points of Light Foundation, established by former President George Bush, and the National Association for Partnerships in Education (NAPE) and its state affiliates, coordinate and expand partnership efforts into businesses, industries, and agencies.

The dynamic nature and scope of partnerships makes it difficult to describe what an educational partnership is. Rigden (1991) organizes partnerships along a continuum that highlights the variety of forms and activities partnerships assume. The continuum moves from "adopt-a-school" relationships, originally proposed to link businesses with urban schools to improve employment opportunities for inner-city youths (Britt, 1985/86) to "great projects" partnerships, in which volunteers from businesses or agencies work with schools for a specific innovation, such as a new reading program or a science fair. A further development beyond great efforts is "reform-based" or collaborative partnerships where businesses or agencies enter into long-term relationships with schools specifically to impact instruction, student learning, and teacher empowerment, with the ultimate goal being to bring about school reform (Rigden, 1992).

Studying such enduring partnerships indicates there are a variety of ways partnerships organize into various types of activities (Sills, Barron, & Heath, 1993). After a decade of working with educational partnerships, I observe some partnership efforts are dynamic and active from their inception, while others never develop. Some partnership teams suffer trauma yet endure, while others disband when faced with stress. The question is what characterizes lasting partnerships (Bainer, 1998)? Are there core characteristics essential to different partnership patterns?

In looking at endurance, the initial research assumes that an enduring effort will achieve its goals more than partnerships that do not endure. Participants in a reform-based partnership program are asked what they thought is essential to a partnership's endurance or demise based on their experience in elementary (K–6) school settings. An interpretation is made between the assumption of singular effectiveness and participants' experiences. The meaning of partnerships changes as varied forms of partnership are considered. Later, partnership endurance is reinterpreted in terms of three organizational forms (Wright 1994, 1996)

For both interpretations, the term "partnership" refers to a relationship between two or more individuals or agencies, at least one of whom is an educator, school, or school district. The term "resource professional" meant an individual involved in a working relationship with educators aimed at sharing expertise in order to impact education. Resource professionals are from businesses, industries, or government, health care, or community agencies but may be private citizens, such as farmers or hobbyists, who know about some aspect of science. The sponsors find mutual benefits from the partnerships and the individual resource professionals reveal a variety of rewards.

## MODELS OF EFFECTIVE PARTNERSHIPS

Cobb and Quaglia (1994) point out that we need to know more about partnerships to ensure successful school reform. The literature offers models of group efforts derived from considering organizational systems (Hord, 1981), interactions during program evaluations (Wichienwong, 1988), and established partnerships between businesses and schools (Cobb & Quaglia, 1994; Sills et al., 1993). These models agree that most effective partnerships are dynamic and interactive, work toward common goals, and are characterized by equality and a high level of commitment among group members (Bainer, 1997).

In contrast, Wright (1994, 1996) presents a model of group efforts derived from mathematical theory. Wright's model provides insight into group efforts to form and sustain partnerships. He develops an approach to describe the different ways groups organize themselves. Partnerships contain individual abilities forming a microstructure that is used to predict overall group effectiveness. "Composition analysis" suggests three organizational patterns for group efforts.

### Packs

Packs are characterized by diversity and independence. Members disagree with each other, but the pack collectively benefits as it works through problems and disagreements, drawing upon the divergent approaches and viewpoints of its members. Because members express more divergent concerns in the group, a pack becomes stronger as it increases in size. A pack succeeds when each individual member succeeds. This configuration works by solving intermediate and hard problems and it functions in difficult contexts. The pack is like an emergency task force, where the most talented people are assembled. Wright (1994) explains that a group of people looking for lost keys is acting like a pack: the keys are found when everyone agrees to disagree about where to look for them. The alternatives to a pack are interdependent roles organized to cover different problems in a chain, or everyone looking for the same answers in a team.

### Chains

Chains are specialized organizations, wherein individuals overcome their own limitations. Mountain climbers are organized like chains. Climbers are roped together; one moves forward while others hold on; and, finally, all climbers know when it is their turn to move and when they need to hold on and serve as anchors. If one climber acts out of turn, the entire group is endangered. A climber who falters is saved by those to whom he is roped. Chains of climbers are effective when each member knows what role to perform and does it.

### Teams

Teams are groups of people who agree with and support each other. Like a well-functioning jury, a team relies on consensus, whereas disagreements paralyze its functioning. The strength of a team comes from its individual members, and the ways these members solve team problems. Individual strengths are stronger than team experiences, making the team decisive. For example, in football, individuals who use their outstanding strength for their own recognition rather than team effort hurt the team. This configuration is effective for problems that are easy, involving routine tasks in problem-free contexts because the group members agree on one obvious course of action. When a team solves a problem, members continue in this formation. If the situation requires divergent thinking, the team is jeopardized by weaknesses, disagreements, or independence of the players.

As a project develops, chains create a cooperative workforce. Later, discord and disagreements harm the chain's efforts. Because of this, the group is threatened because, as the group increases in size, growth increases the likelihood of disagreements. Consider a task force whose large membership hinders its effective functioning. Stressful or difficult contexts limit members' ability in a chain to solve problems, although chains are more effective within difficult contexts than are teams. In theory, chains are connections for imperfect agreements that rely on solidarity (Wright, 1996).

Wright's (1996) model posits that group projects evolve through a core sequence of *pack* to *chain* to *team*. Packs solve the hard initial problems and the transitional chains build solidarity and group structure, while teams ultimately implement and maintain the project. Applying this model to the experience of teachers and resource professionals engaged in educational reform, the question is whether partnerships are organized as packs or teams. An important issue is which configuration enables a partnership to endure in elementary school contexts.

## AN INNOVATION IN TEACHING SCIENCE

A first step in understanding partnerships is to find the common problem new partners explore. Teachers and resource professionals confront the question of enhancing science instruction and improving student learning. Two funded programs are involved: Partnering for Elementary Environmental Science (PEES) and Sciencing with Watersheds, Environmental Education, and Partnerships (SWEEP) (Bainer, et al., 1998). These programs in science education employ partnerships to support the professional development of elementary classroom teachers. The combined efforts overcome teachers' fears (1) by engaging them in hands-on learning, (2) debriefing them about the experience, and (3) separating the learner's point of view and from the facilitator or teacher's perspective. Discussions focus on developing a plan, learning about materials and resources, managing students while involving them in the project, and evaluating this hands-on learning experience.

The program provides a library of published materials that are available and agency-sponsored science and environmental programs. Internationally recognized programs such as Project Learning Tree, Project WET, and Project Wild are presented, as well as trade books. Participants use these materials to plan lessons, engage in activities to "get a feel" for them, and purchase selected ones from funds provided by the project.

In order to overcome teachers' lack of science knowledge, individuals are paired with science content experts. Most of these resource professionals are employees of the state Department of Natural Resources or county recycling, parks and recreation, soil and water conservation, or health agencies. Other content experts come from the Environmental Protection Agency, local conservation and environmental groups, and science-related businesses, such as Meade Paper Company and Lockheade Martin. A few others, including teachers with strong applied science backgrounds, volunteer.

These specialists promise to help teachers for at least one year and are representatives of organizations in partnership with the teacher's school. The organizations see mutual benefits, such as publicity for themselves, and improved science education for students. The joint goal is to establish reform-based partnerships that create collaborative, school-based projects.

During an intensive summer institute, teachers and resource professionals learn pedagogy and partnering skills, develop their relationship, identify curriculum and learning goals, and plan lessons for the upcoming academic year. Two day-long conferences are held during the academic year to bring the partnership teams together to share, evaluate, reflect, socialize, solve problems, and learn about new resources. Participants receive newsletters and site visits from members of other teams or project staff (available all year).

For five years, the program engages nearly 400 individuals in partnership teams as a result of state and federal funding. Partnerships range in size from two members (one teacher and one resource professional) to seven members (five teachers and two resource professionals). Most partnerships consist of two or three teachers working with one resource professional. Two-thirds of the partnerships are based in rural or small-town elementary schools, with the remainder in suburban and urban settings.

One year after government funding ends, researchers begin to examine why some partnerships are still functioning while others meet an early demise. Was this related to their structure? In-depth telephone interviews with all team leaders and focus groups with selected team members are conducted to understand which partnership teams persist beyond the funding period. In the prearranged telephone interviews, leaders describe the relationship among members, any changes in their groups, and any crises their group experiences. They define which groups continue or falter and relate the reasons for their group's experience. The leaders' reports define which groups continue and are expected to continue. Of the 62 leaders interviewed, 57 were teachers, 3 were resource professionals, and 2 were school administrators. Focus groups, each with 10–12 individuals who participate in partnerships for at least one year, respond to similar questions.

The data are transcribed, content analyzed, and verified by independent researchers. In an ongoing, inductive analysis, interviews are organized by themes. The patterns become obvious as the number of completed interviews increases and interview data is merged with focus group results. Three categories of characteristics are apparent: strong, moderate, and low predictors of a partnership's endurance or demise (Altrichter, et al., 1993). This difference among predictors are based on the judgment of researchers.

## RESEARCH RESULTS

Thirty-one of the leaders report that their partnerships are active. Of these, 6 teams last 1 year; 12 groups complete 2 years, 7 partners are involved for 3 years, and 6 teams continue after 4 years. All of these teams finish an academic year. An equal number of groups disband. Three of these never make it through their first year of partnering. Nineteen groups disband at the end of their one-year commitment to the program. Other partnerships continue before disbanding: 2 for 2 years, 2 for 3 years, and 5 for 4 years. Considering both active and inactive teams, the mean years of partnering is two and the mode is one year.

### Reasons Why Partnerships Endure

Responses to interviews and focus groups suggest seven characteristics of partnerships that are most frequently mentioned as reasons why the partnership endures. These emphasize the importance of impacting students and classroom instruction in an ambitious collaborative, rather than a problem-free undertaking. The seven strong predictors that consistently went together are:

1. *A strong resource professional* who generates ideas, works well with children, gathers resources, prepares in advance for activities, provides access to other resource professionals, provides content knowledge, is enthusiastic, and is a motivator;
2. *Commitment to the program*, including taking the program seriously, determining to finish the year-long plan, and committing time and resources to the program;
3. *Assistance in the classroom*, specifically having the team members, parents, and/or volunteers aid with gathering resources, making phone calls, and doing the "legwork" required of an activity-based, thematic curriculum;
4. *Collaboration* and interaction with other adults (teachers and resource professionals) who serve as sounding boards, enjoy working and learning from each other, fill in gaps in each others' knowledge of science and pedagogy, share similar expectations, and are trustworthy;
5. *Commitment to science education* and the environment, including a desire to make science learning fun, to provide an educationally sound program, to meet the district and state science objectives, to share a love of science and the environment and, ideally, to instill environmental stewardship in students;
6. *Benefits for children*, such as challenging them toward higher order thinking and problem solving, providing resource professionals as role models, providing positive learning experiences to enable them to learn content more readily, to work with students from other grade levels, and to relate concepts they learned in science to the "real world" of the environment; and, finally
7. *Positive relationships among partners*, including shared interests and age cohorts and compatible philosophies, attitudes toward children, and instructional approaches. Team members share the idea that collaboration is easy because team members enjoy working and learning together and because they think alike and support each other in solving problems. Consequently, strong friendships form.

Four "moderate predictors" or qualities are mentioned less frequently as reasons why partnerships endure, focusing on individual benefits:

1. *Excitement and satisfaction* with the program because of the hands-on learning and field trips it encourages, the questions it raises in

students' minds, which they subsequently explore, the positive reactions of students to the program, and the longterm changes seen in students' behavior and learning;

2. *Professional growth and development*, especially in student management, science content, and teambuilding. Expanded community networks help teachers learn about professional development opportunities and resources;
3. *Parents*, who share excitement for the program, support and volunteer for the program, and request that their children be involved in the program; and,
4. *Administrative support*, providing program visibility within the building and district and facilitating the expansion of the program to include additional teachers and classrooms.

Five "mild predictors" of partnership endurance are far less frequent than moderate or strong predictors. They emphasize broad conditions in the school and society: equal relationships among team members; flexible scheduling and communications; teaming relationship in working with children; school fundraising and professional development opportunities; and community benefits from recycling and removal of debris.

### Reasons for Partnership Demise

While personal benefits and broader conditions reinforce the seven conditions for partnership, immediate conditions negate partnerships. The characteristics that lead to their demise speak of a troubled work arrangement in which members lack commitment to the group, program, or sponsors, or are disrupted by personnel changes. The challenge is to reestablish social relationships. Five problems, which are also linked together, involve the daily interaction of partnerships and cause more stress than the partnership can handle:

1. *Lack of commitment by the resource professional* is demonstrated by not wanting to partner, working with children, or making long-term arrangements because of competing demands for time;
2. *Job change for the resource professional*, such as being transferred to another position or shifting job responsibilities, often leading to withdrawal from the partnership;
3. *Lack of commitment by the partnering agency* is illustrated by a lack of long-term support, especially for the time off required by resource professionals to participate in an extended partnership;
4. *Job change for the teacher*, including moves to another grade level, content area, or building or in order to reorganize the school or teaching location; and, lastly,

5. *Lack of relationship among partners*, experienced as incompatibility of philosophy, energy level, personality, or "power level," lack of common interests, lack of consideration and mutual support, lack of critical mass and support in small partnerships, and lack of communication. Leaders observe that partners "just didn't click."

"Moderate predictors" of problems cover less frequently mentioned work conditions, including proximity and lack of shared responsibility. The first set of problems could be overcome by a partnership with a supporting cast, but deaths, competing loyalties, or feuds among staff are permanent barriers to a well-established partnership, but they are the odd occurrences:

1. *Trauma or drastic change*, such as the loss of a teacher or resource professional as a team member through staff changes, loss of a classroom through school reorganization, loss of a land lab, or strike threats;
2. *Lack of commitment by teachers* because of competing demands of programs already at the school, misunderstanding about the length of the program commitment, or a mismatch with the program's goals;
3. *Proximity*, that is, teachers are located in different buildings or the resource professional is distant from the school; and,
4. *Lack of equity* is demonstrated in a partnership in which all team members did not share the responsibility for planning, preparation, and communication, and they do not share professional knowledge;

A host of other problems leads to the demise of partnerships, involving anyone affecting the relationship, including parents, curriculum changes, or lack of continuing challenges from the partnership. These six problems could become excuses for those who would abandon partnerships: resource professionals who do not flexibly relate to children or the team; school administration who do not see the program as important; other teachers who resent not being involved; teachers who believe the partnership has served its purpose; curriculum changes or unrealistic plans that involve too many people, grades, or courses of study; and parents who complain about the activity projects, or those who want their children transferred into the program.

## CONSEQUENCES FOR THEORY

If a partnership's endurance is a proxy for its effectiveness, it is important to understand what contributes to endurance or demise. Reviewing the predictors of partnership endurance in the light of

Wright's (1994) model helps us understand the organizational patterns of the partnerships in this funded program. Recall the program's target reform-based partnerships, which, by definition, are long term and are supported by multiple levels within the school and partnering agency. Enduring partners are goal-oriented, collaborative, and focused on enhancing science instruction.

The characteristics identified as qualities of continuing partnerships demonstrate that these groups are examples of teams. Teams are comprised of strong individual members. The most frequently cited predictor is a strong resource professional. Fifty-seven of 62 team leaders are teachers who hesitate to characterize themselves as strong, or to identify teacher strength as a reason why the partnership endured. The strength of the members and their commitment to the program and to education is pervasive in this list.

Members help each other to reach the team's goal. Leaders of the enduring teams speak of the resource professionals and teachers providing classroom assistance for each other—gathering resources, making telephone calls, cleaning up after activities, managing students during activities, paperwork, and routine classroom chores. One of the main roles for the resource professional is to connect teachers with resources from their agency and the community, thus enriching the science curriculum. Mutual help, characteristic of teams, is revealed by the enduring team members' commitment to the program—developing and carrying out the year-long curriculum plan.

As the theory predicts, interviews reveal that enduring teams are compatible, homogeneous, and "just plain liked each other." Members of partnerships that endure share a strong commitment to the program, to science education, and to the environment. They arrive at mutual goals, drawing upon the strengths of the group. Members of enduring teams enjoy having other adults in their classrooms because they are about the same age, sharing the same interests and love for science. The theory posits that the amiable team's structure is most effective in relatively problem-free contexts. Leaders relate the support and enthusiasm from their students, administrators, parents, and the community as reasons teams "work" in many elementary schools.

Were the partnerships that meet their demise not organized as teams? The list of qualities that lead to a partnership's decline reads like a mirror image of the endurance qualities. The list suggests that these teams have weak resource persons or lack commitment by the resource professional, teacher or teachers, partnering agency, and/or school administration. A poor initial match is later compounded with disagreements to make the relationship more difficult. Leaders of demised teams speak of incompatible philosophies and energy levels. Individuals from partnerships with only two members cite the "lack of critical mass" and support.

Another explanation is that the disbanded teams are originally teams, but that they become inflexible. Perhaps some members of these disbanded partnerships expect the group to work like a team but the group has some independent individuals posing different viewpoints, challenging other team members' thinking, wanting to fill more specialized roles, or resisting social interactions with the group. Some resource professionals bring different perspectives to the partnership, do not interact amiably, and are not accepted by elementary teachers.

During the first year of the partnership, diversity creates discord. If the partnership is inflexible and restricts itself to a team, demise follows. If the group acknowledges its diversity and changes to a pack pattern, the partnership may endure and perhaps flourish. The lack of ability or willingness to modify the partnership's organization explains the breakdown of a partnership team.

## SPECIFIC CASES

An adaptable partnership is formed by a fifth-grade teacher and a resource professional who was director of a historic farm. Many local residents oppose the state's proposal to refocus the farm into a living museum. Nancy, the teacher, is outspoken in the effort to preserve the farm and its herd of cows. Bill, the farm manager, removes the cows, leaving a trail of resentment in the community.

Soon after their pairing, it is obvious that Nancy and Bill are not a match for a partnership, but the partnership enables them to achieve mutual goals. Although they are not friends, they determine to work together in spite of their differences. The partnership is active, provides programs to Nancy's class and others in the school, and leads to professional development for Nancy and Bill. At the end of the year, they agree to disband their partnership.

Bill and Nancy part on good terms, yet disagree on issues related to the farm. Nancy and Bill discover that, although they share many educational goals, they organize their partnership as a pack. The strength and energy of this partnership is rooted in its diversity and synergistic thinking. The pack enables both members to benefit. If such people organize or present themselves as a team, their partnership fails.

Another interpretation is that the disbanded teams are organized as teams, but function in a negative and stressful context. Members of defunct teams describe adverse working conditions: lack of support from school administrators and partnering agencies and parents or teachers who complain about the program. The distance of the resource professional from the school creates stress; one partner drives two and a half hours to the school site. A pack allows divergent thinking and role specialization to solve situational problems.

A fourth possibility is that the now-defunct partnerships are unable to solve problems involving job changes. For example, three teachers in one partnership are transferred to different grade levels and buildings before the end of the summer, and they stop cooperating at the beginning of the school year. Curriculum changes account for other demises. Partnerships with teachers from many grade levels from different courses of study tend not to endure, nor did those that develop curriculum plans too grandiose for the allotted time.

Two exceptional partnerships function as packs rather than teams. The first such partnership, dubbed the Central partnership, is comprised of Kevin, a male sixth-grade teacher; Stacy, a female sixth-grade teacher in the same building; Linda, the curriculum director for the school district who works out of the central office; and Donna, an enthusiastic resource professional. Team members work together and became good friends. Their enthusiasm for the program leads to a second partnership at another school in their district. Donna serves as the resource professional for that team as well, and Linda joins with two female third- and fourth-grade teachers from that school to form the new partnership. During the second year, Kevin dies. The remaining members of the partnership are devastated. The original partnership disbands for the remainder of the year, but reorganizes into a three-member team, partly as a tribute to Kevin.

A second unique case is the Brooks–Brooks team, named for two of the members, Bobbie Brooks, a fifth-grade teacher, and Dick Brooks, a sixth-grade teacher, who are married. Also part of the partnership are Sharon, a fourth-grade teacher from another building in the district, and two resource professionals, Roberta and Cheryl. From the beginning, this partnership experiences difficulty. Cheryl wants to withdraw from the summer institute because she sees no reason to partner, did not like the program, and wants no direct involvement with children. Although she provides little input, she stays. Cheryl is upset by multiple grade levels, different courses of study, and conflicting personalities, which cause problems in developing a year-long, innovative science curriculum.

The Brookses began the school year with a bang; they knocked down the wall separating Bobbie and Dick's adjoining classrooms to make one learning area, although they had no approval for this change. They forge ahead and gain permission to combine classes across the two buildings for many activities, using school buses and parent volunteers. This group communicates across buildings as pen pals (the rural schools had no computers), sets up buddy systems across grade levels, and establishes collaborative learning activities among the classes. They rotate locations and times for team planning sessions, for combined class activities, and for field trips. The energy and enthusiasm of those in the partnership spreads to the students and parents. Cheryl is won over and becomes a vital and enthusiastic team member.

The Brooks group experiences difficulties: Cheryl changes jobs and works farther from the school; Roberta's work changes, limiting her availability to the partnership; and a new resource person joins the group, but is a weak member. District budgets tighten and buses are no longer available. The Brooks–Brooks partnership endures and flourishes for years. Group members provide in-service to other district teachers relating to hands-on science and partnering. They establish additional partnerships within the district, write and win grants to purchase equipment and develop land labs, present papers at professional conferences about their partnership experience, and experience professional and personal growth.

The Central and Brooks–Brooks partnerships exhibit both characteristics of partnerships that endure and the characteristics that lead to a partnership's demise. The reason they endure difficult contexts and serious problems when other teams did not is they are organized as packs rather than teams. The leadership of teams is different from that of packs. A team shares leadership through the year—a facilitator rather than one chief. Because of the homogeneity and agreement among team members, there is no person who is the dominant leader.

In contrast, a pack has a distinct leader; not a master, but one who listens to and responds to all members, then motivates group members to move toward their common goal. A recognized leader is necessary to moderate the disagreements and divergent thinking within a pack. Dick assumes the leadership role with the Brooks–Brooks partnership, while Linda moderates the Central group.

Some individuals function comfortably in teams, while others prefer packs. For teams, individual strengths are stronger than the problems the team experiences. The team configuration is too restrictive for some individuals. In the Brooks–Brooks team, Cheryl changes when she realizes she possesses unique knowledge and "connections" to contribute to the partnership. She discovers a distinctive and vital role. The learning styles of sanguine individuals lead them to collaborative efforts, but independent people, who are divergent thinkers and relish the challenge of resolving conflicts. The only person in the Central and the Brooks–Brooks partnerships who is not independent is the resource person added to the Brooks–Brooks partnership.

## IMPLICATIONS

The model of different types of partnerships cannot be tested because the partnerships are based on a reform innovation and the evidence is exploratory. The insights gained from Wright's model and from the interviews and focus group data suggest alternatives for partnerships. Should partnerships be built as teams or packs? Most partnership efforts are based on a team configuration. Is this the best approach? This study suggests building packs instead of teams—at least in difficult educational contexts.

Who is placed on teams should be considered in terms of the people with whom they will work and the context in which they will collaborate. Early in our summer institute, "job alike" groups are conducted. The teachers form one group, and the resource professionals meet in a separate room. They brainstorm what they want the other group to know about their work environment. Later, the two groups come together and share their lists. Similarities and differences of the two lists summarize the activity. This project enables group members to correct misunderstandings about the others and begin to understand their roles.

How partnerships are organized needs to be examined. Does an individual prefer group work, or is independent problem solving his or her forte? Does the individual need the approval of others, challenges, or space? Availability of time, compatibility, and commitment are critical considerations for teams. Individuals entering an educational partnership require partnering skills. Partnership members might form teams or morph into packs as the context changes or as situations demand. Flexibility rather than rigidity is the key to partnership endurance.

Case studies can target how partnerships are composed, functioned, and endured. How do partnership members interact with each other? How and when do partners change the structure of partnerships? Are individuals with different learning styles more effective in different organizational structures? Is one organizational structure better than another at bringing about educational change?

## EDITOR'S NOTE

The author has a number of ideas that should be linked and developed: business partnerships and partners for science; her study and Wright's theory; and the meaning of endurance and flexibility or further development. Business partnerships involve paternalism with few joint aims, but when they are linked in a comprehensive plan, they will appear as packs. The Atlanta Project, which brings businesses together with schools and community agencies, is a pack trying to become a chain with schools as the linchpin for over 17,000 volunteers in Atlanta (Mitchell, 1996).

Most business partnerships do not involve this combination of agencies and expertise. The adopt-a-schools program seldom becomes a complicated project, certainly not a comprehensive reform plan. However, the Galileo network has moved in this direction. The number of sponsors grew as it moved from one school to a larger network.

The writer links her theoretical interest in forms of partnerships with a study of two to seven individuals in schools. Teams and packs are considered in her case description and the possibility of chains is omitted. It is not clear that she has followed the mathematical conception of Wright nor that he means for it to be so limiting. Individuals and small groups form larger movements. Chicago reform is an example of such a movement that enlisted the commitment of individuals into broader coalitions (Mitchell, 1996). Individual concerns, then, became political efforts.

The evidence in this study suggests that effective partnerships are influenced by the efforts of students and parents. There is more to reform than links among individuals, no matter how expert they are. In this study, professionals initiate the activities, but students are expected to respond and parents create problems. In successful teams, professionals need to make commitments, but their positions move others to action.

Though a lack of dedication could lead to job changes, this study tells us job changes are the major constraints for teachers or professionals. The distinction between dissatisfiers with immediate conditions in work and motivators for the growth of individuals has a long history in psychology (Herzberg, 1966). Current educational reforms show that growth can be related to broader concerns about inequality. If people are mobilized in a movement, this is not the case. In a broader context, links among schools, as well as within them, provide support for teachers and resource professionals to achieve equality.

Some of the cases suggest more extensive developments. Three individuals, Kevin, Linda, and Donna, develop their own support structure. They cross three different fields: teaching, curriculum planning, and resource work. Though the author sees this partnership as a pack, it could be a chain. If this effective partnership is a chain, then upon the death of Kevin it becomes a pack. In contrast, chains are a link to broader areas.

Though they can expand, partnerships are very unstable and are never to be taken for granted. They last two years or less, depending upon the commitment of the teachers and resource professionals. In Chapter 3, partnerships that develop more varied allies have more possibilities of continuing support, but a basic change is required every three years.

In this chapter, the problems of individual resource personnel part-nering with teachers is as limited as the original parallel to adopt-a-school business partnerships. Neither begins to expand the scope of educational reform. It is not a question of studying partnerships that result from innovation or participants knowing about the theory that is important. It is how these partnerships are linked to their communities and expanded to different settings that is critical.

The context of partnerships is ignored in this study. The rural and small-town places of Ohio provide these partnerships with more than farm animals. Chapters 10 and 11 explore the limits of a rural setting. Chapter ll shows that available partners and subsequent relationship are different. Partners in other rural areas travel thousands of miles in order to meet and plan, more than two and a half hour's drive away from a partner, which is said to be a limit in this case.

The team structure is a result of the more informal and family-like, or "gemeinschaft," structures in rural areas. The friendships that form easily would be consistent with this view. The team structure relates to the communities as well as elementary schools. Packs would emerge if links are established with other schools and other communities, as described in Chapter 11. The limited concern for equity in relationships is a reflection of the limited life in elementary schools and the lack of political direction for the partners.

Chapters 5 and 6 show simple structures suffice for technological or business partnerships. Multiple community relationships become packs and chains in Chapters 7 and 8. In Chapter 9, complex reform efforts for dealing with education, health, and social deprivation sug-gest chains (Mitchell, 1998). Large-scale reforms require complicated structures, but simpler teams suffice for classroom changes in tradi-tional settings.

# II

# Advocating Specific Changes

Are we in partnership with the schools? We have a very close relationship with the schools, the teachers, but we are not partners. We are the providers and they are the purchasers, which is not exactly a partnership. The schools did not come to us and say, "We need you to do this, so let's do this together." We created it, and they bought it (Mark Schubert cited in Remer, 1996, p. 160)

Mark Schubert was the founding director of arts education for the Lincoln Center. He raises the essential questions for promoters of any kind of packaged programs. Are you sharing common goals with those you claim to serve? Are there complimentary functions for your activities and theirs? How do you change your strategies?

Computer technology has become a basic skill for students in schools, and adults in the workplace. The planners of these programs often are administrators of institutes. In Chapter 5, the case of EnterTech offers virtual school training helping clients to obtain employment. The male experts make little attempt to understand mothers on welfare. The programs are often changed on the basis of technological thinking, but the experts do not try to get beyond this approach. Unlike expert-based partnerships discussed in Part I, where the directions are often unknown, EnterTech combines scientific thinking with business goals to produce clear strategies.

Similar strategies are the environmental basis for combining a market-like relationship with community improvement and education of students. Reclaiming building materials has meant current builders save on the cost of removal, customers for materials at another site save, schools create job-related training for at-risk students, and, most of all, the environment is saved from filling available dump sites. For Enviroworks, the choice for a profit program, rather than a non-profit one, initially was simple since the schools was acting as an agent for others (Mitchell, 2000). Over time, Enviroworks found tactics, such as networking, became crucial for both their profit and community improvement goals.

Community partners are a direct basis for a partnership created by university students. Students have taken the lead in developing service projects for communities (Mitchell, 1998). These students are aware they have to understand people very different from themselves. In order to develop a list of specific programs, students consider the needs of the community and relate to a host of organizations, trying to work within the same neighbourhood.

The biggest problem for Neighbors Project is their own parent organization, the university. Students at one university attempt to work with the organization of students at another university. The same university that supports them in working with a host of community organizations does not know how to modify its own organization so the students can work with a rival. University hierarchies are not attuned to service partnerships.

The test of idealism becomes more definite when a university is one of three recognized and respected organizations working together. Though the university, a symphony orchestra, and school systems share a commitment to music education, these partners experience the instability characteristic of developmental partnerships discussed in Part I. The Kingston Symphony Educational Partnership is shown to develop very specific strategies to survive longer than more global partnerships. For example, music students must work in teams on music in the curriculum and with supervising teachers. In addition, the supervising teachers must integrate the work of student-teacher teams with their own teaching as well as contributions by symphony members to individual classes.

Arts education in this case becomes more than the selling of a packaged program. Like the other arts, music education can not match the support other projects obtain. Neither government support for the technology of EnterTech, government and business support for Enviroworks, nor foundation support available to the Neighbors Project are available to the Kingston Symphony Partnership. Not even the traditional patron sponsorship is available to the music partners.

The strength of the Kingston partnership is based on the people involved. University students are serving the less fortunate people in a poor community. Computer training by planners is very distant from welfare recipients. Students in the retrieval enterprise are a mystery; only the exchange of goods and services is clear. A grass-root organization can develop multiple relations and a number of specific strategies with its partners.

All of the partnerships develop ties with their environment. Organizations must be as varied as the demands placed on them by their communities, organizations must change their level of expectations (Morgan, 1997). The music partnership grows by going into small towns with its existing program; it does not connect with the other arts. The university student program tries in vain to connect with another university. EnterTech plans its universal expansion while Enviroworks seeks international recognition. There is no attempt to integrate any of these specific programs, and no integrated effort results from their individual organizations.

# 5

# Research Guides Education for Employment: EnterTech

Joseph W. Hauglie, Deaton Bednar,
Melinda Jackson, and Jordan E. Erdos

EnterTech is a unique collaboration between business and education partners in Texas. During the pilot phases of this program for high technology industries, some problems arose involving the adaptation to at-risk employees and the software behind EnterTech. Replication of this program could show its effectiveness in high technology and the kinds of strategies that partnerships could use in the future for different students. Results from pilot testing the current program are suggestive for those who would make future efforts.

During recent years, there are an increasing number of efforts to align business needs with the processes and outcomes of public education. Many industry and manufacturing alliances with school districts and community-based organizations are sponsored by government commissions. The common vision of these partnerships is to ensure that the community, state, or region has a viable pool of potential employees who will be capable of actively participating in the area's economy. From a business perspective, this goal translates to framing higher standards for incoming employees, while allocating fewer resources for bringing new workers to minimum skill levels. The educational partners establish clear justifications for certain types of vocational skills training, while offering students strong incentives for completing their schooling.

One of the greatest concerns for such coalitions is the relevancy of available skills instruction to the actual workplace environment. Recent secondary or technical school graduates find they did not receive adequate training on current tools, or their training emphasizes only a handful of skills required for entry-level work in a given industry. Basic employability skills, such as punctual attendance and good interpersonal communication, are overlooked. Many employers report that the lack of basic skills and adequate training are the reasons for turnover among their entry-level workers.

## ENTERTECH

The EnterTech Project is one collaboration that overcomes both of these obstacles. Through the medium of a computer-based virtual environment, EnterTech offers strong evidence that it is possible to create, design, implement, and support technology-based learning to target learners with the skills needed to gain and retain employment in the new economy.

This coalition consists of 23 employers, 31 educational entities, 10 government agencies, and 20 nongovernmental organizations (NGOs). They collaborate in the development, production, testing, and implementation of an innovative Web-based training program. The EnterTech model aims to provide a workforce to meet the labor needs of technology where unemployed and underemployed workers can earn adequate wages. Businesses and local education providers support this competency-based program.

EnterTech utilizes a realistic, interactive, Web-based simulation training program. Each learner acts as an employee with peers and supervisors in a virtual technology company. By recognizing and accommodating learner needs in a holistic and supportive learning environment, students achieve success in the EnterTech training program and bridge into better jobs, continued education, and sustainable futures. This program is a model for designing solutions to dual problems through stakeholder participation and innovative design.

## NEED ANALYSIS

A 1997 Texas Technology Survey conducted by the Texas Governor's Science and Technology Council found a growing workforce shortage among high-tech industry across the state, with more than 60 percent of the participating companies reporting unfilled jobs at various levels (Governor's Office, State of Texas, 1998). Many of these vacant positions offer opportunities for improved employment outcomes for at-risk populations by providing sustainable wages, career pathways, and continued skill improvement. While most service sector jobs begin at the federal minimum wage level, $5.15 per hour, the average starting wage for positions in the high-tech industry is $9 per hour or more (EnterTech Project Report, 1998). Entry-level jobs for high-tech firms include positions such as assembler, machine operator, manufacturing associate, material handler, production associate, or warehouse/shipping clerk.

Effective training is critical to obtaining these entry-level positions. Businesses and local educational institutions aim to find capable people for such jobs. Communication problems and different approaches of businesspeople and educators obstruct progress in understanding the needs of the other side. One group may criticize the ineffective efforts of the other, resulting in the unemployed individual losing an opportunity.

EnterTech Project coordinators recognize that to resolve this issue it is imperative to examine both the social and business sides of training. Project leaders understand it was crucial to state explicitly the objectives of job training for each concerned stakeholder: the employer, the educator, the state government, and the NGO. The common needs of the coalition members are in the foreground to frame the immediate vision and build support for the program.

## EMPLOYER'S PERSPECTIVE

The 1990 research study conducted by the (U.S.) National Alliance of Business identifies particular educational deficiencies that affect entry-level training, higher education, the education–work connection, continuing or on-the-job training, and life-long learning. The study estimates that by 1995, 14 million Americans would not be prepared for available jobs (Sharp, 1990). This estimate is accurate for many regions of the United States.

Austin, Texas, is one of the most rapidly growing areas of high-tech development in America, with several major employers such as Dell Computer, Motorola, and IBM. Over 200 computer hardware and support companies and 400 software companies are in and around the city. These employers seek key attributes among their incoming workforce: a willingness to learn and work in teams, adaptability, and individual reliability. They believe these "soft skills" are more important than a technical background.

From a business perspective, it is important that potential employees understand *a priori* that they are expected to fulfill certain responsibilities. Prospective employees must know there are consequences for not fulfilling those obligations, or for making poor choices in daily situations. A willingness to obey instruction is a fundamental requirement for all employees. Without skills and a positive attitude, it is difficult for applicants to hold positions that lead to definable career paths in high-skill, high-wage occupational areas.

A 1996 report produced by a key local semi-conductor industry coalition projects a need for 5,000 skilled workers in the following three to five years to meet the minimum expectations of regional industry growth (Squires, 1996). Many of the workers who would be hired to fill these positions would likely be unqualified, needing to acquire skills as they work. This lack of workplace readiness requires additional investments of time and resources that most employers would rather not make with new workers. Employers want assurance that the employees they hire understand the reality of their job so they know the expectations and perform accordingly.

## EDUCATOR'S VIEW

More than ever before, today's educators are being challenged to validate their students' abilities against local and national performance norms. These criteria are based partly on economic data, which indicates job skills most likely to be necessary or valuable in the future. Ultimately, educators want students to learn skills that enable them to adapt to workplace variety for their careers. Many school districts and local programs understand the need to prepare students for the changing workforce. A comprehensive summary of the underlying need for a program such as EnterTech underscores the imperative for education to respond to industry's needs for qualified workers that cannot be met by the existing workforce or by current training programs (Erdos, 2000).

## GOVERNMENT'S POSITION

Recent U.S. state and federal welfare reforms mandate that aid recipients make a transition from welfare as quickly and efficiently as possible. Such legislation aims to leverage the current national economic surge by creating further opportunities for former welfare recipients to reenter the workforce. In Texas, there is great pressure to implement welfare policy changes. The administration of former Governor George W. Bush identified recipients of Texas Aid to Needy Families (TANF) as a large, untapped potential pool for employers, and devotes significant resources to finding ways to help individuals on public assistance or those who otherwise do not see themselves as part of the new technology-based economy. Increased opportunities for education and training are being offered as paths for individuals to move into employment in the technology sector and to make greater progress toward self-sufficiency.

## NONGOVERNMENTAL ORGANIZATIONS (NGOs)

As a result of the government's shift in social policy, there are demands being placed on many NGOs to assist in the process of moving people from welfare to gainful work. NGOs in the central Texas area specifically address the needs of incumbent workers, TANF recipients, and unemployed or underemployed individuals. Their primary concern is linking people coming out of a NGO's workforce development program with jobs that pay a living wage and hold advancement potential. NGOs address issues, such as transportation and childcare, for their program participants to make successful transitions.

These organizations recognize the difficulties faced by target populations. Each NGO seeks innovative ways to address them. Like employers and educators, NGOs recognize the importance of teaching and encouraging personal responsibility skills in addition to basic math and reading skills. They want to introduce at-risk populations to technology and computers. Without such knowledge capital, no employee in today's workforce can succeed or advance.

## BUILDING PARTNERSHIPS

While their various perspectives on training may be distinct, the goals of the stakeholders are similar. The question faced by many members of the Austin business, government, agency, and higher education communities is how to assemble a coalition of representatives that would not only address these issues, but resolve them more effectively than before. In 1995, Dr. George Kozmetsky, founder and chair of the $IC^2$ Institute of the University of Texas at Austin, began a series of informal meetings with high-level training representatives from local high-tech companies. (The institute's name stands for Innovation and the square of Creativity and Capital.) Dr. Kozmetsky's and the institute's reputation, which was established over 22 years, is effective in calling businesses together.

The businesses are aware of a growing problem of training new employees to participate in the surging technology-based economy of central Texas. Conventional methods for training new workers were ineffective. Most new employees still took several months to reach expectations in a high-tech workplace. A persistent theme of meetings with businesses is Kozmetsky's position that the economy is moving toward being knowledge-based. The working group focused on employers, not educators, developing a common training curriculum for new employees. If this premise is correct, effective training could be done faster using a different approach. This alternative is a step to increase the local labor pool available to all employers. In 1995, the area's semiconductor industry wants to bring in 500 technicians annually. Only about 100 students, or one fifth of this industry's demand requirements, are successfully completing a program each year at a local community college.

The early stages of the partnership move toward overcoming the communication barrier that exists between educators and employers. The style and feeling of the project make it difficult to establish consistency among the coalition members. One of the group's leaders is an extremely talented individual on the technology development side, but weak at communicating information to a corporate audience. Some of the business members offer less-than-enthusiastic participation, and express concern the project is solely another education initiative in search of money from the private sector. According to one participant, there is a lot of interest, tempered by skepticism, at the meetings.

The group meets quarterly through 1996, but there is little progress made, other than naming the project. Throughout this early development period, coalition partners repeatedly emphasize the group's purpose is to find new ways of training entry-level employees to enter technical fields. The eventual name, "EnterTech," symbolizes this purpose.

## TECHNOLOGY-DRIVEN TRAINING

By early 1997, many coalition members agree that whatever form the project would take, it must be valid for the high-tech workplace. By definition, content-validity would include both a relevant context and a delivery mode consistent with the industry. This decision meant the eventual program would be delivered via interactive multimedia and computer based training.

A 1996 study conducted by AMR Training and Consulting Group demonstrates that interactive, computer-based training involving multimedia delivers a potential return on investment of up to 400 percent (Price Waterhouse, 1998). A review of video games, computer games, instructional television, distance learning models, presentation formats, and WebTV narrows the discussion to the final delivery model. EnterTech produces a web-based program for direct computer instruction, with an option for a disk that is not dependent on Internet connections (CD-ROM).

A prototype model of an interactive multimedia program is developed by one consortium member, and provides a conceptually intriguing vision of how learners could experience a virtual work environment and perform their learning tasks. The five-minute prototype offers a broad variety of activities such as basic skills applications, including reading memos, making simple calculations, and completing simple forms. The learner is required to interact with virtual team members by using suitable language. The coalition immediately grasps the concept, and momentum builds.

The end result of these early decisions is the unique integration of the EnterTech learning environment. Work simulation and compelling narrative drama combine with group projects and workbook activities to create an integrated interactive learning experience, one that promotes both community learning and individual success. Instructors facilitate the students' learning through technology.

## CREATING NEW ALLIANCES

In late 1997, the $IC^2$ Institute identifies a new project director, Deaton Bednar, who devotes her full attention to making EnterTech a reality. The coalition needs to be drawn together more tightly. One of the director's first tasks is to revitalize the group, renewing the common vision of EnterTech. By placing the group's project and mission squarely in the forefront, the director generates interest in the project, and participation at quarterly meetings increases. Regular, well-organized meetings helps reassure some of the more tentative coalition members. The director's office becomes the focal point for all communication. A consistent approach satisfies the employers, who had complained of redundant requests for information. This central focus on the director's office maintains closed-loop communication, ensuring that team members act on items.

One of the reasons for success of the coalition lies in the diversity of its membership. Different groups bring their separate expertise. The coalition is a "knowledge community" that takes its diverse experiences and works together to achieve the same objectives. Responding to a post-meeting survey, one coalition member wrote, "The collaboration partners resist the [traditional] turf war issues and contribute in the spirit of solving a statewide issue."

## TIME LINES AND FUNDING

Two clear stages are identified for the project, both requiring funding to proceed. The first phase, development, is estimated at $1.2 million.

This is followed in the second year by delivery and testing, which is estimated at $1.5 million. Initially, several government agencies are identified as potential funding sources. Project coordinators meet with the Texas Department of Commerce and Texas Workforce Commission representatives. While both offices express excitement regarding the project, each agency turns it down because of costs.

Coordinators approach the state Governor's Office, who responds favorably to the group's proposals. Three key changes are required by the executive office. First, the overall budget is reduced to $2.1 million. Projected savings result from reduced development costs and increased "in-kind" contributions from coalition members. Second, the program gives priority to training welfare recipients, public assistance clients, and teen parents. This realignment means that EnterTech would focus on entry-level training rather than higher-level technical training, as first projected. Third, the revised proposal identifies strategies for increasing the likelihood of maximum participation by particular target groups. These efforts include close collaboration with several NGOs and state-funded incentives to find individuals who have the work ethic to complete the program.

As a result of these revisions, the time line for the project and the necessary funding are altered. "Year One" runs from June 1998 to September 1999 and is funded for $1.4 million. "Year Two" runs from September 1999 through August 2000, and is funded for $500,000. The state funds are seed money, and not for ongoing development. While this designation is restrictive, it enables the project leaders to focus on the original vision of EnterTech. The project director generates additional funds from the state during 1999–2000, for a total budget of $2.1 million.

By Spring 1998, the first phase of the EnterTech Project is complete. This involves taking Kozmetsky's vision, fleshing it out conceptually so potential coalition members could understand it, selling the vision to interested parties, and forging a working coalition. Phase 1 includes writing the grant proposal and obtaining the initial funding. The second phase of development focuses on research, analysis, and design. Project staff concentrate on identifying competencies and performance objectives by relating the curricula of each coalition member. An analysis of current delivery platforms and emerging technology trends is conducted.

By November 1998, an evaluation system for learners, employers, and the program is in place. The competencies, performance objectives, and assessment strategies for entry-level positions and continuing education are designed, although only the entry-level positions are in the actual program. The fundamental research phase closes with the completion of five reports in January 1999, relating to evaluations, content, and delivery (EnterTech Project Reports, 1998–1999). By summer 1999, the support system, referral system, and graduation procedure are in place, and instructional design is complete. By December of that year, the computer-based training workbooks are available, and initial testing reveals results. The final phase, from January through August 2000, involves pilot testing, statewide deployment, and full deployment plans. Feedback from learners, educators, employers, and other stakeholders is incorporated into the curriculum and program delivery.

## INNOVATIONS

EnterTech's approach to entry-level training is *sui generis*, both in the manner of its creation and in its objectives. The project is the first multimedia program to combine personal skill building with professional skill building. It is the first Web-based program to use a virtual company, complete with a story line, job duties, and virtual coworkers, to prepare students for work in a real company. Rather than focus on "job-getting" skills, EnterTech prepares students with "job-doing" skills, providing the industry with graduates who can enter the workplace with the positive attitude and flexibility for which employers are searching.

EnterTech seeks to provide "trainable" employees who are ready to enter the workforce and succeed. For such a program, the project leadership selects a local multimedia company as the prime contractor for design and production. The design team, comprises both project leaders and employees of the prime contractor, pursues a four-track method of development. A complete description of this decision-making process is available in Erdos (2000).

## TECHNOLOGICAL CONSIDERATIONS

The most constraining aspect of technology is enduser bandwidth availability, or the sustainable rate of downloading a user's computer. Because computers change so rapidly, it is quite difficult to imagine what the standards will be in a few years. Project coordinators determine 18 months in advance that there would be sufficient bandwidth in computers at delivery sites to support full Internet-based implementation. It appeared that a 28.8kbps modem would still be the lowest common denominator in Internet connection in the near future. The team decided the program should first be available for both Web-based from the Internet and a combination of Internet instruction and a disk (hybrid CD-ROM/Web CBT). The combination is to be phased out when there is no prospect that direct computer connections are a problem.

Bandwidth concerns determine many options during development. EnterTech designers make choices regarding programming languages, graphic design, plug-in use, streaming media, and other tools that could increase computer speeds. Designers hope to avoid making temporary additions to existing computers to overcome the bandwidth problems. Such additions would enable streaming animation or video to run on an Internet site. When actual programming begins, the contractor notes it would cost an additional $100,000 to $150,000 if additions or plug-ins are not used, based on the additional time needed to work on the total programs.

There is always the question of production costs. Custom video production is expensive, as are streaming media network servers. Creating a simple audio file to accompany the typed computer program increases costs. To resolve these problems, EnterTech uses "puppet characters"—still photographs of actors that shift and change to reflect the characters—monologues to the learner. To reduce large audio files, the programmers choose plot developments in printed text, concentrating on the use of audio on tasks the learner is to carry out.

## IMPLEMENTATION

Prior to implementing the program, EnterTech Project coordinators conduct a number of background studies, including an examination of the targeted learner populations, solicitation of employer input regarding the curriculum, and an assessment of the technology infrastructure of Texas. Project coordinators identify potential EnterTech learners: TANF recipients, mature and dislocated workers, incumbent workers, unemployed workers, and the underemployed. The project's researchers interview 10 instructors with experience teaching welfare-population students and conduct a focus group of six TANF recipients and three program instructors at the Austin Area Urban League, one of the coalition members. Focus group participants provide information about their personal, educational, and work experiences. Instructors contribute information about their experiences teaching and supporting TANF learners.

In Texas, the typical welfare or TANF recipient is a single mother in her 20s or 30s with one or two children. Most recipients have some work experience within the past two years, and almost two-thirds have high school or alternative certification (State of Texas Department of Human Services, 1997). From 1997 to 2000, over 59,000 TANF recipients are expected to be removed from the welfare system, with many of these individuals living in the metropolitan areas of the state and the southernmost parts of Rio Grande Valley bordering Mexico (Lawson & Lawson, 1998). Based on recommendations from coalition members, research targets learners' abilities in specific areas: reading for information, following instructions, teamwork, applied math, and listening. Instruction must emphasize context for learning, learning styles, self-esteem, and computer facility.

A recent study conducted by the Center for Law and Social Policy (CLASP) examines welfare-to-work programs across the United States for effective strategies to break the cycle of welfare. This research identifies three ways for welfare-to-work programs to be successful. First, these programs needed to know how to help the most disadvantaged recipients for whom a job search is not promising. Second, the programs need to help recipients find better jobs. Lastly, successful programs know how to help recipients sustain employment (Strawn, 1998).

In light of these findings, the EnterTech Target Learner Characteristics Report recommends the project develop a support model to connect learners with community resources. Instructional models develop to encourage individual resourcefulness in seeking multiple options and solutions for problems or barriers, and in creating and participating in natural networks of friends, family, and coworkers in order for participants to become self-sufficient through mutual support (EnterTech Project Reports, 1998–1999).

This report recommends the project provide realistic simulations of high-tech work environments, which incorporates the sights, sounds, language, and culture of the high-tech industry workplace into video segments and the thematic content of the curriculum. Additional recommendations suggest EnterTech should:

1. provide models for engaging in workplace culture and activities that foster successful behaviors within the work setting;
2. place a strong emphasis on the collaborative and interpersonal skills required by all employers;
3. provide for individual differences among learners; and
4. provide an instructor guidebook to accompany the computer-based and student workbook training materials.

Project coordinators conduct in-person and telephone interviews with key individuals in a number of technology and communication companies operating across Texas, including Dell Computer, IBM, and Texas Instruments. The interviewees represent a broad range of job descriptions and responsibilities, and include managers, trainers, and researchers. Results of the interviews verify that the workplace and educational skills targeted by EnterTech are highly relevant to high-tech work environments.

The project leaders utilize Work Keys™ to conduct the profiling. Work Keys identifies a generic employability skill level in eight distinct areas. The skill levels in applied technology, for example, range from 3 to 6. The skill levels are transferable across occupations and are tied to the job profiles (skill level requirements) for particular jobs or occupations. The Work Keys skill levels translate skill requirements for individual jobs into "levels" of proficiency so that a job can be profiled to determine generic skills, such as applied technology or applied math with observation. From the skill levels studied, comparable employability skills are measured for individuals. Results for these levels are reported in Table 5.1.

When first developed, the competency matrix includes more than 160 objectives. To reduce and synthesize the matrix, tasks appearing across the core job functions of the profiles are prioritized. Next, Work Keys job profiling is performed by subject experts to select other priority tasks. Finally, the entire matrix is sent to EnterTech employer coalition members to rank tasks on a Likert scale to indicate which tasks are most often necessary for their entry-level jobs.

Based on this cumulative analysis, a new matrix emerges, consisting of 44 performance objectives. It is organized into eight learning areas: job skills, personal skills, organizational skills, communication skills, reading and writing skills, number skills, strategy skills, and growth skills. Within each learning area, competencies, performance objectives, and subskill sets are detailed. Table 5.2 shows how these categories are used to report results.

The program designers want to measure both the cognitive complexity and the learner's independence in completing tasks. The goal is to create a challenging learning environment that meets individual learner

**TABLE 5.1**
**Percentage of EnterTech Completers Performing in Eight Skill Areas by Levels**

| Skill Areas | Level 3 | Level 4 | Level 5 | Level 4 or 5 |
|---|---|---|---|---|
| Job | 4.0% | 49.5% | 46.5% | 96.0% |
| Personal | 5.0% | 50.5% | 44.6% | 95.1% |
| Organization | 5.0% | 40.6% | 54.5% | 95.1% |
| Communication | 11.9% | 51.5% | 36.6% | 88.1% |
| Reading/Writing | 1.0% | 45.5% | 53.5% | 99.0% |
| Numbers | 1.0% | 34.7% | 64.4% | 99.1% |
| Strategy | 7.9% | 58.4% | 33.7% | 92.1% |
| Growth | 4.0% | 60.4% | 35.6% | 96.0% |

(Rounding at .75; $N$ = 101)

**TABLE 5.2**
**Mean Performance of EnterTech Completers on Eight Skill Areas**

| Skill Areas | Mean | Std. Dev | Min | Max |
|---|---|---|---|---|
| Job | 4.63 | 0.40 | 3.43 | 5.00 |
| Personal | 4.51 | 0.48 | 3.00 | 5.00 |
| Organization | 4.62 | 0.44 | 3.00 | 5.00 |
| Communication | 4.39 | 0.71 | 0.00 | 5.00 |
| Reading/Writing | 4.70 | 0.33 | 3.67 | 5.00 |
| Numbers | 4.73 | 0.35 | 3.60 | 5.00 |
| Strategy | 4.53 | 0.49 | 3.00 | 5.00 |
| Growth | 4.48 | 0.65 | 0.00 | 5.00 |

($N = 101$)

needs, but would not be so difficult that it would cause frustration or failure. This approach gives rise to the EnterTech motto, "Say it. Do it. Use it," and results in the adoption of a skills transcript that provides potential employers with information on the skills and skill levels achieved by the EnterTech graduate.

With an embedded assessment, student skills are evaluated as they interact with instruction. Rather than periodically interrupt the story for a true–false, multiple choice, or other traditional type of assessment exercise, students are continually assessed as they problem solve and select or input solutions for the computer. The learner's strengths and weaknesses are identified, enabling employers to match learners with job responsibilities and identify in which areas they need additional training. The skill's transcript provides employers with a well-defined list of the performance objectives and student results in each learning area.

Once designers create this integrated, interactive learning environment, it is time to test EnterTech with the target populations. The test focuses on the nature and scope of possible program revisions to increase its effectiveness in advance of a large-scale evaluation of program implementation and learner outcomes. Two education sites in the Austin, Texas, area are selected for this testing: the Gonzalo Garza Independent High School (an inner-city alternative education facility) and the Kyle Learning and Career Center (a NGO located in a rural area). Five learners at Garza High School and 10 at the Kyle Center participate in the evaluation. Each site offered EnterTech a three-week, half-day schedule. Both instructors and students at these sites are paid a small hourly stipend for their participation. Project coordinators collect and study data pertaining to five stages of the evaluation design: entry, reaction, learning, performance, and continuation.

Because of the small sample size in the implementation testing, the EnterTech staff performs only descriptive analyses. The results of this testing indicate that program is effective in providing the skills and knowledge necessary for successful entry-level employment. The ranking of learners through a three-tiered process proves to be informative about learners' performance and the evaluation of the EnterTech curriculum. Aggregated instructor assessment and computer-embedded tracking data measure learners' knowledge, skills, and abilities to perform at an entry-level job position. The important lesson learned during the pilot implementation testing is the program needs to be more user-friendly, particularly for instructors. Project coordinators learn more data review could be done on-line, especially in the area of student evaluation. It is important to work closely with sites from the beginning in order to avoid simple technical problems that result in user dissatisfaction. The program needs to be offered in different schedules, like other program options at such learning centers. Nonetheless, the learners overwhelmingly enjoyed using EnterTech.

Pilot testing for the program occurs at 13 sites throughout Texas from March 2000 to October 2000. The training sites consist of one high school, 6 community colleges, and 6 community based organizations. Of one hundred twenty-one learners who enroll in this program, 101 complete training. Of those completing training, 65 are employed or continuing their education, while 19 are unemployed. Among the unemployed learners, 15 have difficulty gaining employment due to transportation, childcare, and/or health problems, but they attain the skills necessary to succeed as entry-level employees. The remaining unemployed learners are actively applying for positions.

The performance objectives for each of the eight skill areas are assessed at three levels (3–5). A learner performing at level three is able to state, describe, or explain procedures and concepts. Level four represents a learner who is able to correctly perform tasks without significant help from others and without significant errors. A learner performing at a level five is able to integrate skills into problem resolutions. Learners averaging 3.75 to 4.74 on a skill area are categorized as achieving an overall level 4 performance on the skill area. Learners averaging 4.74 to 5.0 on a skill are achieving an overall level 5 performance on the skill area.

Table 5.1 reports the levels at which learners performing at levels, 3, 4, or 5 and levels 4 or 5 combined for the eight skill areas. For example, on the reading/writing skill area 1 percent of learners attained a level 3 performance, 46 percent attained a level 4 performance, and 54 percent attained a level 5 performance. The skill areas—reading or writing, numbers, growth and job skills—show high performance with 96 percent or more of learners performing at level 4 and 5. Table 5.2 shows the mean performance, standard variation among learners or deviation, minimum performance and maximum performance of learners in the eight skill areas. On average, learners attained a mean performance of 4.39 or higher on each of the skill areas, indicating learners are able to correctly perform tasks without significant help from others and without significant errors.

Consistent findings appear, including key information about the system as well as the software itself. User interfaces need to be simplified for instructors, and the administrative back-end of the system (record collection and student tracking) needs to be strengthened. Changes are currently being made, and some demonstration sites are implementing these changes. Graduates of the pilot sites are tracked during employment to determine learner and employer satisfaction, job and knowledge retention, and potential reductions in turnover rates. EnterTech is both an adaptable and improving program for entry-level employees.

## SUSTAINABILITY AND REPLICATION

Project coordinators are considering the sustainability and replication of the EnterTech program. The current model is supported by employers, ensuring a closed loop between education and employment. Funding to underwrite portions of this adoption process is available through governments or education systems as well as from interested employers. Multiple support sustains EnterTech.

EnterTech Project coordinators see the national need for a similar program since similar problems should respond to a single solution: employers need more workers, and the targeted learners need jobs. An ever-increasing number of people in the targeted audience find themselves without the skills, competencies, and personal abilities to become and remain gainfully employed in entry-level positions. The lack of electronic literacy skills, problems with transportation, and dependent care prevent many of the most motivated learners from attending traditional site-based classes. We need to broaden the capabilities of "anytime, anywhere" training available via the Internet.

With respect to replication, EnterTech is designed to be a process, not a product, in order that the product might be recreated time and again, adapting to different sets of circumstances and needs. As one coalition member states: "The big thing that distinguishes EnterTech [from other programs] is not the content; it's the delivery mechanism and the contextual aspect of it." Project coordinators have always thought about transferring this program to a variety of contexts.

There are three identifiable levels in transforming the program:

1. Translation—changing the language of the program;
2. Localization—altering the visuals and story line to appropriately reflect people and customs in a different context;
3. Customization—transforming the product to teach the same or different skills in a different virtual environment.

To maximize the potential for transferability, designers try to reduce the program to the minimum number of necessary components. EnterTech designers recognize that in order to transfer to other contexts, the program needs to provide for local variation. The solution is to utilize computer-generated text for much of the program, so that text could be replaced by new information, rather than having to generate completely new artwork. Likewise, the use of "puppet characters" makes transferability simpler because the characters' lips do not move, facilitating the insertion of new audio in any language. The administration accommodates new media, while the computer program can be manipulated separately.

## LESSONS LEARNED

The mission of the $IC^2$ Institute, which oversees the EnterTech Project, is to discover, explain, test, and disseminate breakthrough knowledge that accelerates wealth creation and prosperity sharing. The EnterTech Project combines all facets of this mission, resulting in an improved economic environment, by creating a larger pool of potential employees for businesses (wealth creation) and increased career opportunities for those who successfully complete its training program (prosperity sharing). EnterTech can go beyond providing entry-level employees to the high-tech industry. Its curriculum design units, such as materials handling, would be used in product shipping for any company involved in manufacturing. The program is applicable to other areas, such as vocational schools or community colleges. It could teaching necessary soft skills through a virtual classroom instead of a virtual company.

Reflection on the EnterTech process suggests five specific strategies:

1. *Construct the membership of the coalition with the end results in mind, and carefully maintain the coalition.* The makeup and maintenance of a successful partnership or coalition endeavor is critical to its overall success. Members' needs and desires must be understood and clarified. Moreover, it must be made clear to members how participation in the coalition will help them achieve their goals. Information exchanges should be simple, direct, germane, and consistent. Members need to know that they have been heard.
2. *Know who the customers are and understand what they want.* The customers are the employers and learners in the community. A

motto that was developed in the formative stages of the project captures this belief: "Learner Success, Employer Satisfaction." In Texas, the current workforce development system is still encumbered by a great degree of bureaucracy. Strengthening partnerships among the local economy and labor market, as well as the interested community-based organizations, will increase success of efforts by the parties involved.

3. *Hire independent, specialized consultants to review the work of contractors.* A curriculum expert or Web-based delivery specialist is essential. EnterTech project coordinators utilizes subject-matter experts successfully, which led to early detection and resolution of many critical issues. Using these experts leads to further contacts and possibilities for development with many NGOs.

4. *Ensure the instructor customizes the product and that the products are altered to response to different customer needs.* One strong appeal of EnterTech to instructors is the straightforward interaction between the program and the instructor. The instructor continues to be the most important component of the program. The ability to override or customize various program features is essential, as is the ease of operating a self-management environment. Automating many report functions through Web-based tools frees time for instruction and changes rather than paper-based tests.

5. *Determine how sustainable the project is; plan in advance of product rollout.* In business terms, this is a critical aspect of good financial modeling. With a coalition, the same principle enables members to stay informed and involved throughout the product rollout and latter planning stages. The numerous and often odd-shaped pieces of a sustainability puzzle are difficult to fit together. Consequently, determining the end model sooner allows energy and resources that can be directed toward one established goal, as opposed to trying to define and select a model.

A team of stakeholders that shares common interests and concerns can create, design, implement, and support a program for the new economy.

## EDITOR'S NOTE

A classic description of technological impacts depicts the tendency to generalize findings as a result of abstract formulations (Wolcott, 1977). Revealing flow charts are available from the authors, which show the emergence of the project and the influence of every factor on the students. The science and technology basis of the project is taken further by the formulation of this program as a general answer to the problems of the unemployed and underemployed and their expectation for the discovered solution to be replicated.

The logical reasoning about the problem does not include the welfare mother, other than as clients to be provided with computer education. Resistance to abstract solutions to educational problems is repeatedly shown in the literature, and either active or passive resistance to this innovation should be anticipated. It is strange for mostly male experts to plan a program for largely female workers. The active opponents of change, counterpreneurs, will not occurr without advocacy organizations. The authors claim that competency-based instruction is successful. Poor and pregnant women may not be able to offer as much resistance as teachers, but some resistance is possible.

Though there is no slave revolt, there is an enormous distance between those pushing the project and those to be trained. The ideas for the project are those of George Kozmetsky who has built a reputation that makes this approach acceptable. The partners in government, business, agencies, and education accept his agenda. Though this program is modified in a few ways, it is a determinist way of thinking about the problem, which indendent people would not accept.

InterTech has merged a deterministic or scientific approach with business reasoning. Literature is cited to claim a "potential return on investment of 400 percent." The name of the founding research institute, which squares two cs of creativity and capital to combine with specific innovations, is revealing. Without evidence, it is claimed EnterTech is a unique program and their preliminary results "were highly relevant to the typical high-tech work environment." There is no question in the minds of the writers about their ability to deliver the goods for employers.

Supreme confidence is typical of expert innovators until they encounter major opposition. Ironically, such confidence is the source of the authors' greatest strength, providing clear directions on how to deliver a similar program. The chain of decision making is based on very specific aims. Many partnerships are an adaptation to extreme uncertainty where partners are drawn on, when they do not know what they are doing. This program sets one aim and brings in expert consultants and makes adaptations to learner needs as required. Alternatives do need to be considered. Could web-based instruction be combined with classroom education as suggested in Chapter 3? Could employer evaluations be combined with those of instructor which is discussed in Chapter 6? Can virtual schools be used to overcome social differences, including rural deficiencies discussed in Chapter 10? Technology can be used in other ways, but this study makes clear how successful one directed effort is.

# 6

# Retrieving Resources: Enviroworks

## Michael Zanibbi

> Enviroworks certainly exhibits very high qualities of innovative ideas, organization wide impact, collaboration, sustainability, and outcomes that meet ongoing environmental challenges
> —Dawn Ralph, Executive Director of the Peter F. Drucker Canadian Foundation (personal communication, October 27, 1997)

Enviroworks is a program of the Limestone District School Board (LDSB) in Kingston, Ontario, Canada, which is receiving national and international attention as a partnership model. It pools the resources of the private sector, the public sector, the education system, and the community. The alliance among these groups benefits its partners because students are being better prepared for the changing world of work, local businesses are reducing costs, and the community is addressing important environmental issues. The program started four years ago with only 15 partners and grew to over 300.

## LOCAL CONTEXT

The Enviroworks program is an example of how an entrepreneurial partnership starts when problems are seen as disguised opportunities. Immediate problems are caused by the city of Kingston's growth. During 1997, the area experiences its greatest construction boom ever, led by the industrial, commercial, and institutional sectors. From 1996 to 1997, building permit values for construction more than double, which greatly increases the amount of construction and demolition waste. The Kingston community is concerned because of the increased pressure on local landfill sites; the cost of disposal soars, increasing by 30 percent. This cost affects local businesses and Kingston residents.

The environmental crisis is matched by the difficulties encountered by the education system. Schools in Ontario are feeling the effects of a new provincial government whose mandate includes large cuts in grants to Ontario school boards. Increasing pressure from the business community calls for young people to be better prepared for the workplace. The education system is challenged to become more innovative and entrepreneurial.

## THE PROGRAM

Any group can augment its effectiveness through the formation of powerful alliances (Cramphorn, 1999). The issues faced by the education system, the private sector, and the community are difficult to address individually. Under the direction of the LDSB, a partnership is created to pool resources and address all the issues simultaneously. The end result is the formation of Enviroworks, a used building materials store that is owned by the LDSB and operated by the students on the board.

Enviroworks attracts extra funding to the school board and provides a unique vehicle for training students. This program is modeled after many of the used building material stores that are starting all over North America. What makes Enviroworks unique is that it is owned by a school board and operated by students. The program is based at Queen Elizabeth Collegiate and Vocational Institute (QECVI).

Although Enviroworks is based at QECVI, it is not run from there. Enviroworks is in an 8,000-square-foot warehouse. The program is coordinated by Mike Zanibbi, a business teacher at QECVI, and Steph Running, a former Enviroworks student who now manages the store. The primary goal of the program is to divert construction and demolition waste from Kingston's landfills. The program obtains materials, such as doors or sinks, from households and contractors who are disposing of them, and sells them back to customers, who will reuse them.

Enviroworks provides students with a learning opportunity to operate a business. There are 15 to 20 students from several different schools in the program at any one time. Participants gain valuable experience in a number of areas, including marketing, sales and customer service, accounting, human resource management, computers, technological studies, and entrepreneurship. Young people develop the skills and attitudes established by the Conference Board of Canada's *Employability Skills Profile*: problem solving, responsibility, adaptability, teamwork skills, communication skills, and positive attitudes and behaviors (Corporate Council on Education, 1998).

### Topics

The Enviroworks program runs for two semesters. Students are at the stores all day and receive four credits a semester in different subject areas (marketing, accounting, computers, entrepreneurship, management studies, business communications). These courses relate directly to the operation of the business. When performing duties, such as making the budget, entering information into the computerized accounting system, or producing monthly reports for the school board, students earn credits in accounting. When working on the marketing plan, conducting market research, or creating advertising (TV, radio, and newspaper), students are earning credits in marketing.

There is no distinction between the business and classroom; *business is the classroom*. Students have an opportunity to gain excellent work experience to put on their resumés while completing their academic requirements. Young people are in a better position to sidestep the Catch 22, "No job without experience, and no experience without a job."

Like a company, extensive planning and research *are the beginning*. The very first class of 11 students plan and prepare business for the students who participate in the following years. Table 6.1 shows the many activities the first class performed as well as the continuing work of later students. The program challenges them to become entrepreneurs and solve business problems. Students become entrepreneurial when stimulated by more innovative students and through working with businesspeople.

Students are encouraged to become "intrapreneurs" (entrepreneurs within an existing organization) and are allowed the freedom and resources to develop their ideas. A special budget is available to students who have ideas to make a business operate efficiently. Such students suggest ideas relating to operational planning, cash management, financing, advertising, public relations, or sources of supply.

### Proving Themselves

Enviroworks uses a combination of traditional and nontraditional methods of evaluation. Students are given tests, exams, and assignments as a means of measuring how well they learn the material

**TABLE 6.1**
**Student Activities for Enviroworks**

*Stage 1: Starting Up (1995–96)*

Performing industry and market analysis

Conducting market research—competitor analysis, supplier analysis, market survey

Determining pricing policies

Advertising and promotion

Finding a facility

Purchasing and leasing equipment

Implementing the education and awareness campaign

Financial forecasts

Analysis of critical risks and problems

Planning the store layout

Developing the business plan

Creating the accounting system and cash controls

Recruiting suppliers

*Stage 2: Continuing Work*

Maintaining the computerized accounting system

Overseeing sales and customer service

Developing the adertising campaigns

Creating the budget

Public relations

Operational planning

Coordinating pick-up and delivery schedules

Supplier recruitment

Strategic and long-range planning

Generating quarterly and annual reports

Market research and analysis

Creation of advertising (radio, television, newspaper)

Preparing for trade shows

Developing and maintaining the web site (www.enviroworks.org)

Managing the new deconstruction and demolition division

Recruitment of new students

Networking with local businesses

Staff training

required by curriculum guidelines. Curriculum requirements are integrated into the program. For example, if the marketing guidelines specify that students must learn about the marketing environment, students do an assignment identifying and evaluating the political, economic, social, and technological factors affecting Enviroworks.

Students are also evaluated on how well they demonstrate the skills outlined in the Conference Board of Canada's *Employability Skills Profile*. These skills are measured from both a classroom and work perspective. Communication skills are measured by written and oral presentations and reports in the classroom. These skills are observed by studying students' phone manners and interaction with customers. Members of the business community conduct "performance reviews" in the store. Local businesspeople listen to student presentations or observe how they deal with customers. The businessperson's assessment is combined with the teacher's mark. Both evaluators provide feedback and instruction for the student.

Enviroworks combines assessments into a portfolio. An inventory is made of students' projects during a semester. The portfolio includes the address of the web site they design, a copy of an advertisement they create for the local radio station, or a newspaper clipping of an interview they did promoting the program. This portfolio augments their resumé as well as their grades. Students are evaluated on the extent to which they display entrepreneurial skills, which show creativity or problem solving. These two skills are measured by looking at students' ideas for improving the store's customer service, sales, or operational planning.

## FOCUS PROGRAMS

Enviroworks is part of a large partnership model that makes up the Focus Program system in the Limestone District School Board. Focus Programs are packages of courses offered at Limestone District secondary schools. They concentrate on a particular field that will give a foundation in a career or area of study. These special programs enable students to come together to benefit from specialized equipment and training. They are to help high school students make well-informed career decisions to post-secondary education or the world of work (LDSB, 2000). There are over 50 programs, ranging from business and construction to theater and art. A student from any of the 11 schools in the LDSB can enroll in a focus program; LDSB absorbs transportation costs.

Enviroworks fits well into the innovative school environment because of their emphasis on "at-risk students." Other programs are at the same location, Queen Elizabeth school. QECVI is under the leadership of a principal, Dick Mulville, who rejuvenated a school that was once on the verge of closure. In 1989, this school had 450 students, but by 1995, there were 1,100 students in 20 focus programs. Programs include Theatre Complete, the Building Construction Internship Program, Creative Arts, Marine Technology, and the Second Chance Program. These varied curricula attract students from all over Frontenac County.

## VISIONS

Through an addition to the Focus set, Enviroworks is a new approach to developing community partnerships and a radical departure from traditional education. It illustrates a proactive approach to develop employment opportunities for today's youth. The world of work is undergoing a major transformation, shaped by the globalization of labor, technological change, growth of the service sector, and corporate downsizing and outsourcing. Young people have to be taught not just how to "get" a job but also how to "make" a job.

For LSSB, this means teaching a new set of student skills: opportunity identification, idea evaluation, literacy skills, technical skills, and thinking skills. It also means a new set of student attitudes: creativity, initiative, responsibility, collaboration, and learning as a way of life and work. The Board generates additional resources by developing community partnerships. Enviroworks provides a model, which pools the resources of the education system, private sector, public sector, and community. The government supplies the initial funding, the private sector provides the training, the education system makes available human resources, and the community donates the materials.

## LIMESTONE SCHOOL BOARD'S INVOLVEMENT

When the approval for Enviroworks to proceed with a program is given, a major stipulation is that it could not cost the LDSB any money. When the LDSB is approached about Enviroworks, a grant from Human Resources Development Canada for $103,000 is already in place. The school board provides the salary for one teacher, myself, and this is conditional upon attracting 20 students.

My role is to coordinate all business operations in addition to developing and teaching the curriculum. As I am already being paid as a business teacher at QECVI, there is no additional expense incurred. Enviroworks generates other funds to support the program either through revenue generation, grant support, or in-kind donation.

Although they do not provide financial support, LDSB is supportive of the program. Negotiations with the City of Kingston are required to alter a city by-law, which states schools can not be located in industrial zones. Enviroworks needs to operate out of a warehouse and most warehouses are zoned industrially. The board's organization resolves this problem and its staff establishes accounts and monitors purchasing activities for this project. Enviroworks uses busing, which is in place for Focus programs. At the school, the project teacher is supported by the principal of QECVI for student discipline, or to maintain academic performance.

## REASONS FOR BUSINESS SUPPORT

An effective partnership is mutually beneficial to all parties involved (NBEC 1999). Private sector giants, such as DuPont and Alcan, are leery of entering into partnerships with the LDSB since for them partnerships mean financial commitments. Most school principals and superintendents think that anyone who gives them money is a partner. For such partnerships, the benefit to business is good corporate citizenship. This benefit is available from donating money to any one of the thousands of organizations constantly soliciting big businesses. Companies do not want to be only a funding source for education. From a public relations standpoint, many companies try to spread their philanthropic activities around, supporting an organization for one to three years at most and then moving on to another organization.

School boards must learn there are other resources in the community. More and more businesses are seeking to donate their human resources and look forward to the opportunity to do so. Many members of the private sector believe that while their money is welcome in the classroom, their employees may not be. Enviroworks include human resources by involving partners in a number of ways. Some, like Human Resources Development Canada, provide funding for the program's training component. Others, like Cataraqui Cabinets and Queen's University, donate materials. Still others, such as Vista Enterprises and the Greater Kingston Chamber of Commerce, advise the students and the LDSB.

When Enviroworks conducts market research and needs help in developing the survey, several marketing research firms, like Thornley Stoker Advertising, volunteer. Local companies such as CKWS Television and GTO 960 help the students develop TV and radio advertising. Partnerships with the Enviroworks program are beneficial in three ways: (1) by providing free consulting and market research services, (2) by saving organizations money in disposal costs, and (3) by providing employers with better-trained students.

The Greater Kingston Chamber of Commerce, which represents over 900 businesses in Kingston, as well as the Junior Chamber, is proactive in providing businesses to work with the students when needed. Business "mentors" donate their time to students. They help Enviroworks in the areas of marketing (advertising, promotion, pricing), accounting (checking financial statements and budgets), computers (web page development and use of computer hardware such as LCD projectors), and place students on various Chamber committees. Their input leads to a new environmental business and technology curriculum.

Business partners realize that young people are the future for economic and community development. The benefits for company time and effort are in the development of a pool of skilled employees. Small business operators want generalists, people who have experience and skill in many different areas of business. In most small businesses, employees are required to do many different tasks. Our program gives students the opportunity to perform many tasks owners themselves would do: marketing, bookkeeping, sales, customer service, strategic planning, and networking.

Potential employers are free to watch the students operate in a real business setting before hiring them or taking them for a work placement. In both cases, LDSB invests in the training of students before sending them to potential employers. The business community is impressed because education is taking responsibility for the preparation of their students in a realistic learning environment.

Organizations realize the cost savings a partnership provides. Disposal costs are a great expense to many businesses and nonprofit organizations. The Enviroworks program works with local businesses to save them hundreds of thousands of dollars in disposal costs. Manufacturers are stuck with products, such as doors, counter tops, and windows, which have minor defects or have been cut to sizes other than specified. These companies cannot sell these products and either store them or have them removed at a cost of $90 per ton.

Environworks does not charge for a pickup. The companies who partner with us are seen by the community as environmentally responsible, and supportive of the education system. In both instances, there is publicity generated at no cost to the businesses. Large corporations, such as Alcan, Dupont, and Bombardier, and small companies, like Bathworks, Cataraqui Cabinets, and Lowen Windows, participate. Every year more businesses utilize the services the program provides.

## COMMUNITY ASSISTANCE

The free pickup service is a great advantage to many nonprofit organizations. Nonprofits, especially those affected by government cutbacks, save significant amounts of money in demolition and disposal costs. Queen's University saves over $35,000 a year in disposal fees. Before Enviroworks, this university ran its own small reuse center where the public could come two days a week to take away materials.

They used to pay someone to run the reuse center and organize the materials. If materials did not sell, they stored them in needed space. By allowing Enviroworks to take the material, the university disposes of a large volume rapidly. Fewer materials are taken to the landfill, which upholds Queen's environmental reputation.

Some other examples of nonprofit partnerships are the City of Kingston and its townships. The roads department provides Enviroworks with items and phone numbers of residents needing a collection. Enviroworks contacts people with reusable building materials, collects discards (saving the roads department work), and diverts materials from the dump. Before our project residents waited as much as two months to have their materials removed.

Enviroworks partners with city agencies such as the Kingston Area Recycling Corporation (KARC). KARC is in charge of the blue box program in Kingston. They recycle paper, glass, plastics, and even hazardous materials. Many Kingston residents call about disposal of materials that KARC does not take, including building materials. When calls such as this come in, KARC refers them to Enviroworks and we arrange to collect the material. Conversely, when we receive calls about recyclable materials, we refer these people to KARC.

## NEW SERVICES

In an effort to offer greater cost savings to local businesses and community organizations, Enviroworks is starting a demolition and deconstruction operation, which works with local renovators and homeowners to save them money and remove the materials in better condition. Our deconstruction team, students and a supervisor, goes on to renovation job sites to dismantle and remove materials or to demolish smaller structures. This service is offered free to contractors. We only ask that they give us the materials removed or demolished. This new service expands our training program.

Expanded services are especially attractive to small businesses and nonprofits that are financially strapped. The students are developing web sites for several different organizations in both the private and public sectors. They provide consulting services and market research. Like the demolition and deconstruction services, assistance is offered free since students gain excellent experience in exchange for their work.

In the early years, Enviroworks frequently worked with nonprofit groups constrained by finances and expertise. Many nonprofit organizations need assistance with the challenges they face. Students in the program need real problems to solve. Organizations, such as Kingston General Hospital (KGH) and Hospice Kingston, organize fundraising events. Hospice Kingston operates Chilifest and KGH organizes the Festival of Trees. In order to gauge the success of these events, survey research is conducted. Staff cannot tally the results and generate reports. Our students create the database needed to analyze the results. A report for both events summarizes their results and makes recommendations. Organizers of the two events tell other nonprofits that contact Enviroworks to do similar work for them.

Other examples of partnerships include one with the Voices, Opportunities, and Choices Employment Club, which seeks to develop employment opportunities for psychiatric patients being reintegrated into the community. We develop a business plan for a store operated by the patients. We provide a solid waste disposal resource, which is available to every person in the city of Kingston. Students study solid waste recyclers in the community.

Partnerships are developed with the St. Lawrence II, Kingston's tall ship. The St. Lawrence II offers sailing trips where people learn to operate the ship, learn teamwork, and learn discipline during an adventure. The organization that operates the ship wants to attract consumers from a younger age segment. Enviroworks tries to come up with a strategy to promote both itself and business studies to younger students. The combined result is the Enviroworks Elementary School Business competition, which involves students from surrounding schools who are in the target market for St. Lawrence II. The goal is to have the students create a radio commercial that would appeal to the 10- to 14-year-old youths. Enviroworks coordinates this day-long event in conjunction with the Kingston Tourist Office, the Greater Kingston Chamber of Commerce, Vista Enterprises, and Country 96 FM.

Students hear from representatives from the Kingston Welcome Center concerning the importance of tourism in Kingston, Brigantine Incorporated about the St. Lawrence II and their market, and Country 96 FM on how to make a radio commercial. The winning group is invited to Country 96's studio to record their commercial, which is played free on the radio during Tourism Week. The advertisement increases the number of young people and adults who use the St. Lawrence II and younger students learn about Enviroworks.

## GROWTH IN PARTNERSHIPS

In the first three years of Enviroworks' development, partnerships are initiated by Enviroworks. Recently, because of our reputation, companies are approaching us. A proposed partnership is between Robinson's Solutions, the City of Kingston, and Enviroworks. Robinson's Solutions, a multinational firm of more than 1,000 employees in three countries specializing in janitorial and property management services, asks us to consider a unique partnership. Robinson's is trying to develop a private/public partnership with the City of Kingston. It wants to take over the collection of garbage and recyclables and believes it can save the city at least $1 million per year. The company promises better service, new equipment, and less garbage going to the dumps. Since building material makes up 30 percent of the waste stream, Enviroworks would take these materials.

Some of the other opportunities that we are investigating include partnerships with companies in both the movie and call-center industries. Kingston is one of the oldest cities in Canada and is the first capital of the country. Its well-maintained historical architecture makes it very attractive for movie companies shooting historical films. Last year, *Vendetta*, a movie starring Academy Award winner Christopher Walken, was filmed using parts of Kingston and the City Hall area. Elaborate sets were built to remake Kingston into New Orleans during the 1800s. The same production company is filming the CBS miniseries, *Feast of All Saints*. The production staff spends about $200,000 for construction of the sets. After a movie is finished, the sets are torn down and brought to the dump. The producers are happy to let Enviroworks take the materials.

Enviroworks is seeking to develop a partnership with the Kingston Area Economic Development Corporation (KEDCO) that, in turn, is seeking to market the area as a film location. Another joint investigation with KEDCO involves the growing call-center industry in Kingston. Bell Canada has a call center in Kingston, employing approximately 350 people. KEDCO makes call centers a priority, and five other companies are looking at opening call centers in Kingston. What these companies want is an employee who has customer service and organizational skills. Call Centre Expo, held in Kingston, is an opportunity to plan a training program that would make Kingston more attractive to call centers. The reputation of Enviroworks would grow with the number of call centers.

## PRIVATE AND NON-PROFIT MODELS

A business owned by a school board is a radical departure from traditional education practices. A not-for-profit enterprise of this size and scope is a new attempt by a board of education. Since there was no model to use, we combine business and education perspectives. Should Enviroworks be organized as a nonprofit or for-profit enterprise? In Ontario, eight stores (four nonprofit and four private sector) were studied.

The nonprofit stores know how to find financial support. Their experiences suggest environmental initiatives can be funded by government organizations, including the Ministry of the Environment, Human Resources Development Canada, Industry Canada, and Ministry of Northern Development and Mines. Possible private foundations would be Laidlaw Foundation, Canada Trust's Friends of the Environment Foundation, and the Allstate Foundation Environment Program. The nonprofit stores are adept at creating free publicity for themselves through special events such as the recycled building material art show. Their stores offset slower sales in building material during the winter months by taking in furniture. In the different ways they find to survive, nonprofit stores promote the environmental benefits of their work.

On the other hand, for-profit stores demonstrate a marketing strategy that emphasizes cost savings to the customer. For-profit stores have strong accounting systems and controls in place, together with business plans that they follow closely. Stress is put on minimizing waste by being very selective in terms of the material they accept and marketing the business effectively. Operations and financial management are not the strong suit of nonprofits. Though nonprofit leaders could be joiners, it is the private sector owners who network with the community and join organizations like the Chamber of Commerce.

By working through the education system, Enviroworks secures advantages that are not available to the private sector. Our store benefits from the tax-exempt status afforded to schools. Enviroworks pays no business tax or property taxes. In addition, it gets a portion of its sales tax back because of the tax exemption. In terms of purchasing, it buys equipment, materials, and advertising through the LDSB. This practice allows the business to take advantage of the huge discounts given to the school board because of its purchasing power. Our store takes advantage of the board's charitable status and its ability to issue tax receipts. By issuing tax receipts, we get donors to lower their taxable incomes.

## SUPPORTING EVIDENCE

Enviroworks measures its success by monitoring its objectives:

- Average classroom attendance among students increases 100 percent from the previous year in the regular school.
- Employment rates for our students at Enviroworks are among the highest in the county.
- Enviroworks diverts over 70 tons of construction and demolition waste from Kingston area landfills. This number is expected to jump to over 100 tons a year.

- This program helps LDSB bring in over $1 million in additional funding from both the private and public sector. The store itself generates gross sales of over $40,000 per year.
- The number of business partners in the program grows from 15 to over 300 in the space of four years.
- Local businesses save hundreds of thousands of dollars in disposal fees.
- Kingston residents are encouraged to change their disposal habits. Over 3,000 Kingston residents divert materials from the landfill every year by using Enviroworks.
- With the help of its business partners and the community, a new environmental business and technology curriculum is developed.

Those who benefit from the program highlight the impact this project has. Terri Flindall, Programming and marketing coordinator for the Greater Kingston Chamber of Commerce, says:

> The Enviroworks program has taken all aspects of running a business and handed it over to the students. With this hands on experience, the program is training students to become competent businesspeople of the future. (Interview, September 18, 1998)

The specific waste management is discussed by John Rhodes, public works manager for the City of Kingston:

> Enviroworks is a component of our comprehensive waste management system and occupies a valuable niche in the management and diversion of solid waste in the Kingston area (Interview, March 12, 1997).

As a business mentor and potential employer, Matt Hutcheon, president of Vista Enterprises, believes:

> The instruction that students receive . . . allows them to leapfrog their peers by being able to understand cash flow forecasts, conduct strategic planning, and sell products to real consumers. (Interview, September 16, 1998)

The benefits of Enviroworks are summarized by Roxanne Flynn, vice principal of QECVI:

> It is incredible to see students who have had a history of attendance problems, and who have lacked motivation in the classroom, now volunteer after school, on Saturdays, during March break, and even in the summer. (Interview, September 15, 1998)

## NATIONAL AND INTERNATIONAL AWARDS

The value of the program is recognized at the local, national, and international levels. In Kingston, Enviroworks is the winner of the Local Industry Focusing on the Environment (L.I.F.E.) Environmental Award from the Greater Kingston Chamber of Commerce, the first school board program to win a major business award in Kingston. It is also the winner of the Ontario Waste Minimization Award as the outstanding nonprofit organization in the province, an award bestowed by the Recycling Council of Ontario. At the national level, the program receives the National Partners in Education Award in the "Broad Community Collaboration" category. This award recognizes the Enviroworks program as one of the best partnerships in Canada. It receives the Honorable Mention Award in the Peter F. Drucker Canadian Non-Profit Award competition.

At the global level, Enviroworks receives the internationally acclaimed Nova Corporation Global Best Award in the "Caring for the Community and the Environment" category among entries from 13 countries. We are awarded the United Nations Global 500 Award. Enviroworks is one of 17 individuals and organizations recognized worldwide for outstanding contributions to the protection of the environment and success in mobilizing community resources to address these problems, the only winner from Canada.

Impressive recognition comes from Japan for the United Nations award. Phil Lalonde, a student, and myself are invited by the United Nations and the Japanese government to receive the personal congratulations of the Japanese prime minister and the Emperor and Empress of Japan. Keizo Obuchi, the former prime minster of Japan, said he admires our enthusiasm, creativity, and teamwork. He believes our accomplishment will encourage young people around the world to act for the environment (Letter, June 16, 1999).

Klaus Topfer, executive director of the United Nations Environment Program, states:

> As a defender of the Environment, Enviroworks has often been a 'silent partner' in the struggle for environmental protection. Its members do not seek awards, but their achievements richly deserve to be recognized. (Letter, April 16, 1999)

## STRATEGIES

While maintaining its positive reputation, Enviroworks is working toward self-sufficiency through its revenue generation. The program attracts a great deal of financial support from both the public and private sectors. Enviroworks does not need the community's money to survive, only its waste! Enviroworks receives more material every year, which converts into funding for the school board.

To increase the number of partnerships, LDSB takes a more proactive approach in terms of its involvement in the business community and develops several strategies to ensure the development of successful partnerships. To increase its partnership base, LDSB joins the Greater Kingston Chamber of Commerce. For a program of this size LDSB looks to the business community for assistance because of its greater experience and expertise. Seeking new partnerships at every level, Enviroworks seeks to implement four strategies: (1) networking, (2) diversification, (3) strategic fit and (4) duplication and expansion.

## Networking

It is people, more than financial resources, that are our most valuable resource and the key to the survival of the program. Students and teachers take an active part by attending business mixers and breakfast meetings and help to organize Chamber events such as the Home and Leisure Expo and Golf Tournament. Students work with the Kingston Jaycees, a leadership group for young professionals. Students participate in, and help organize, the St. Lawrence Fishing Festival, the Polar Plunge, the Over-the-Hill Soap Box Derby, the Green Expo, the Santa Claus Parade, Chilifest, the Festival of Trees, the Citizen of the Year Awards Dinner, and the Young Entrepreneur's Networking Dinner.

These high profile events let students network on behalf of Enviroworks. The public highlight of the year is when Enviroworks student, Charles Wilson, is named the Kingston Jaycee Rookie of the Year, the youngest winner in the 55 year history of the Kingston Jaycees, and is also selected as the winner of the Mayor's Youth Award for Volunteerism.

## Diversification

Previously, two examples of diversification were mentioned: the deconstruction and demolition service and market research service. A number of groups are insisting they would be willing to pay for our services. A new project is to form a product assembly division. When people buy something, such as exercise equipment, sometimes they want it assembled for them. Our students could assemble these products for the retailers and learn a new skill that could translate into their own small business.

## Strategic Fit

Enviroworks approaches businesses in the community that have a "strategic fit" (Bloom, 1993). Home Depot can be a valuable ally in helping to train the students and for the materials they are able to give to Enviroworks. Their corporate philosophy supports both the environment and youth at risk. Home Depot can help us teach students in the areas of customer service, client interaction, product knowledge, selling skills, retail calculations, and stock control.

Since Home Depot is well known for their employee training, our students could participate in training sessions along with their employees. Taking advantage of Home Depot's installation services, we could divert some of the old materials that they remove. The students could help remove the materials. Home Depot might inform customers that Enviroworks is available to take their used materials. This company benefits by training young people; perhaps the most promising graduates of the program could be employed by the company. A pool of workers would be created, trained jointly by Home Depot and Enviroworks. This partnership is an ideal pilot project since our services and organizational interests are similar. The long-term goal is to duplicate our program in cities where a Home Depot already exists.


## SPREADING THE PROGRAM

There is interest in duplicating our model. Groups from across Canada and North America come to see the program. Several different countries are interested in our initiative. I was invited to Japan, Norway, and Scotland to talk to business, education, and government leaders about Enviroworks. Representatives from other countries arrange to have information sent to them. Entrepreneurial training is attractive to nations concerned aboout high unemmployment rates among their youth: Argentina, Great Britain, Greece, Malaysia, and Poland, for example. Other countries, including Australia, Belgium, and Italy, are more interested in the program for its environmental benefits. We are investigating the development of a compact disc that takes interested parties through the process of starting a used building material store. Duplication in other countries expands the possibilities for partnerships to benefit Enviroworks.

Developing a similar program would require varied funding. Our program relates to several areas of funding: environment, job skills training, and youth. Our initial funding came from Human Resources Development Canada through the Youth Internship Program and was followed by a grant from the Ministry of the Environment. The Canada Trust Friends of the Environment Foundation, Shell Environmental Fund, and Community Foundation of Greater Kingston donate to our project. Since Enviroworks is close to being self-sufficient ($30,000 deficit annually), we are increasingly attractive to funding groups.

Enviroworks uses human resources within the school system. Students from various LDSB construction programs, including Renovations Plus and the Building Construction Internship program, perform the renovation work needed for our building. Students pour the concrete floor, frame the building, drywall the classroom and bathrooms, and paint the finished facility. This learning experience for the students saves our project money.

The success of Enviroworks helps LDSB to attract funding for other board initiatives, such as the Bridges to Employment. The Bridges program, a provincially funded initiative, requires school boards to develop organized school-to-work programs. LDSB, in conjunction with the Algonquin and Lakeshore School Board, concentrates on the retail and tourism sectors. As a result of its retail emphasis, Enviroworks helps this new project obtain a grant of $175,000 each year for three consecutive years from the provincial government.

Our project can be duplicated by other school boards and communities. Although there is a need for funding, the business can be started for a relatively low cost if the school board, its business partners, and community are committed. Warehouse space may be donated or rented at a very low price; trucks can be donated if a promotional arrangement is made, and the manager can be a teacher or a volunteer. The labor force consists of students who are paid with academic credits rather than money.

Financing is not the most important factor in duplicating the Enviroworks model. There needs to be an entrepreneurial mindset at the administrative level. A teacher/director needs to understand both the business and training aspects of the Enviroworks model. It is essential that market research be conducted in order to determine the supplier potential and market demand. Nine months of research was undertaken before the doors of Enviroworks opened.

Analysis of the competition is another key factor in order to obtain help from government funds and business volunteers. There is only one other used building material store in Kingston and it does not offer free pickup of materials. Our competitor pays for material, whereas we do not. Our source of material is mostly residential, while our competitor's is mostly commercial. Enviroworks is organized with these differences in mind to avoid competition with a private business. Private business support is needed through marketing, promotion, finance, and strategic planning, and they would not provide this help if we were openly competing with another private business in a small community.

## CONCLUSIONS

Enviroworks is a model for entrepreneurial education. It pools the resources of the community, the education system, and private and public businesses. Although it was initially a school board initiative, Enviroworks grows to become a broad community venture. It provides an opportunity for young people, donors, and business partners to feel proud about contributing to the betterment of their community and its young people. Enviroworks plans to measure its success by the number of students it encourages to stay in school, the tons of material it diverts, the amount of funding it attracts, and the number of businesses, organizations, and individuals who become involved in its program. It is an attempt by a school board to develop human resources through business planning.

## EDITOR'S NOTE

Educators lose sight of academic achievement as they pursue practical benefits. Finding ways for students to carry on construction and building the quarters for Enviroworks raises the question of whether dependency is being nourished inside an institution. The author's emphasis on strategic fit for the program inside the school system and with companies like Home Depot begs the question of whether there is a new educational philosophy involved in this program.

If the program uses the same discipline procedures and the same authority structure, how can it possibly revolutionize a system that diverts most changes? Innovations are similar to diversions to the landfill from new construction in that they extend their lives. Enviroworks is a part of the Focus program, but these changes reach a small number of students. How is the lesson being developed within LDSB for most at-risk students?

An entrepreneurial way of thinking involves combining approaches and trying new initiatives, but it must be the rule rather than the exception. Economist Joseph Schumpeter stressed that entrepreneurs use existing resources for new purposes (Mitchell, 1990). New links are brought out in this chapter, particularly in terms of selling both an environmental program and cost reductions for organizations. The new perceptions do not go beyond the established positions of businesses, for example, avoiding competition with them, and never seeks new recognition within the system for Enviroworks.

Perhaps without realizing it, the program has changed the meaning of partnerships as it developed. The original meaning includes anyone who is prepared to enter a relationship with the school. These relationships are instrumental and temporary. As the networks develop and strategies are formulated, partnerships become more mutual and binding. The difference between nonprofit organizations and for-profit ones are reduced but still significant. Environworks acts as a cooperating non-profit within the school board, but is a calculating competitor outside of the system.

The Neighbors Project in Chapter 7 is a community nonprofit effort, which wants to develop a reciprocal relationship with a similar student organization from another university. It enjoys varied reciprocal ties with people and social agencies in a poor community that both student groups serve. In contrast, Enviroworks wants to keep its competitor at a distance while building partnerships to increase its pool of allies and its own reputation.

The environmental program has won every honor, but we do not hear the voices of students or their parents. We learn that younger students are being attracted to the program and the current students are paid in academic credits rather than money. The students are pawns in the business game. They may be very willing players, but we know no more about them than the welfare mothers who are in the virtual training program discussed in Chapter 5. The students need to be a part of the loop or circle and seek to improve themselves.

# 7

# Student Service in a Nation's Capital: Neighbors Project

## Melinda Pollack

For two years, I was the coordinator of the Neighbors Project, a student-led service program at George Washington University (GW) in the District of Columbia (D.C.). My work is part of an effort by dynamic, thoughtful, and compassionate student leaders and community partners. The services provided to the community are one of the most extensive student projects in the United States. The service project is a reciprocal approach in which students gain as much as they give. It takes many forms but essentially divides into regular activities, such as mentoring younger students, and major events, like a celebration of outstanding volunteers. GW is one part of a web of social services that has emerged in D.C.

This joint program, the Neighbors Project, went through a series of changes in goals and challenges. These changes occurred when I was a volunteer and professional within the Shaw and Columbia Heights neighborhoods of Washington, D.C. My experience together with that of the people in the community is the primary basis of this report. The program had begun in 1993, a year before my start. Other documentation from project reports and accounts of previous community projects are used (Neighbors Project, 2000).

Much of the historical information results from listening and speaking with individuals raised in the neighborhoods; these individuals speak on behalf of community residents, provide historical tours, and are political activists. When not specifically documented, my description of current life in the neighborhoods draws on teachers, doctors, volunteers, youth, parents, social workers, and community organizers. These people are dedicated to the communities in which the Neighbors Project serves.

The Neighbors Project partners with community organizations, including public schools, health clinics, community development corporations, day care centers, and senior service providers. The Neighbors Project operates in collaboration with a sister program at Howard University, one of the United States' most prominent historically Black institutions. Many of the efforts take place in conjunction with Howard University. Student leaders from both universities identify and address community needs.

The Neighbors Project deeply values reciprocity in the work that we do. The essential theme that runs throughout our program is the understanding that while we have a lot to contribute, there is also much to learn. No individual is simply a server, and no individual simply receives service from another. The Neighbors Project aims to build relationships and understanding, and through reciprocity, we make social change happen.

## HISTORY

George Washington University (GW) is located in the heart of downtown Washington, D.C., surrounded by the White House, National Mall, the fashionable Georgetown neighborhood, and homes of the city's high powered businesses and lobbying firms. There is another side to the city: its city government has a notorious history of mismanagement, moving from local to congressional control and back on several occasions. Plagued with poverty and issues that surround life in the inner city, its government and its citizens face an uphill battle to provide quality education, adequate housing, job opportunities, health care, and other social services to a large, predominantly Black population. While many students enter GW, a private nonprofit university, having seen the marble buildings and other tourist attractions, but through the Neighbors Project they will understand the social issues facing many of D.C.'s residents and bring about social change.

Prior to 1993, GW students worked independently throughout the city to address D.C.'s social concerns. With rising numbers of students involved in community service and service-learning, a small group began to create a network that would focus GW's service efforts into one neighborhood. The intention is to relate different community projects in order to create change in the community over time. With the support of GW's Human Services Program, a university major that affords students the opportunity to connect service to the academic curriculum, the Neighbors Project is born. The Project is awarded funding through the federally based Corporation for National Service and became a Service-Learning Corps focused on serving the underresourced Shaw community of northwest Washington.

## MISSION

The Neighbors Project tries to have a sustained and profound impact in the Shaw community. In doing so, the students and staff who guide the Neighbors Project work with community agencies to ensure that the needs of the community are heard and addressed through student service. The Neighbors Project is guided by the voice of the community through its ongoing partnerships with schools, community centers, health clinics, and social service agencies.

In addition to working toward community impact, the Neighbors Project serves as a valuable co-curricular learning experience for the hundreds of students who are involved as leaders and volunteers. The Neighbors Project provides orientation and ongoing opportunities to reflect and learn throughout the service experience. Orientation and ongoing reflection is significant for the quality of the service experience, and in reaching the Neighbors Project mission. Educating students about race, class, and poverty is a part of this mission in the inner city.

## GOALS OF THE NEIGHBORS PROJECT

The Neighbors Project is committed to serving the Shaw community. Shaw lies close to the White House and influential government as well as private industry, but in many respects it is worlds away. During the first half of the 20th century, Shaw was renowned as "the Harlem of Washington, D.C." because of its rich culture and influential African American community. Shaw was a segregated community and home to Howard University, several major theaters, community centers, and restaurants. Famous African American poets, actors, musicians, leaders, and activists, including Duke Ellington and Langston Hughes, visited Shaw often and many made it their home.

The end of the era of racial segregation is the major turning point for the Shaw community. With the doors open for African Americans to live in other neighborhoods, many middle class and affluent African Americans relocate in Washington's booming suburbs and outskirts of the city. With the departure of many residents, the Shaw community loses businesses, cultural activities, and socioeconomic diversity.

By the 1960s Shaw is an impoverished community, lacking essential resources, quality education, and well-maintained housing. The riots in the late 1960s, which mark the close of the civil rights era in cities across the United States, affect the Shaw neighborhood profoundly. Today, burned buildings, including important cultural and recreational centers, are still found in shambles throughout the neighborhood.

Though Shaw was stagnant during the 1970s and early 1980s, in the 1990s, the people in this community begin to see new possibilities for themselves. The building of several subway stops within the Shaw neighborhood renews interest in the community; people begin to see the potential of the community. With new interest, nonprofit organizations struggling for resources start to obtain funding. Additionally, many new nonprofits are started. Shaw continues to be a primarily low-income, minority community. The gentrification of the neighborhood, which is becoming more and more desirable to young professionals, is changing the community.

While meeting the needs of the community, the Neighbors Project works with 15 local organizations that serve individuals and families in Shaw. Fourteen Neighbors Project student leaders serve as staff members of community partner organizations and work with them about 20 hours each week. Additionally, the student leaders serve as liaisons between the campus and the community. Students work to deliver university resources to the community organizations to foster a sense of trust between parties that have experienced mistrust and differences in priorities. The most valuable resource that student leaders bring is the volunteer efforts of their fellow students. Approximately 700 GW students volunteer in the Shaw community.

The Neighbors Project's community partners are extensive:

- *Bright Beginnings*: a Head-Start program for children who are homeless or living in transitional housing. *Bright Beginnings* serves nearly 100 infants and preschool age children, providing full day care, education through a creative curriculum, and emotional support. The student leader housed at *Bright Beginnings* serves as the volunteer coordinator.
- *Northwest Settlement House*: a community center with infant, preschool, after-school enrichment, and senior service programs. *Northwest Settlement House* serves children, families, and senior citizens through a year-round infant care center and preschool, a school-year enrichment center, full-day summer camp, and weekly programs that engage senior citizens in community activities. The student leader housed at *Northwest Settlement House* coordinates volunteers for the early childhood programs and assists with senior citizens' programs.

- *New Community After-School and Advocacy Program*: an after-school program for children and teens focusing on literacy and school achievement in order to help students excel and pursue higher education. *New Community* serves children aged 5 through 17 and supports them to grow academically and artistically throughout their development. Children attending *New Community* show high levels of achievement in school and many continue to volunteer with the organization as they become adults. The student leader at *New Community* plans and teaches lessons within the teen program and tutors teens and children.

- *Calvary Bilingual Multicultural Learning Center*: a community center with preschool, high-tech after-school, and a wide range of culturally focused programs for children and families. *Calvary* focuses on serving a diverse community and is a leader in service as well as advocacy. *Calvary* is a large organization and continues to expand as the needs of Washington's Latino community develop. The student leader at Calvary works as a counselor in the after-school program and assists in developing the computer lab curriculum.

- *Martha's Table*: a community center that includes after-school activities, one-on-one tutoring, and teen programs and provides access to basic needs, including food, clothing, and laundry services. *Martha's Table* is a strong voice in the Shaw community and receives national recognition for its diversity of services. The student leader at *Martha's Table* serves as volunteer coordinator for the nightly tutoring program and is a counselor in the daily after-school program.

- *For Love of Children*: provides comprehensive services to the Shaw community, including literacy training, focuses on a neighborhood tutoring program, an alternative high school for teens, foster parent programs, services for teenage parents, and an outdoor retreat center for community children. Four student leaders work with *For Love of Children*. One works with the alternative high school, coordinating a program that bring teens to the GW campus twice each week for tutoring and mentoring with GW students. Three coordinate community tutoring programs in elementary and junior high schools, utilizing a structured curriculum, which results in students' mastery of reading and mathematics skills.

- *Local elementary and junior high schools:* student leaders and volunteers provide a range of services, including classroom assistance, instruction of a service-learning violence prevention program, and after-school tutoring programs.

- *Bread for the City and Zaccheus Free Medical Clinic (B&Z)*: a community resource center that includes a full-service health clinic in addition to legal and social services, emergency food, and clothing.

*B&Z* has actively served families for 20 years in two community locations. The health clinic serves individuals and families who do not have health insurance and do not qualify for insurance according to city and federal assistance laws. The student leader serves as a medical clinic coordinator and facilitates volunteers in all divisions of *B&Z*.

- *Emmaus Services for the Aging*: a senior citizen outreach center, provides services for seniors such as food shopping, medication delivery, supplemental food delivery, cleaning, and friendly visiting for companionship. *Emmaus* concentrates on services that allow seniors to continue to lead fulfilling, independent lives. The student leader works individually with seniors and recruits teams of volunteers to serve on Saturdays.

- *Manna* and *Shaw Eco-Village*: community development-focused organizations work to bring community voice to the forefront for decision making about the future of Shaw. The student leaders serve both organizations for youth development. Both recruit GW students to work with community youth to address issues the students identify as important. Previous projects include the redesign of a local playground, landscaping of the neighborhood library, and the institution of a community festival for children.

Because the service at each organization is unique, the role of each student leader links the needs of the organization and community to the skills of student volunteers. The staff of the Neighbors Project works with a designated site supervisor at each organization to ensure that the student leader is learning as well as contributing. The staff, site supervisor, and student leader develop programs that involve volunteers to the benefit of the community.

As the following comments from site supervisors about the Neighbors Project reflect on the student leaders and their community partners.

They have helped build bridges, not only between generations, but across cultural, class, and racial divides as well, delivering crucial services and genuine caring with creativity and unflagging energy. . . . I have seen how the experience has transformed the students themselves. By stepping out of the comfortable bounds of typical student life to encounter the realities of aging, mortality, poverty, and racism in D.C.'s inner-city, all [students] have become more thoughtful, caring, and active citizens. (M. Anderson, personal communication, 1998)

Community is an essential component in the success or failure of our children. [The Project has] engaged my students with neighborhood cleanups, intergenerational programs, hearing-impaired programs, and through these experiences the children gained greater self-awareness, greater appreciation for their community, and a cleaner and healthier environment in which to grow and develop. (L. Bunch, personal communication, 1998).

## LEADERSHIP OPPORTUNITIES

These comments, and others like them, reflect the reciprocity present in the ways Neighbors Project volunteers interact with community partners. Students involved in the Neighbors Project benefit from the strong ties between the university and community. Each year, 14 students are choosen to serve as student leaders on the basis of their previous service, commitment, and understanding of community development, and their potential to lead their fellow students. The process of selecting the team is competitive and entails a series of steps involving the Neighbors Project staff and the community partner organizations.

Diversity among the Neighbors Project student leaders is valued. Students of a wide variety of cultural, racial, and religious backgrounds are chosen to lead service efforts. By working together as a tightly woven community, Neighbors Project student leaders experience and explore issues surrounding diversity, both as a small group as well as within the community.

Student leaders participate in a series of diversity-focused workshops designed toexamine the experiences and personal history that form unique individuals. By learning to appreciate each person's characteristics, students are able to learn to work together, appreciating both similarities and differences. Student leaders are trained to facilitate discussions about diversity with volunteers. The volunteers are supported to work on the ongoing issues that are a natural part of the intense intercultural experience.

Students selected to lead the Neighbors Project begin their service with a two-week "preservice training" that builds comradship among students, introduces the community, and provides skills. Community partners play a primary role in the initial training of the student leaders, leading sessions focusing on the four core areas of the Neighbors Project: health, community development, education, and senior services. Neighbors Project members visit community partner organizations, take tours of Shaw and its adjacent neighborhoods, and participate in community service projects.

## COMMUNITY PARTNERSHIPS

The Neighbors Project's partnerships with community organizations are developed throughout the year. A site supervisors' training is held each summer preceding the start of preservice training in order to familiarize community partners with changes in Neighbors' structure and expectations as well as to discuss mutual goals and expectations, and build partnerships between and among community partners. The site supervisors play a primary role in the selection of student leaders as well as the initial preservice training.

As the year progresses, the Neighbors Project staff visit the community partners while student leaders are in action, attend special events, call at least once a month to speak with site supervisors, and meet for a mid-year evaluation of the performance of the student leader. The actions of Neighbors Project staff represent the university's commitment to the community. As a result of consistency and passion for the service taking place, successful and constantly deepening partnerships are fostered.

## EMPOWERING GW STUDENTS

To reach out to as many students on campus as possible, the Neighbors Project forms partnerships with student groups seeking to participate in service. The Neighbors Project serves as a catalyst for service for students and student groups throughout the university. Through the Neighbors Project, student volunteers blanket the Shaw neighborhood with information on services. Most participate on an ongoing basis, for a semester or the entire school year, while others participate on a one time or periodic basis. Students' ongoing service includes:

- Delivering supplemental groceries to senior citizens residing in subsidized housing on Saturday mornings.
- Implementing a community development program for local high school youth, focused on creating and gaining city approval on a plan to renovate Shaw's largest playground and rehabilitate the landscape surrounding the neighborhood library.
- Dispensing medication to patients at the neighborhood free health clinic.
- Tutoring junior high school students twice weekly; enabling students to reach grade level proficiency in reading and math.
- Developing curriculum and facilitating a weekly service-learning program at an elementary school focused on violence prevention for sixth grade students.

## ENTRY POINTS FOR SERVICE

Several special events are planned by student leaders under the guidance of site supervisors. Special events are usually linked with national or local initiatives and offer an opportunity to open the door to service for students who have not previously been involved. These one-time service projects provide major service in a short period of time and bring in hundreds of students. The following are special events that took place during the 1999–2000 school year:

- *Make a Difference Day* is a national service sponsored by *USA Today* newspaper and other organizations each fall. Neighbors Project student leaders coordinate a "Volunteer Week" on the GW campus coinciding with Make a Difference Day. During the week, the efforts of GW students are highlighted and recognized through a "Neighbors Project Prize Patrol" that delivers donated gifts to volunteers and a free barbeque for all volunteers. The culmination of the week is a day-long service project during which children who participate in after-school programs come to GW's campus for an afternoon of arts and crafts activities, including pumpkin painting and macaroni art.
- *Walk to Help the Homeless* is a D.C.-based annual event that focuses on raising funds for local organizations that serve homeless and low-income families. Neighbors Project members recruit several hundred students to collect pledges and walk the 5-kilometer event. All proceeds benefit the GW community partner organizations. One team raises $15,000, the single largest donation made to the organization.
- *National Youth Service Day* is an annual event sponsored by Youth Service America to raise awareness about services provided by young people throughout the United States. They are recognized during the second weekend in April. A Neighbors Project leader is rewarded who coordinates a service project to refurbish the playground at Bright Beginnings preschool and organize a library out of hundreds of donated children's books. Volunteers from GW, Georgetown University, and local nonprofit organizations are recruited by this leader.
- *Hands on DC* is a local event organized each year in order to renovate D.C.'s public schools. This year, a team of 70 GW students spent the day at Shaw Junior High School, where the Neighbors Project leads an after-school tutoring program. GW volunteers paint the exterior doors and the hallways of the school, which staff in facilities management had not done due to budget constraints. This event is run by volunteers, but community members coordinate it. The yearly event rehabilitates dozens of D.C. public schools.

## COMMUNITY IMPACT

The Neighbors Project accomplishes its mission by working with students, community members, and affiliated organizations. The Project is practical, results based, and is an ideological effort. The results of these collaborations are abundant. Neighborhood parks are cleaned, the neighborhood library is filled with flowers in bloom reflecting each season, community festivals are staffed with volunteers, medication is dispensed to patients at the local health clinic, and senior citizens receive visitors and helping hands to collect groceries and medication, clean their apartments, or deliver supplemental food. Children from first grade through high school are tutored in a one-on-one supportive atmosphere during and after school, and preschools drastically lower their child–adult ratio with the assistance of a large group of weekly volunteers.

Community change is difficult to quantify, but the results of D.C.'s 2000 standardized testing of public school students are slightly higher than last year, and a *Washington Post* article (Blum, 2000) notes that the school system attributes the rise in large part to extracurricular work being done with students.

One Neighbors Project partner organization, For Love of Children, which oversees three after-school programs at two schools, measures the progress that students make by grade level through periodic diagnostic exams. On average, students enrolled in a For Love of Children/Neighbors Project tutoring program improve between one and two grade levels in their reading abilities. In Washington, a large proportion of students perform below grade level, and the proportion grows as students grow older. Working with children at the elementary and junior high school level helps to ensure that more students will not fall behind.

On an organizational level, the collaborative work of the Neighbors Project allows local organizations to meet their service missions. Many organizations, especially those that provide early childhood education, have highly transient staffs. The Neighbors Project tries through continuity-provided student leaders is a stable force in the neighborhood, supplementing the efforts of our community partners.

Through its community ties, the project breaks down barriers often assumed in D.C.'s politicized, racial and economically divided climate. The Project builds bridges of mutual respect and understanding between community residents, organization staff, and GW students. Successes are achieved through varied programs, formal training, consistency, and dedication.

Strong relationships are built between young parents of children and the GW students who organize the programs. The parents and the GW students are similar in age, but otherwise would not have the opportunity to meet and learn from each other. The Neighbors Project works to break down preconceived notions that are brought into the relationship. The goal is for each person to view themselves and offer others individual contributions in order to learn from each new experience.

## BECOMING CITIZENS

The impact of the Neighbors Project on GW student leaders and volunteers is difficult to quantify. One 1999–2000 Neighbors Project student leader wrote:

> The biggest improvement that I have seen in myself this year has to be my sense of accomplishment. . . . I have learned that one person can make a big difference! I've learned how to recruit, train, organize, and maintain a force of volunteers [and] how to keep people coming back. I've learned better communication skills [and] to be aggressive when the situation calls for it. I've learned how to be more flexible [and] how to take complements, and how to take criticism. I've learned about how a nonprofit works and how to be an administrator. I've learned how to lean on other people for help when I need it. I've learned how to plan humongous projects that actually work [and] how to get 18 crazy three-year-olds to listen to me, and how to dodge baby throw-up. I've learned from my Corps members [fellow Neighbors Project leaders] about their lives and about diversity. . . . I've learned how to balance my life. . . . I've learned about leadership and most importantly about friendship. (A. Crowell, personal communication, May 2000)

> I have been inspired. I have faith in this world. I believe that there are enough people in the world who will make a difference. I believe, more than hope, that poverty will be overcome. There will be a guarantee of healthcare. (A. Geiger, personal communication, June 1999)

> Because I did not come from a poor family, I have grown to understand the less fortunate. When I first came to this school I was exposed to for the first time to the homeless and the poor. Today, my primary objective is to pull out of people's minds the ignorance of the poor by educating them and showing them that the less fortunate are not as society sees them. (J. Lee, personal communication, June 2000)

Students leave the Neighbors Project with an understanding of civic engagement. As a result of their service, many students pursue careers as teachers in inner-city schools, social work, nonprofit administration, psychology, law, and medicine to help communities and people in need.

## FINDING NEW AND CONTINUING SUPPORT

While the Neighbors Project has many strengths, it also faces several limitations. These limitations include reliance on grant-based funding, the transient schedules of college students, and the challenge of supporting a large number of community and institutional partnerships. The Neighbors Project is funded by the Corporation for National Service, which is the umbrella organization for AmeriCorps, otherwise known as the U.S. domestic Peace Corps. The Neighbors Project is supported by the Cafritz Foundation, which makes a large number of social investments in the Washington, D.C., community.

The grants supply funds for the salary of a Neighbors Project Coordinator, stipends for Neighbors Project leaders, funding for retreats, training, supplies, and recognition activities. GW supplies many in-kind resources, including office and meeting space, phone and computer access, and technological resources. Various university departments including athletics and recreation, catering, and the student union donate tickets to events, food, and space for children to come to campus. While support, both in-kind and financial, is strong, the challenge of funding remains. Because the Neighbors Project is not institutionally financed, external funding must constantly be sought.

Like many university programs focusing on community service, the Neighbors Project faces the challenge of educating student participants about service learning and the philosophy of volunteer work. The GW campus highlights the exceptional work of students through its own version of the Academy Awards, a formal evening affair that includes a reception and ceremony. The Excellence in Student Life Awards program recognizes students involved in campus life through student government, the yearbook, Greek life, and community service. Many students involved in community service programs do not want to be thanked for their service. The Neighbors Project encourages student leaders to develop and implement creative ways to maintain a high level of energy and motivation among student volunteers.

Many volunteer students find their education is more meaningful because of the academic link to the Human Services Progam. These classes require students to participate in service as a part of their learning experience. While the support that the Neighbors Project receives from the Human Services Program is strong, additional linkages with academic departments are needed. Further university support for service learning enhances the experiences of other students.

The Neighbors Project is successful because of the commitment of its staff to write and maintain grants for funding. Reliance on grants requires a large portion to writing, editing, and communication. The reliance on grant funding makes long term strategic planning difficult because grantors often change priorities or grants are written in order to fill expectations of a grantor, thus requiring changes in the program based on regulations rather than identified needs. An increase in institutional funding for service initiatives would alleviate this problem and enhance community belief in university commitment.

The transient schedules of university students are an additional limitation of the Neighbors Project. Students come to spend their four years at GW from across the nation and the globe. Few students are from D.C. or its metropolitan area. Numerous students study abroad during their undergraduate years, and many leave the University during summer and the month-long winter break. The university year is two distinct periods: September through early December and January through April. During the time beyond the semesters most students take on internships and part-time jobs as a result of the abundant opportunities in Washington.

Midterms and finals are obstacles because they do not correlate with breaks in the public school system calendar. When breaks and scheduling conflicts are considered, there are only about six months during which student volunteers are involved in service. Student volunteers are seen as inconsistent members of the community, unable or unwilling to make service a priority. This problem is confronted through open communication with community organizations and planning programs to follow student schedules and to meet neighborhood needs, such as scheduling major events.

## A NEIGHBORING PROJECT

GW's Neighbors Project operates in collaboration with a nearly identical program, Project C.H.A.N.G.E., based at Howard University. Partnership between GW and Howard was a natural fit because of Howard's location adjacent to the Shaw community and its longtime commitment to community development. Since 1997, the Neighbors Project and Project C.H.A.N.G.E. have shared the responsibilities and resources of the Corporation for National Service grant. Student leaders from both campuses have been trained together and serve together at seven community organizations. Because of the depth of the partnership with Howard University, a great deal of staff time is devoted to cultivating this partnership.

The partnering of two large educational institutions is difficult because both campuses have bureaucracies that operate very differently. Also, the goals of both campuses and the offices within which Neighbors Project and Project C.H.A.N.G.E. are housed are different, with GW focusing largely on student development and Howard focusing more on community development. General differences in office cultures at both campuses create challenges for the staff of both programs as well as the student leaders. As a result, decisionmaking is a lengthy process.

Ongoing communication and weekly meetings for members of both campuses' staff are maintained. Strategic planning meetings are held several times each year with stakeholders from both campuses. Both campuses agree that the partnership is worth the extra work because of the added impact on the student learning experience as well as the community's sense of strengthened support.

Student leaders believe bringing together two distinct groups from culturally different campuses initially leads to misconceptions and miscommunication. The combination forces discussion of societal issues such as racism. However, friendships and partnerships are also formulated among students from the two campuses. The students exchange views. A GW student, Alyssa Heresberger, believes Howard students help them gain entry into a community, while a Howard student, Rachel Hunt, thinks both student groups develop tight bonds (Lechner, 1999, p. 4). AmeriCorps, which sponsors both universities, is a national and local partnership that allows individuals to explore themselves within the bonds of the community.

The community organizations that house the Neighbors Project need more direct support if they are to assist more students and universities. Staff turnover affects the work of the Neighbors Project because of the need to rebuild positive relationships with new staff members. Most staff of the partner organizations do not have time to further develop the relationship with volunteers from the Project. These staff already work far beyond 40 hours each week at their organizations, and it is an extra effort to work with the Project.

## CONCLUSION

The Project faces several challenges and limitations that are similar to those faced by all universities seeking strong community ties. The Neighbors Project is a program that links people who otherwise may not build relationships with each other. The individuals, who lead the project in their passion for social justice, are what makes this program valuable and substantial. Student leaders, staff at community partner organizations, community members, and university staff, working in collaboration, each play an important role.

The Neighbors Project is reciprocal; the community, the students, and the university as an institution profit in different ways. The community gains hands needed to provide essential services on an ongoing and periodic basis. The students have a unique experiential learning opportunity, which develops their sense of civic responsibility and their understanding of complex social issues, which influences their future career plans.

The program helps the students achieve an important but neglected mission to serve as a member of the community, while providing them with an opportunity to learn and grow as citizens and leaders.

## EDITOR'S NOTE

The program at George Washington University is similar to widespread efforts by students to become active in the social life of communities (Mitchell, 1998). Though these approaches were typical of the 1960s, college students are now pioneering in service projects. Some college graduates pursue teaching with at-risk students in continuing project, such as *Teach for America*. The efforts of college students are emulated by high schools who are requiring service for graduation.

This study of college volunteers reveals how community development is carried out by diverse organizations in large urban areas. Education is one part of a larger problem. Child care, medical services, student tutoring, programs for elders, and provisions for survival are the services provided by students together with a variety of community organizations. The efforts are partially unified by the ceremonies and forms of recognition within the community and at the university.

The coordination of efforts and the host of efforts provided are both activated by the sense of crisis in American cities. Students in rival universities develop common ties as they work together with community organizations. The common efforts are similar to the unity based on shared relationships that rural communities possess. Though poverty is greater in rural areas, they are not receiving the same attention. Chapters in Part III explore rural communities and the possibilities they offer.

Aside from rural areas, many communities that are designated as "emergencies" are not able to bring bureaucratic organizations together or encourage community efforts outside of them. The continuing problem with student initiatives: How are schools or universities going to control them if they become controversial? High schools avoid this problem when they administer the service program rather than let the students do so. Control denies the students the opportunity to be empowered as citizens. Letting students make decisions always involves risks for the institutions and the young people, but there is no other way to learn decision making.

The institutions themselves often act on the basis of inertia and need the challenge that students can provide. It is likely that cooperation between the student organizations at George Washington and Howard University is limited because their respective universities provide no model of cooperation. Indeed separate identities are a problem that reform in higher education must confront. There is also the continuing separation of community service projects in universities with those in schools. The students in different universities and the two educational levels may be interacting, but the institutions are not.

Community service, with all its specific goals, reveals as many problems for cooperation involving tertiary education as did professional development partnerships discussed in Part I. The universities usually have more problems in providing minimal community and health services for those directly affected by their existence. Integration of social and medical services around schools, as discussed in Chapter 9, requires grassroots community efforts. Chapter 8 shows how a program for schools by a symphony association and a university can become such an effort. The surprising example of the arts shows how communities can be unified by ceremonies and strategies that bring community organizations together.

# 8

# Community Support for Music: Symphony Education Partnership

Roberta Lamb

The gymnasium is already buzzing with wiggling, whispering girls and boys. Will they, can they, sit still long enough to get through the program? How will they like the show? Those of us who feel inclined chat a bit. "Which school are you from? Wow, you've traveled all that way! What pieces were you and your teacher working on? Hey, I think we're playing that this morning. Maybe you guys can join in . . . This is a viola . . . . Yes, I've been playing a long time. What kind of music do you like? Ah, I think I can play 'My Heart Will Go On' . . . I'm not sure about "Blue," how does it go again? Oh, looks like I'd better get ready. Nice talking to you, have fun." Wiggling, fidgeting, poking, and giggling—will they last? . . . "Are those guys really going to play sandpaper?" They laugh. Their faces light up, more poking—"Hey, that's the song we did in class!" They're quiet, they're right there, captivated by the music. They know what's coming next: the clarinet, the flute, the piccolo. It doesn't matter where these kids are from, their reactions are the same: they enjoy the concerts because they can participate. They're not just hearing us play, they're playing with us. They become the stars, and they love it! That's what we're here for, isn't it? (J. Coles, personal communication, June 2000)

These children are brought together because a symphonic triangle exists among the Kingston Symphony Association, the Limestone District School Board, the Algonquin and Lakeshore Catholic District School Board, and Queen's University School of Music. The triangle is the Symphony Educational Partnership (SEP). The metaphor of the triangle can reveal the partnerships as a stable, balanced, yet flexible geometric form. This partnership consists of three equal partners: the schools, the university, and the orchestra in a Canadian city, and the surrounding rural area. The triangle attempts to remain equilateral, although at one time or another, any one of the three segments (schools–orchestra–university) may be greater than the others are. The triangle suggests the competing values that may be found among various combinations of partners as they work together. Although the focus is on the symphony triangle, attention is given to some of the social context that affects, applies pressure, or activates the triangle.

The orchestra partnership tries to build support in and arround the city of Kingston in the Canadian province of Ontario. Descriptions of this city and Ministry of Education and Training policies and practices provide a frame for portraits of the partners. Both conflicts and consensus are involved in the development of this partnership. From reflections by the partners on its evolution, principles emerge. The principles and their implementation enable this grassroots partnership to garner community support for music in the schools.

## LOCAL CONTEXT

Kingston is a small urban center (about 120,000) in a rural region. Though it is a city equidistant from Toronto, Montreal, and Ottawa, rural communities look to it as their cultural center. The first European settlement of this city was the French Fort Frontenac, but it is the English descendants of the Loyalists who fled the American Revolution who dominate the city's history. The second largest ethnic population is an older Portuguese community. There is a continuing French community, an established Indian (Hindu) community, and a growing Asian community. Queen's University, the Royal Military College, a community college, half a dozen hospitals, and as many prisons are located in Kingston.

The region is hard-hit by government cutbacks because much of the economic base is public institutions (the university, hospitals, prisons) and government. Grants from arts councils are reduced by cutbacks. Provincial grants that municipalities used to have to give, in part, to the arts, are decreased. Unlike, Montreal, Toronto, or Ottawa, Kingston boasts no major fully professional orchestra, dance, or opera company. The city struggles to support major performing arts organizations.

The Kingston Symphony Association (KSA) is unique in Canada. The association includes the professional orchestra, a volunteer choral society, a youth orchestra, a junior strings training ensemble, and an avocational adult string orchestra. The KSA sponsors unusual annual performances, such as the Canada Day *Beat Beethoven* "run." KSA plays a Beethoven symphony in the city park and nearly 1,000 runners and walkers attempt to complete the 8- or 4-kilometer course before the last note is heard. *Beat Beethoven* includes playing the 1812 Overture as Old Fort Henry fires real cannons, and the opera-in-concert presents feature singers, such as Jean Stillwell.

During 1998–1999, the Kingston Symphony premiered seven new Canadian works for orchestra. The KSA is the only symphony in Ontario to win two Lieutenant Governor's Awards for the Arts (1996 and 1999), a competitive award for an arts organization showing exceptional community service and private-sector support. Kingston Symphony remuneration for services is not enough to be the musicians' sole source of income. Musicians must engage in additional paid employment as high school music teachers, adjunct music instructors, or other careers completely outside of music (K. Carleton & J. Coles, personal communication, June 2000).

The second point of the triangle, Queen's University, is a research-intensive university with a small School of Music and a medium-sized Faculty of Education. The School of Music has links with community arts and education organizations and with professional musicians. Just as Kingston does not have the resources of larger cities, Queen's University does not have the resources of prestigious music schools. Seventy-five percent of School of Music students become music teachers, although students are not streamed. Though the School of Music tries to improve the quality of music teacher preparation and strengthen music in the region's schools, the responsibility for teacher certification belongs to the Faculty of Education. The medium-sized Faculty of Education has fewer full-time music education professors than does the School of Music. Cooperation between the School of Music and the Faculty of Education ebbs and flows.

The third partner, the Limestone Public School Board, is centered in Kingston but includes Frontenac, Lennox, and Addington counties. Rural schools are included in this board as are those in the publicly supported Catholic system. The Algonquin and Lakeshore Catholic District School Board is the largest separate school board in Ontario, expanding over 200 kilometers. Both school boards stretch from Lake Ontario in the south to north of the Trans-Canada highway. In addition, one county within the area of both school districts has the highest long-standing unemployment rate in Ontario.

Locally, the quality of arts (visual art, music, drama, and dance) teachers is left up to each school board, but it is limited by the provincial funding formula and related regulations. A historic custom affects arts education. Elementary teachers are generalists; secondary teachers are likely to be specialists. Music education programs at universities are originally for training high school specialists, while normal schools included some music in their programs for elementary teachers. In 1950, the first music education program began at the University of Toronto for the preparation of high school band or orchestra directors (Green & Vogan, 1991).

Very few arts specialist teachers remain in either school district. Elementary students in both school boards receive little music instruction within the schools. Classrooms present a wide range of teacher and student capabilities and experiences. This variety makes it difficult to achieve a cohesive music curriculum.

## DEMANDS BY MINISTRY OF EDUCATION AND TRAINING

The way the Ontario Ministry of Education and Training defines adequate subject preparation for teaching music limits the quality of music teaching in the schools. Elementary teachers are not required to have any preservice preparation in music, although they are required to teach music as part of what appears to be a fairly rigorous arts curriculum. During the past decade there are three major curriculum shifts, so it is difficult for anyone to know which curriculum is used in any particular class or school.

In 1998, the Ministry of Education and Training implemented a new elementary curriculum that requires much greater musical knowledge (as well as much greater knowledge in all subjects) from teachers than their education provided. This curriculum requires stringent reporting on specific outcomes, which creates new problems. For example, identifying the instruments of the orchestra is required in grades 2 through 7, changing to "identify tone colors in various performing ensembles" in grade 7, a task that is likely easier than the grade 2 requirement to identify families of instruments. Grade 4 students are required to "demonstrate correct embouchure" even though instrumental music instruction does not begin until grade 9. Prescribed "creative activities" include limited skills such as reading standard music notation (*The Ontario Curriculum*, 1998).

In 1998, the government amalgamates school boards, which increases the number of students and the geographic area for each board. In addition to amalgamating school boards, the legislation micro-manages the decreased powers of the local school boards, prescribes standardized testing, specific standards for specific marks, and a provincial report card; increases assigned teaching time; decreases teacher preparation time; and reduces professional development. As a response, teachers engage in a province-wide political protest against the provincial government, closing the schools for several weeks. Currently, teachers are scrambling to keep up with the government-imposed changes, though some try to teach what they think is important in spite of the government.

The stages of the Symphony Education Partnership (SEP) are not easily defined since it arose from community need rather than grants council or governmental agency regulations. The initial stage ends when all the current partners become active participants. Future commitments are still being developed. Challenge, conflict, change, and consensus flow through each stage in retrospect, although the partners were not fully aware of the processes at the time.

## PLANNING (1991–1995)

The music director, the symphony manager, the recently retired school board arts coordinator (a KSA board member and symphony violinist) and the author, a music education professor, formed the first Symphony Education Partnership (SEP) Committee. These three people are the committed leaders make this project succeed. The KSA music director is flexible and humble, willing to collaborate with school and university personnel, while encouraging the musicians. The violinist-retired teacher is an orchestral musician who worked in the schools in this region for many years, and is a great facilitator, knowing how to communicate educational policies and practice to other musicians and to bureaucrats. The music education professor is the catalyst to involve potential teachers and plan for the project's future.

Initially two partners, the Kingston Symphony and the School of Music, want to work together beyond the common promotional activities, such as reduced price tickets for music students, volunteer experience, and scholarships. Prior to 1991, these were the typical activities of the players. The school boards take some time to join. The public school board's arts facilitator hesitates due to a previous frustrating experience with the School of Music. These doubts dissipate as the program develops connections with the elementary curriculum and a school board representative joins the committee in 1993. The Faculty of Education music education professor declines an invitation to join. From these first steps, this partnership is envisioned as one of collaboration, as defined by Nierman:

> . . . both organizations take an active role in formulating the goals or objectives that are mutually beneficial. A "We" process mode develops. Leadership is shared by individuals from both organizations. Both groups

contribute staff time, resources, and capabilities to accomplish the task. (1993, p. 26)

Of course, the SEP involves three distinct organizations rather than the two referred to in Neirman's model.

According to the KSA, educational concerts provided in past years were always successful but were discontinued. The music education professor suggests a program to combine preservice teacher education with symphony school concerts. University students could present sample lessons to the elementary students to prepare them for the symphony's education concerts. Elementary lessons would be drawn from the curriculum in order to ensure symphony concerts become an integral part of that curriculum, not merely a field trip. With proper planning a program provides a meaningful field experience within the music degree, improves the quality of music instruction in the schools, and the symphony encounters a more receptive young audience for its concerts.

Acting upon the music director's suggestion, the partners decide the Symphony Education Partnership should target elementary students in grade 4. The partners agree on an essential component: grade 4 students would perform with the symphony in some musically and pedagogically meaningful way. The Symphony Education Committee implements the program for the 1993–1994 academic year, with only the public school board participating. The committee feels some urgency to begin the program with a minimal plan in order to prove its viability, rather than wait until all protocols are in place. The separate, or Catholic, school board joins the program in the second year. During 1993–1995, the music education professor shepherds the academic course requirements through various levels of university governance.

The music education professor provides participating grade 4 teachers with copies of lesson plans and an audiotape of orchestral selections that university students will use in their classrooms. The university students facilitate a curriculum follow-through in each grade 4 classroom after the symphony concert and with the guidance of the music education professor. During their previous university class session, the students practice peer-teaching the lesson. The university students then teach the grade 4 classes. At the conclusion of the project, the music education professor sends evaluation forms to the participating grade 4 teachers.

## EARLY CHALLENGES AND CONFLICTS

Comments are collected from teachers in 1995, 1999, and 2000. In these evaluation forms, teachers talk about grade 4 students attending a symphony orchestra concert: "Most had never been to a symphony concert and they were surprised by the pleasure it gave them." The symphony's value to elementary students is the beginning of consensus in the first year of the partnership.

For the orchestra, the primary reason for scheduling school concerts is to develop a future audience. Unfortunately, the Canadian Opera Company chorus singers, who perform in the second season, do not understand the pedagogical import of their presentation or the purpose of the partnership. The opera singers are focused on their roles as highly trained opera singers. Professional performing artists often focus on the quality of the performance rather than the educational process. Playing for a young audience is not valued artistically.

This attitude is a by-product of professional training and subculture, which traditionally values the soloist or virtuoso much more highly than the orchestral musicians or the audience. The same attitude could be seen in many musicians, who view the school concert as primarily a performance. Some of them see the performance as entertainment rather than education. This attitude is reflected in one musician's comments:

> I prefer to focus on the orchestra rather than providing accompaniment for something else [like dance or opera]. We should wear a tux to bring the atmosphere of the concert hall to the gymnasium. (J. Coles, personal communication, June 2000)

Teachers provide the most varied, challenging comments to the partnership. Their responses often conflict with the musicians, the SEP Committee, and other teachers. This is due to the many educational philosophies and practices of the profession. One teacher raves over programming and the preparation of the university music students in an evaluation form comment:

> My students were most enthusiastic about opera. It was great for me, too. I was very impressed with my two first-year students: comfortable, fun, informed but properly controlled learning environment.

Another teacher tersely dislikes the concert program and criticizes the university music students' skills: "No opera. Better classroom management." Teachers are consistently making concrete suggestions for improving the overall educational value of the partnership. These suggestions are often things the committee had not considered, but worked to implement the next year:

> The classroom teacher—if aware of the details of program content at the outset—could increase the merit of this opportunity through integration of its content. The more lively the music the better.

Teachers provide insights into equity issues that raise awareness among some of the SEP Committee members: "I like having a male and female QU [Queen's University] student together, as students often perceive music as a female subject."

These insights provide thoughtful commentary on authenticity and cultural practices.


## DEVELOPMENT (1996–2000)

The Symphony Education Partnership builds on the previous year's concerts, curriculum, and experiences. Each year features different content, albeit based on similar procedures and structure. Flexibility comes from the SEP Committee's problem-solving approach to the partnership.

The school board representatives take on the tasks of confirming which teachers in specific schools are willing to take a pair of university music students, thus centralizing the placement process. They take over the responsibility for distributing and tabulating the project evaluations. The school board representatives and music education professor work together to write a curriculum that grade 4 generalist teachers could use in preparing their classes for the concert, especially if they did not have university music students placed in their classroom. These curricular materials are provided to all grade 4 teachers, whether or not they elect to attend the professional development workshop given by the SEP Committee.

Changes to the university curriculum have an impact on the program. In order to ensure university students know more music, the Introduction to Music Education/Partnership Program is moved from a first-year to a second-year course. Although the students are much more knowledgeable and better prepared to teach, fewer university students register for the course, decreasing the number of grade 4 placements. The university course materials are placed on the Internet, allowing all classroom teachers access to the lessons the university students are teaching.

The school board SEP Committee members want to expand the project so that those grade 4 students in outlying areas would have the opportunity to participate in the concerts. Distance limits the scope of university student participation, since they only have one time slot scheduled for this purpose, and it was impossible to preplan who might have a car available for transportation. All grade 4 classes within the two participating school boards are given the opportunity to participate every second year. Simultaneously, all university students are placed in schools accessible to them within their course timetable.

By 1998–1999, teacher demand for music practice teachers exceeds availability, so the following year the university music students are placed individually in grade 4 classrooms in order to provide instruction in more classrooms. Individual placements proves a failure. The failure is due to lack of immediate peer mentor's support and shared perceptions of classroom experience. Another factor contributing to this failure is the mistaken belief in the university music students' advanced musical knowledge. They are often viewed as experts in a curriculum-driven classroom taught by a generalist. These novice university music students have no experience with classroom management, modification of curriculum for children with special needs, or the realities of school culture. Following the principle of mutual benefit for each of the partners, paired placement is reinstated in order to promote a comprehensive music experience in the grade 4 classrooms.

In contrast to the problems of placing teachers, there is a challenge, which the SEP Committee enjoys, to find ways for the elementary students to perform with the symphony. The value of an authentic musical experience is identified by most teachers as the key to the program. One comments: "I *loved* doing the Orchestra Song—giving kids a chance to participate!"

The different capabilities, experience, and expertise of partners are a problem for the Symphony Education Partnership. The university professors and orchestra musicians are skilled and experienced professionals in music. The university students are focused on becoming professional musicians and music specialists. The school teachers are skilled as educators.

Musicians' and teachers' understandings of music education through the partnership often conflict:

> The *Young Person's Guide* (Britten) is an excellent thing to do [musician].
> I don't think it was necessary to do *Introduction to the Orchestra* (Britten) as a performance piece, if teachers already cover it in the presymphony package [teacher].

The SEP Committee tries to include teachers in the planning and implementation of the curriculum. Generalist teachers have limited musical knowledge. This makes it imperative for the SEP Committee to consider their feedback in order to develop a curriculum that encourages teacher growth.

The curriculum package must be one that is self-explanatory because not all grade 4 teachers will attend the voluntary professional development workshop. A teacher who may need the professional development workshop says:

I wouldn't have started a recorder unit if I had known this was happening in February. As a result, I didn't teach my class the Orchestra Song in time for the Symphony. Yikes! It would have been great if a Queen's student could have been able to come up to our school—even for half a day.

Teachers who do attend the workshop and have come to understand the program express concerns about those who do not in the evaluation forms: "It should be ESSENTIAL that the curriculum package is addressed by all the classes attending. Only then do the students realize the full impact of the performance."

The school partners want every school to have equal access to the concerts and university music students. The schools seek equal access to the orchestra and the university, but the resources of these two partners are limited. A school principal may want to place a university music student in a classroom that needs the most support in the arts, and some teachers want university music students to relieve them of teaching responsibilities. Both of these situations constitute inappropriate placements.

## UNIVERSITY MUSIC STUDENTS

Unlike the teachers, the music students are in a dilemma as a result of the education they do have. Their music professors and professional musician mentors see them as just beginning to learn their skills. Some orchestra musicians identify those music students who take music education courses as less talented or musical than those who take music to become professional musicians. A musician-teacher-researcher comments:

> I was thinking about the project in terms of teacher as learner and teacher as expert. The success of the step dancing part of the project depended on the teachers' willingness to become learners. . . . This is especially true in areas like music and dance, where you can't prepare yourself with just research. (S. Johnson, personal communication, June 24, 2000)

Simultaneously, when these university music students arrive in the schools, they are identified as a talented elite. To generalist classroom teachers music students are such experts that the teachers forget that they are still students lacking classroom experience. When the music students are placed in classrooms with experienced and highly competent teachers and given support as beginning teachers, they begin a successful teaching career:

> I was able to take what I was learning in my lectures and implement these new and different teaching techniques into the classroom. The practical

classroom experience I received from this program was a great asset for future educational endeavors. When attending the symphony presentation students said to me: "Look, that's a cello!" or "Did you see how fast the timpanist played?" or "I really liked the Stravinsky piece." (D. Clarke, personal communication, June 15, 2000)

Most music students are motivated and enthusiastic. They want to please everyone—professors, musicians, teachers, children—and end up tripping over all the contrasting and contradicting expectations. For them the Symphony Education Partnership is a balancing act among their music education, the curriculum they teach, and their transition from university to schools.

## THE MYSTERY OF THE ORCHESTRA

The traditional symphony orchestra structure that includes the practice of only the music director making decisions is not conducive to cooperative and collaborative efforts. This traditional structure does not work with a small symphony orchestra composed of a combination of contract players, university music students, and per-service players. Most of the KSA contract players teach as applied music instructors in the university or in high schools.

The part-time work and low wage require that the orchestra management not make excessive or autocratic demands on the musicians in order to maintain a skilled, cooperative, functioning, and musical ensemble. A small orchestra like the KSA runs on volunteers and the good will of its musicians. An autocratic music director can destroy such a group, but aspects of the "maestro myth" live on and are cherished (Lebrecht, 1991).

The male, typical "maestro" can limit an orchestra's repertoire. Many musicians and traditional audiences favor the "great music" composed by dead, white, European males. It is difficult to introduce cultural diversity and new pieces in a small orchestra. As the SEP develops, the Kingston Symphony takes risks in programming new music for the schools, including one piece commissioned specifically for the educational concerts. The composer of this new work ignores time requirements and expectations for an easy-to-sing melody.

Since Western classical music training begins as training toward a soloist career, the same problems composers encounter with young audiences are found among orchestral musicians. This attitude can be exacerbated if the musicians believe that "those who can do, and those who can't, teach." It may be that some orchestral musicians are shy people who much prefer being part of an amazing wall of symphonic sound than to interact.

Professional development for musicians as educators assists the transition from solo-musician to musician-teacher. It is also a change of orchestral culture to develop a musical organization that is as pedagogically effective as it is artistic. In 1999, the Kingston Symphony schedule a series of workshops to develop musicians' improvisational skills and increase their interaction with students and audience. The KSA sponsors the same workshop for classroom teachers and university music students. Some orchestra musicians participate in these workshops, Babineau (2000) and Weigold (1999).

The musicians no longer see the SEP concerts as children's entertainment, but recognize the educational value, so the "orchestra participates in local education out of its unique capacities and concerns." (Myers, 1996, p. 102). The orchestra representatives on the SEP Committee believe: "We used to hear condescending comments about the 'kiddy concerts' but that attitude has disappeared." The concertmaster writes:

> The preparation for the concerts is crucial and makes it much more meaningful. The choice of music is largely very good. The involvement of the kids in the concerts has been central to their success. We're doing a really good job.

He now identifies the forging of musical quality and pedagogical value into one.

Many musicians participate with a whole-hearted sense of community that is reflected in the subscription concerts. One university music student puts it:

> The Kingston Symphony is definitely a strong part of the community in Kingston. Whenever I go to the symphony now, I recognize former instructors, students, and faculty members. I have been to several community events where the symphony has played. I never get this sense of connection in Toronto. I feel there is a larger attachment to the community here. (P. Kole, personal communication, June 14, 2000)

Community support for music grows in direct proportion to SEP's progress.

## RENEWED CONSENSUS

By the end of February 1999, SEP completed seven years of programming and was ready to examine the terms of the alliance. The SEP Committee holds a series of planning and reflection meetings. The Faculty of Education music education professor again is invited to participate, but withdraws after a few meetings, citing research priorities as the reason. The planning and reflection process continues. During this time, the SEP Committee identifies six principles underpinning the SEP practices and program, and makes commitments to continue developing the partnership.

## SIX SEP PRINCIPLES

The principles that are selected are defined after a lengthy process that highlights the differences among the partners and test their commitment to collaboration. The partners acknowledge that the musical and marketing interests of the symphony may not always coincide with the pedagogical concerns of the schools, that the interests of the university are different from those of either the schools or the symphony.

The review discussions did not proceed in a linear fashion, but rambled from success to failure, favorite projects to pet peeves, or to impossible dreams. Achieving consensus in this review process enables the SEP Committee to articulate priorities and direction.

These principles-by-consensus are:

1. The SEP is a partnership of mutual benefit to which each partner contributes substantially in different but equally valuable ways;
2. The Kingston Symphony performs a concert designed to meet objectives chosen from the Ontario Ministry of Education and Training grade 4 music curriculum by the Symphony Education Committee;
3. The grade 4 students must participate musically in the concert;
4. University music students teach preparatory and follow-up lessons, based on the provincial music curriculum, to grade 4 students in a supervised classroom placement that introduces them to teaching;
5. Grade 4 teachers enhance their professional development through a prepared music curricula and a music workshop focused on the symphony experience and related curriculum;
6. The Kingston Symphony reaches an extended audience of elementary students and teachers.

Each of the six principles now appears self-evident. There is not one principle that any member of the SEP Committee would leave out or diminish. Keeping the principles in the forefront of SEP planning is necessary, because it is easy for individuals to slip into representing the self-interests of their group more highly than the principles of the partnership. When the SEP Committee experiences difficulty—plans that have run amok, concerts that do not quite work, lessons that fall flat—it is because one or more of the principles is neglected.

The first principle of mutual benefit functions for the Symphony Education Partnership as a test; it is the one that resolves difficult issues. How is a new or different policy mutually beneficial? How does each partner contribute to the revision? When these questions are answered, the problem can be solved. This principle of mutual benefit is the result of having a clear vision of each partner's role in making the partnership work, nurturing flexibility and grounding the partnership in community (Boston, 1996).

The second principle, choosing the repertoire and designing the supporting curriculum, is the major focus of the SEP Committee. Involving all the partners exemplifies the principles of high-quality teaching and learning that Myers identified. These include professional development for teachers, the many challenges and strategies of curriculum, teaching, and musician training, and performances. Myers argues this will happen:

> . . . when teachers—those closest to the children—are involved with each facet, from selecting age-appropriate concert repertoire to sharing successful teaching strategies with their professional colleagues. (1996, p. 105)

This is how teachers are involved in the Kingston Symphony Education Partnership.

The third principle of grade 4 participation ensures meaningful engagement with the music through experiential learning. It emphasizes the value of musical learning. This principle distinguishes the orchestra concert from other assemblies or field trips. The authentic participation of grade 4 students convinces some of the more resistant musicians and teachers of the program's value.

The fourth principle extends professional development to the preservice teachers, musicians, and university music students. This principle is one way the partnership supports existing programs and sustains relationships among those participating, while the fifth principle addresses the more obvious professional development of classroom teachers, and the sixth principle shows that "the role of education is valued within the orchestra" (Myers, 1996, p. 101).

## A UNIQUE PROGRAM

As review and reflection continue, including examining reports of other orchestra partnerships, it becomes apparent that the Kingston SEP differs from other programs. The following characteristics appear to be unique to the Kingston Symphony Education Partnership: the structure; elementary student performance; preservice teacher education; focus on music; the manner of funding; and grassroots solutions based on partner-identified principles. Other partnerships have some of these elements.

The three-party structure of schools, symphony, and university is unusual. Other arts education partnerships present a package to the schools, who purchase it as-is. (Myers, 1996). The SEP Committee develops their program to meet the needs of their constituencies. The schools, university, and the orchestra contribute to constructing the curriculum (Boston, 1996). Creating a unique package marshalls a cohesive community behind the program.

This partnership differs from other similar symphony concert experiences or orchestra partnerships because elementary students prepare to perform with the symphony. This performance are in different ways—singing, dancing, or composing. Grade 4 students know from the beginning of the six-week study unit that they will be performing with the symphony. This performance is a major goal and motivator. The program combines important music and significant pedagogy (Boston, 1996). Singing a song with symphonic accompaniment signals that the partners function in relationship to the community.

The university music students who practice-teach are the link between performance and continuous education (Myers, 2000). The first level of music education courses are in conjunction with the placements for practice-teaching. These courses are open to any student with adequate music preparation, whether or not they identify themselves as music education majors. Some students are pursuing the Bachelor of Music degree; others the humanities-based Bachelor of Arts Honors with a music concentration; others a music minor. While most of the students in the course plan on becoming teachers, a few see themselves as performers, composers, or music history majors.

These introductory music education courses function as the university students' first exposure to teaching in a classroom setting. The courses are required for anyone who pursues further courses in music education. The placement is part of a structured, regular course within an academic degree. This is an example of how partnerships can "foster sustained relationships and programs" (Myers, 1996, p. 103).

Music and education are combined. Though this program does not include the other arts, it provides connections with other arts. One of our most successful programs (1997) involves dance in an intrinsic relation to music. Each program includes connections to other areas of the curriculum, for example, dance, art, drama, science, geography, or history. Although music is taught in a social context, the focus is always music. The concern is specifically music performed by the instruments within a symphony orchestra. This direction creates the opportunity for an intense and deep artistic and educational experience with music (Boston, 1996).

This unique music program is created from existing resources by SEP; an occasion when "resources and funding constitute a shared enterprise" (Myers, 1996, p. 108). Neither grants nor a wealthy benefactor are involved. One possible reason is the strong leadership from the orchestra manager. The performing and rehearsing expenses constitute a portion of the Kingston Symphony's education budget (Boston, 1996). The schools provide the buses to concerts, release time for teachers who play in the symphony, reproduction of curriculum materials, and facilities for meetings and professional development workshops. The university contributes the student practice teachers, curriculum development, and facilitators for the professional development workshop.

SEP is built from existing resources, a direct solution to the problem of relating the interests, needs, and skills of the individuals present within the orchestra, the schools, and the university music department. The partners come together as a result of common concerns: music education; the precarious position of the arts in schools and universities; the partners understanding of and experiencing the arts are critical.

Budget reductions to arts agencies/organizations, the schools, and universities require partners to find innovative ways to engage in the artistic/creative, educational/pedagogical, and professional projects vital to people who believe the arts as expressing their values and social significance. This grassroots solution exemplifies the direct relationship that others find between the strength of the partnership and the degree to which it is grounded in the community (Boston, 1996).

## COMPARISONS AND CONCLUSIONS

Many orchestras maintain some type of partnership. Orchestras Canada provides models from major symphony orchestras around the world to its members (Orchestras Canada, 2000). Some of these partnerships are more technological, such as the MENC–New York Philharmonic partnership (MENC, 1996), which provides curriculum materials to accompany a PBS broadcast, which is available through the *Music Educators Journal* and/or a web site (Myers & Young, 1996). In addition to the Kingston Symphony's, Orchestras Canada reports the following Canadian orchestras with partnerships: Toronto, Scarborough, Saskatoon, Timmins, and Edmonton (Babineau, 1998).

Orchestras participate in educational programs in Canada throughout their history, but contemporary practitioners ignore this history. During the 1920s and 1930s, symphony orchestras framed educational concerts within the rubric of music appreciation. The Women's Committee of the Toronto Symphony administered Music Memory Test contests as part of the concerts for secondary students. Winners of these contests were announced at the next concert (Green & Vogan, 1991). Connecting the repertoire to the required secondary curriculum was a feature of the 1942–1957 annual school concert series.

Although the Women's Committee saw the program's purpose as audience development (Millar, 1949), the participation of secondary students in post-war era Toronto Symphony Orchestra education concerts extended past contributions to planning the concerts and into promotional and fundraising activities for the orchestra (Rowe, 1989). Similar activities are possible today, such as school-to-work, required volunteering, or community night concerts (Allen, 1997).

The high point of current community support for SEP is the feature report in the city's only daily paper (Brousseau, 1999). Teachers, school board personnel, musicians, the music director, music professors, and students are interviewed. The reporter visits to one of the schools and observes a lesson taught by the university students. Several photos of both the elementary and university students accompany the story.

The Symphony Education Partnership is now established as a component of each partner's curriculum. Not one of the partners would consider pulling out. Each year more people want to participate than can be accommodated. Each year something new and different is added to the way the partnership works. Each year the direct benefit for the orchestra, the schools, and the university increases. The commitment is unquestioned and growing.

The Kingston Symphony Education Partnership is a grassroots model that mutually benefits the groups involved, where no organization is short-changed, and that respects all those directly involved. Each group is valued, listened to, and shares ownership of the project. The commitment to collaboration through the principle of mutual benefit is the essential factor ensuring the partnership's continuity and longevity as a music community and as a part of the larger community.

This partnership went through several years of planning and programming prior to the appearance of handbooks for planning arts partnerships (Remer, 1996) and research on music education partnerships (Allen, 1997; Boston, 1996; Cutietta, 1997; Hamilton, 1999; Lippert, 1999; Logan, 1997; Myers, 1996, 2000; Rodgers, 1999; Tambling, 1999). SEP did not have the advantage of access to this body of thought, but it might not have become so unique if they were initially consulted.

From our perspective, Remer's (1996) work is invaluable for bringing together the procedures used by different arts organizations and arts administrators as an organizational or advocacy tool. Remer does not deal with the same kind of partnership structure or specific subject discipline as the SEP. For SEP, Myers's extensive research on orchestral partnerships in the United States is much more pertinent (1996, 2000, and as reported in Boston, 1996). The National Endowment of the Arts tries to identify principles for effective programs. Their principles are based on the study of model programs (Myers, 1996). These models are not grassroots partnerships. When others move in our direction, we will be able to learn and partner with them.

## EDITOR'S NOTE

The arts are so marginal in our society that community support for the symphony and its partnership in Kingston is surprising. There are a large number of arts partnerships spreading across North America (Mitchell, 2000). The most important problem is to keep these partnerships together. In this case the Faculty of Education is the lone irregular in terms of supporting a unified partnership.

The dissent among arts groups is similar to divisions among churches. The sects are organizations, such as the Lincoln Center and ArtsVision, who represent leagues of schools in a large number of different cities. Lincoln Center, corresponding to the well-known performing arts center, stresses appreciation of professional performance, while ArtsVision develops community relationships including arts organizations. Other school support groups stress materials, links with museums and arts resource groups, and integration of school subjects.

Most of the warring factions concentrate on obtaining business, foundation, or government patrons. The Kingston group builds from the people, involves students, and tries to become better known for its accomplishments. It is less likely to be destroyed when accidents befall its patrons. For example, the once-dominant Rockefeller alliance disappeared when its patron, John D. Rockefeller III, died in an automobile accident a few days before he was going to sign the papers for a permanent endowment.

A critical question for building support is the role of volunteers. Symphony members can themselves be said to be volunteers. Certainly, the key organizers of the partnership are committed people who follow their calling, rather than a career. However, more active roles are needed for parents and community members in order to enhance the future support of the community for music education. Just as roles are found for students, roles for volunteers need to be expanded. Festivals provide an opportunity for such expansion, particularly when they are combined with school programs. The performance of students with the symphony is an event to celebrate.

In contrast to a grassroots effort, top down arts education is in love with professionals. Professionals in other fields seem to have the status that artists, musicians, and arts educators lack. When professionals are combined with business support, as among the scientists who provide individual partnerships in Chapter 4, then schools have a double halo for support. People with varied talents are the base from which a wider sense of music community can be built. The arts could have many other supporters to speak with them and for the arts.

> The challenge to arts educationalist is to create a dialogue between the education of young people in the arts, professional artists working in the arts today and the body of artistic achievement that is past. . . . the power base will vary, but ideally student and artist are engaged in a dialogue about the relevance of particular art forms in the modern world (Tambling, 1999, p. 156)

# III

# Spanning Boundaries

> Besides establishing objectives, that address the desire to reciprocate in concrete ways, the advisory committee usually sets a goal of broadening the partnership activities. Expanding to include more schools, district, or even social service organizations within the existing infrastructure is one way for a partnership to continue its evolution and a signal that it has reached the hallmark of collaboration and mutuality (Williams, et. al, 1992, p. 11)

Partnerships are caught on the horns of a dilemma whether or not to expand beyond their existing relationships. Chapter 1 showed the leaders of professional development schools either overlook parents or do not consider them relevant. Other chapters in Part I reveal expertise as a dominant consideration for the formulation of partnerships. The alliances in Part II split between the certain direction of business relationships and the open system of community ties.

There are many limited partnerships, but this section concentrates on attempts to expand beyond the base, urban areas where experts live and specific projects arise. All of the chapters in Part III focus on expanding the scope of partnerships in rural settings.

The first line crossed is between schools and social services. Without a concentrated campaign, school districts resist such an integration. Police or nurses working in schools are asked by educators to teach related subjects. Establishing social programs on an equal basis to academic efforts is a difficult problem.

The issue of crossing boundaries is examined in Chapter 12, which focuses on overcoming racial boundaries in South Africa as well as linking community members and health experts. This is a task similar to integrating health services and education on Native reserves in Canada. In spite of close contact of community members and among the professions, there are far fewer service experiments in the hinterland because of dependency on the metropolis.

Rural partnerships are limited. Chapter 10 shows the success of advanced courses being offered through distance education. The resistance to this effort suggests that social supports and campaigns are needed to mobilize support in the entire community for compensation programs. Small achievements and heightened expectations are needed together with technology and facilities.

Rural communities are capable of new possibilities and visions. Chapter 11 reports promotion by an advocate of partnerships in five separate programs; community development, racial integration, service integration, individual teacher programs, and an international institute. The international effort is based on sixty schools in Nova Scotia and substantial numbers from New Brunswick, New Hampshire, and Maine. An environmental effort for these five provinces or states is built around the common Gulf of Maine, but it is an example of programs constructed from place values (Hass & Nachtigal, 1998). Place visions stress the geography, social continuity and spiritual sense offered by rural communities not yet covered by urban sprawl. Such partnerships are an alternative to modernism.

Rural and community alternatives are not vague suggestions. The chapters in this section stress pre-school education, specialized courses, separate personnel, and comparison of efforts to train doctors in rural areas with those for teachers. Those coordinating efforts in science education produce a startling list of programs around which partnerships form:

institute for professional development of teachers

speakers bureaus

loans and donations of equipment, financial support

scholarships and fellowships

technical assistance—proposal writing, consulting etc

curriculum assistance

program development

public awareness campaigns

legislative/policy advocacy

job placement

career guidance

clearinghouses, databases and hotlines

projects for women and minorities

computer-based telecommunications networks

administrator training

development of elementary and secondary school science programs

school restructuring

(Fowler, 1991, p. 29)

Personal and community programs from rural areas, particularly in Nova Scotia, include many of these options, but others can
be added to a more comprehensive list. Suggestions from this
section include: community organizations, distance education,
cooperative work programs, memorial community services, and
training professionals in rural areas for work in these communities. Just as the problems of poverty are greater in rural areas so
are the opportunities for coordinated social action.

# 9

# Community Agencies Across School Districts

## Lynn Bradshaw

Health and social issues impact a child's education. As these issues have become state and local responsibilities, the shift presents challenges and opportunities for state and local agencies. In North Carolina, Governor Jim Hunt believes that if children were healthy and ready to learn when they entered school, they would become the quality workers needed to sustain the state's economy in the future. To achieve that goal, he established the state's Smart Start initiative in 1993.

Funded by a combination of state dollars and private donations, Smart Start is designed to improve the quality and accessibility of child care, to support preventive health care for children, and to provide education and information to parents. Efforts to form local Smart Start partnerships bring together community and business leaders, child care providers, parents, educators, and health and human services professionals. These stakeholders assess local needs, develop a plan to address them, and seek Smart Start funding from the state.

The Down East Partnership for Children (DEPC) is a Smart Start Partnership that serves a two-county area in northeastern North Carolina. The DEPC is designed to model and support the delivery of integrated health, education, and social services to children and their families. The school districts in the two counties are important stakeholders in the development of the DEPC and its programs. Some of the projects undertaken jointly by the DEPC and one or both school districts are more successful than others, and at times changes in school district leadership and policy pose serious challenges for the DEPC.

This study of the two partnering school districts is grounded on theory and research on organizational collaboration in both education and the social sciences. Data for the study were collected through observations of DEPC activities, document review, interviews, and focus groups. The author, a former central office administrator in one of the partnering school districts, served as an evaluation consultant to the DEPC since 1996. The study is consistent with principles of empowerment evaluation (Fetterman, 1996).

Collaborative evaluation helps the staff, board members, and stakeholders understand how the DEPC develops as an organization and how the interaction of individuals and groups affects the partnership and the achievement of shared goals. The study confirms collaboration among school districts and other community agencies as a developmental process and illustrates the challenges encountered by these school districts and community agencies when they attempt to work together in new ways.

## COLLABORATION THEORY

Some theories of collaboration distinguish between collaboration and cooperation, but Wood and Gray (1991) prefer a more inclusive definition: "Collaboration occurs when a group of autonomous stakeholders of a problem domain engage in an interactive process, using shared rules, norms, and structures, to act or decide on issues related to that domain" (p. 146). The collaborative process is developmental (Gray, 1985; Hord, 1986; Melaville & Blank, 1993), and the early stages of a collaborative effort are particularly important to the eventual success of the initiative.

Reed and Cedja (1987) describe organizational preconditions to support successful collaboration. Partners must recognize both what they need and what they can contribute to the collaborative effort. When the goals of partnering organizations are aligned and there is support for collaboration and strategic planning during the early stages of a project, participants are more likely to be able to build a strong foundation for long-term collaborative activity.

Organizational collaboration is a unique process depending on the needs and resources of the individual stakeholders in a particular problem domain. Studies of collaborative efforts find a predictable sequence of activities, although the "steps" identified in theories of collaboration differ in number and name (Gray, 1985; Hord, 1986; Melaville & Blank, 1993; Reed & Cedja, 1987; Rigsby, Reynolds, & Wang,

1995; Wood & Gray, 1991). Gray (1985) identifies three stages of collaborative activity: problemsetting, directionsetting, and structuring. These three stages encompass additional steps identified by other authors and capture the prevailing forward motion of collaborative activity as new partnerships develop.

During the "problem-setting" stage, it is important for stakeholders to recognize the complexity of the problem and the interdependence of the organizations undertaking the joint effort. The degree to which all stakeholders are identified and involved will 'influence the nature of the agreements reached as well as the ease of coming to an agreement' (Gray, 1985, p. 74). Effective problem setting requires asking the right questions. The unique perspectives of multiple stakeholders (Knapp, 1995) enrich problem setting and other stages of collaborative work.

During "direction setting," stakeholders work together to gather information and develop a strategic plan. As the plan takes shape, power must be distributed to allow all stakeholders to influence decisions about the collaborative effort. When the plan is implemented, structures and processes must be established to accomplish shared goals. The context for such "structuring" is complex, and the results will be influenced by the diverse institutional interests of the partners and the needs of the new collaborator (Crowson & Boyd, 1996).

Although the stages of collaboration are incremental, progress often looks more like a spiral than a straight line. When new members join the collaborative effort, old members leave, or changes occur in needs or resources, the partners must cycle back through earlier stages and make revisions before they can move ahead. The challenge requires partners to balance their focus on long-term goals with flexibility in order to knit needs, resources, and preferences into a plan (Melaville & Blank, 1993).

The successful implementation of collaborative agreements depends upon stakeholders' collective ability to manage continuous change. Mawhinney (1996) suggests collaborative efforts are not really systemic reforms, but rather a series of incremental adjustments as projects unfold. In order to sustain a collaborative effort, an "enablement framework" must assure funding and communication linkages, and as the collaborative evolves, environmental scanning and adaptation must continue (Reed & Cedja, 1987).

The business and social science literature describes a phenomenon called "boundary spanning" that takes place at the edges of organizations that decide to work collaboratively to solve a problem. Organizational boundaries define organizations and departments within organizations, and they regulate the flow of information from one to another. When problems extend beyond the boundary of a single organization or department, solutions require activity across organizational boundaries.

Boundary spanners work where these boundaries cross and overlap. They represent their own organizations, facilitate information sharing across organizational boundaries, and help match needs and resources (Reed & Cedja, 1987). Boundary spanning contacts develop formally and informally, depending on the type of project, and individuals are more likely to serve as boundary spanners because of their work-related competence or credibility than because of their position on an organizational chart (Tushman & Scanlan, 1981).

Throughout the life of a collaborative effort, "boundary spanners" communicate frequently within and across organizational boundaries and engage in a variety of activities that support the new organization, protect their own organizations, or link organizations together. Sarason and Lorentz (1998) observe that boundary spanners or "coordinators" were characterized by scanning, fluidity, and imaginativeness. Cordiero and Kolek (1996) describe the individuals who are able to cross the boundaries of organizations and agencies as multilingual and multicultural "compradors." These activists challenge school leaders, look for similar fellows within the organization, and seek permission to travel.

Those who interact across organizational boundaries encounter unique opportunities to create and influence solutions to shared problems. These personal linkages may be "the most likely source of cooperation" (Eisenberg, 1995, p. 104), but because they are also difficult to control, boundary-spanning activities can create conflict for the organization. When boundary spanners understand the visions of their own organizations and the new partnership and build strong communication linkages within their own organizations, they are more likely to anticipate and work through potential conflicts.

## THE DOWN EAST PARTNERSHIP FOR CHILDREN

This study focuses on the Down East Partnership for Children (DEPC), one of North Carolina's early Smart Start partnerships. It is tempting to begin the DEPC story with the date of its incorporation, December 1993. However, such a story would be seriously incomplete because it would ignore the efforts leading to the creation of the DEPC. The early efforts to improve conditions for children in the area and the preconditions established for this collaborative effort form a strong foundation for its continuing success. Significant events in the story of the DEPC are discussed below and displayed in Table 9.1. Stages of collaboration are listed and defined in the first column (Gray, 1985; Reed & Cedja, 1987). Important examples of activities during each stage are in the second column.

**TABLE 9.1**
**Down East Partnership Activities and Collaboration Model**

| Stages of Collaboration | Down East Partnership for Children Sample Activities |
| --- | --- |
| **Establish the Preconditions**<br><br>Prepare for collaborative activity. | Extensive needs assessment.<br>Broad involvement of key representatives of agencies and other stakeholder groups in both counties.<br>Increasing consensus regarding the needs of children and families and their link to economic development.<br>Commitment to a two-county effort.<br>Incorporation of the DEPC prior to receipt of Smart Start funds. |
| **Problemsetting**<br><br>Recognize complexity of the problem and the interdependence of the organizations | Problems evolved from the needs of children from birth to age 5 to the needs of children of all ages and their families.<br>Articulation of a vision of family resource centers that are a "one-stop shop." |
| **Directionsetting**<br><br>Gather information and develop a strategic plan | Adoption of four goals around which Partnership activities have been organized.<br>Broad stakeholder involvement through committee work.<br>Continuing needs assessment, strategic planning, and program evaluation. |
| **Structuring**<br><br>Establish structures and processes to accomplish shared goals | Policies established as needed (e.g., referral guidelines, personnel policies, etc.).<br>Increased staff.<br>Increased budget and accountability.<br>Contracts management software developed and used for DEPC and shared statewide.<br>Standing Evaluation Committee established in 1995.<br>Training for grantees in the development of measurable program outcomes.<br>Helped coordinate disaster relief efforts in response to the flooding caused by Hurricane Floyd, but reaffirmed the original vision and mission of DEPC as opposed to a continuing role in disaster relief.<br>Development and use of Program Review for Internal Self-Management with DEPC and funded programs.<br>Five-Year Strategic Plan, completed in 2000, set a new standard for organizational planning and evaluation. |

## Creating a New Partnership

Historically, there are concerns about the quality of life of many of the residents of Nash and Edgecombe counties. Just as the governor saw a connection between the condition of children and the future of the state's economy, business and community leaders in Nash and Edgecombe counties recognize the need to improve education and quality of life for children and their families in order to attract new business and industry to the area.

## Identifying Needs and Resources

Indicators of child well-being, monitored annually for all 100 counties in the state by the North Carolina Child Advocacy Institute (1995), highlight serious issues related to the health, education, safety, and security of children in the two-county area. In 1995, these indicators show that Edgecombe County ranked among the "worst" counties in the state with respect to infant mortality, child abuse and neglect, and juvenile and violent arrests. While statistics for Nash County are more positive, Nash still ranks in the bottom half of all 100 counties in the state on 6 of the 13 indicators.

Poverty takes on a different meaning in Edgecombe County than in either its adjoining county or the state. Although the median family income is the same in both counties, substantially more children in Edgecombe County are living in poverty and almost twice as many children are receiving aid for families with dependent children. The contrast between the two counties is most pronounced in the area of safety. Edgecombe County's juvenile arrest rate is almost the highest in the state. As a rate per 1,000 youths in the population, Nash is less than one, while Edgecombe is over 93. Edgecombe also has almost twice as many cases of child neglect or abuse as Nash. Although Nash County has no violent arrests, ranking first in the state, Edgecombe County had one of the lowest positions in the state's accounting.

In spite of the enormous security differences in the two counties, their leaders recognize some advantages of working together to address similar needs. They share the city of Rocky Mount, where railroad tracks in the middle of Main Street establish the boundary between the two counties. The former Rocky Mount City Schools served students from both counties, and economic development efforts focused on environmental scanning and school improvement for the region as a whole. Two earlier initiatives to improve economic and social conditions in the area, Project Uplift and Visions 2000, identify serious childcare needs. Although there are an adequate number of child care spaces, their quality is inadequate, and less than one percent of the childcare operations in the two counties are accredited.

Reacting to these inadequacies, a possible Child Care Resource and Referral Program to serve the two-county area emerges. The new state Smart Start program promises considerable new financial resources and other support to communities whose partnership proposals were funded. Once the magnitude of the needs is broadly understood, there is strong community support for pursuing a Smart Start partnership.

## Stakeholders and Boundary Spanners

Education, health, and human service agencies recognize the Smart Start program could provide new dollars to enable them to expand current programs and implement strategies lacking funding. Agencies operating separately in the two counties, such as Social Services, the Health Department, and the school districts, had their own representatives in the early discussions. As one staff member observes, "The group of interested citizens who got together to apply for Smart Start include the heads of all the major service agencies in Nash and Edgecombe counties." Parents and community leaders, including business and industry representatives, were involved in the discussions.

Boundary spanning activities during the early discussions consist primarily of gathering, analyzing, and sharing information. Once the decision is made to pursue Smart Start funding, the representatives of various stakeholder organizations and groups turn their attention to planning and developing the Smart Start proposal. At this point, the planning is sufficiently general so as not to threaten the boundaries of any stakeholder's organization, programs, or administrative procedures followed in day-to-day work. The ease with which the partnering organizations agree on the goals of the DEPC simplifies the work of the early boundary spanners. They could support the new partnership without obligating their own organizations to change the way they do business.

## Articulating Shared Values

The various stakeholders share a strong desire to improve the quality of life for children and their families. They believe both quality education and accessible community services are keys to achieving their goals, and they articulate the link between the condition of their communities' children and families and their communities' economic future. These shared values and perceived links among educational, social, and economic goals are recalled in interviews by individuals who were involved in the early planning efforts.

The proposed partnership is a significant attempt to involve all players in the lives of these children and to improve child care in the two counties. The importance of integrating services to families is recognized. There would be easy access to services through "one-stop-shops" spread out over the region—less shuffling back and forth among agencies, healthier children coming into schools, and better support systems for children in schools.

### Submitting a Two-County Smart Start Proposal

Community groups conduct a multiple, and sometimes overlapping, needs assessment, resulting in a growing recognition that Nash County has some of the same needs as Edgecombe County. Leaders begin "to see a collective or regional effort could accomplish more." Edgecombe County's more serious needs is an "advantage" in a funding process based on need, and it was unlikely that Nash County could receive funding by itself.

In preparation for submitting the first Smart Start proposal, representatives of the two counties met at the Rocky Mount Campus of Edgecombe Community College to present the rationale for a two-county effort. Later, Nash County representatives approach the representatives from Edgecombe County and work out a funding agreement. One community leader notes that it was unusual for Nash County to seek the help of Edgecombe County. Others confirm that the regional point of view would align well with ongoing economic development efforts in the two-county area.

### Responding to Disappointment

The first two-county Smart Start proposal was submitted in 1993. Unfortunately, however, it was not funded. The comprehensive needs assessments and the commitment of so many stakeholder groups in the planning efforts positioned the group to respond proactively to the failure of the first Smart Start proposal. They move ahead with a two-county Child Care Resource and Referral initiative, and the Down East Partnership for Children is incorporated in December 1993 without Smart Start funding and without any other known source of continuing support. A one-time contribution of $50,000 from the business community enables the DEPC to hire two employees, and they develop a long-term funding proposal for the CCR&R. One of the school districts provides office space in Rocky Mount that had been vacated as a result of a recent school district merger.

The failure of the first Smart Start proposal raises questions about the decision to pursue a two-county Smart Start partnership, particularly from the stakeholders in Edgecombe County. The local newspaper published the following account:

Last year Edgecombe and Nash counties joined forces by submitting one application, a move that was criticized after the Twin Counties were not selected for Smart Start. Statistics show Edgecombe has one of the worst child care problems in the state, whereas Nash County ranked in the middle of the pack. Some in Edgecombe County criticized the collaborated (*sic*) effort with Nash, saying Nash weakened Edgecombe's chances of getting the grant. Zalkind, though, said the positives of the joint effort outweigh the negatives. The joint application, said Zalkind, is the right thing to do since "Rocky Mount cuts across both counties." "It is much easier to coordinate if everybody from across the county line works together." (Vinh, 1994)

In Spring 1994, all stakeholders participate in a strategic planning training session facilitated by the North Carolina Client and Community Development Center. The process helps to clarify and reaffirm the focus of the DEPC. It prepares the group of staff, board members, and stakeholders to develop a second Smart Start proposal and additional applications for funding from other groups. With renewed commitment to a two-county effort, a second Smart Start proposal is submitted in August 1994, which is successful. The DEPC receives a Smart Start planning grant and a commitment to fund the Smart Start proposal in the next grant cycle. The request for Child Care Resource and Referral funding is also accepted.

### Understanding the Problem

During problem setting, stakeholders in a collaborative effort deepen their understanding of the problem domain (Gray, 1985). The immediate "problem" for the DEPC is to improve access to child care and the other services needed by children and their families. In the 1994 DEPC Smart Start proposal, the partnership describes the problem as follows:

Through our needs assessment we learned that much work is needed to create a comprehensive early childhood system, and then to develop an integrated funding mechanism to allow all children equal access. We learned that the quality of our childcare is low, but that childcare providers are excited about the opportunity to undergo self-assessment and changes needed to meet high quality, national standards. We learned that the expectations of parents are very different from the expectations of schools regarding what children need to succeed. Our vision addresses the need to increase opportunities for dialogue and sharing between parents, child care providers, and kindergarten teachers. Finally, we learned that there are many barriers to services, but the most difficult to overcome may be the attitudes that many people have toward using those services, even those that will lead to a better life for their children. By including prospective program participants in the design of services, we expect to begin to overcome these negative attitudes.

As the partnership evolved, stakeholders reaffirm the "problem" in Nash and Edgecombe counties includes but goes beyond child care. They want children to be healthy and ready to learn when they enter school, but support is needed for children and their families as long as the children are in school. For the students to complete school successfully, DEPC serves the needs of children of all ages, not just the very young.

The high expectations of staff and stakeholders illustrate their vision for the partnership and their understanding of the problem it was to address. One staff member observes that if the partnership is successful, there will be one-stop resource centers where families with children of all ages can get all their needs met. A board member recalls hearing about family resource centers for the first time: "When [the first chairman of the board] shared his vision of family resource centers all over Edgecombe County, I could see it!" Board members and staff agreed that a successful partnership would improve the lives of families in both counties.

No child would be without health care, and when parents need help, there would be a person to call, classes to attend, and materials available for them to use. Higher quality child care would ensure that every child would be ready for school, and barriers to school success would be eliminated. Parents would be helped to become involved in their children's education.

Gaps between rich and poor are to be reduced together with less racism. The services provided in the two counties are to be more consistent, and the impact of stakeholders' collaborative efforts would have more impact than the separate, individual efforts of each group in the past. Efforts to preserve families, improve education, and increase economic development are the combined aims. When people are more aware of the services available, the quality of their lives improves.

The two school districts continue to be important stakeholder groups as the DEPC began operation. The location of the first office space in the Nash-Rocky Mount Teacher Resource Center was beneficial in several ways. The in-kind contribution reduced operating costs for the new partnership. In addition, the executive director observed that by providing this "incubation space," the school district is a "parent" for the partnership and confers a sense of legitimacy.

Both school district superintendents fill designated positions on the DEPC board of directors once the partnership is established. The early planning and incorporation efforts follow the successful culmination of more than 20 years of attempts to improve education in the two-county area by merging separate city and county school districts in each county. In the early days of the DEPC, both school superintendents were newly appointed leaders of merged districts. Community interest in education and expectations for improvement were high.

Politically, it was important for the school districts to be active partners in community projects including the DEPC. The superintendent's designated boundary spanners kept both superintendents informed of specific program activities. During these early years, relationships between the DEPC and both school districts were generally positive.

## SETTING THE DIRECTION FOR THE PARTNERSHIP

Positive links among stakeholders came from acceptance of four goals for DEPC:

1. Universal access to high quality early childhood education. The Child Care Resources and Referral initiative provides information to parents about the costs, availabily, and quality of child care in centers and family homes. Scholarships are granted to help parents with the costs of child care. In addition, the DEPC provides training, technical assistance, and grants to help child care providers improve their programs and achieve accreditation.
2. Improved parenting and parent involvement in education. The Family Resource Program develops a growing network of family resource centers in the two-county area. Through the centers, the staff works to improve links between those who need health and human services and the agencies who provide them.
3. Eliminate barriers to services. The Family Resource Data Base provides information and referrals for parents who have concerns about their child's growth and development. Standing work groups continue to address the needs for service integration and transportation, and, because of a growing number of Hispanic families in the area, services expand for them.
4. Improve transition to public school. The DEPC supports home school coordinators and parent education in both school districts and actively calls for a strategic plan for early childhood education in the two-county area. Specific programs are implemented to address the quality of care for school-age children, and efforts are underway to empower parents to be more involved in the education of children of all ages.

Parents, representatives of community agencies and organizations, and the DEPC board and staff continue to be involved in the development of strategies for achieving DEPC goals. State auditors describe partnership meetings as "effective forums to exchange ideas and make decisions about what programs will best meet the needs of the partnership's children" (Coopers & Lybrand, 1996, p. 15). There is a strong commitment to involve clients and community representatives in addition to the recognized agency directors and business leaders. The state auditors find extensive involvement in the collaboration process.

By 1996, the DEPC employs 13 permanent staff, additional permanent consultants, and numerous subcontractors. In addition, 33 board members and more than 200 standing committee members work with the staff as partners in the effort to provide high quality education and coordinated community service in these two counties. The need for continuous strategic planning is addressed in a proposal to support the organizational development of the DEPC: "The DEPC needs to look back at the planning it did when it became involved with Smart Start and re-assess it, looking to move on to a new stage." The proposal is funded by the Babcock Foundation, and it provides support for planning, evaluation, and staff development efforts.

## STRUCTURING FOR PARTNERSHIP

Structuring is the most challenging phase of the collaborative process. For the partnership to last, it needs organizational structures and procedures, a group of "believers," effective communication linkages, and sufficient funding (Reed & Cedja, 1987). DEPC structures and policies are established as needed. As the size of the DEPC staff grows and stabilizes at about 30 people, personnel policies and procedures are established. As the annual budget increases to more than $4 million, contracts management software is developed which is now being used by other partnerships throughout the state.

Structures and processes support positive changes. DEPC continues to make grants to community groups "with strings attached" to ensure the groups that are to receive funding will obtain the training and support needed for their programs. Grassroots leaders are identified as "Community Fellows," completing a year-long leadership training program. These Fellows applied for grants to support projects they believe would make a difference in their own communities.

A standing Evaluation Committee is created to develop an evaluation process to maintain focus and ensure Partnership progress. Program evaluation activities focus on two levels: the partnership as a whole and the individual program activities. Training and support for the development of measurable, client-focused outcomes result in more useful evaluation data. A peer review process for DEPC programs and grantees enables groups who receive DEPC funding to develop sound organ-izational policies and procedures so they are able to carry out their programs.

Information is an important commodity in a collaborative setting. In the first DEPC offices, space was "tight" and shared communication was natural. When the school district reclaimed space used by the DEPC, the partnership purchased the former YWCA building in downtown Rocky Mount for office space and a model family resource center. In the new building, private offices are a welcomed luxury, but internal communica-tion requires more effort. Technology, including e-mail, Internet, and web pages, are useful. Newsletters and mailings provide a means of sharing information with the community, and the quarterly evaluation reports generate regular discussion about program outcomes.

Continuing funding is essential for a collaborative project, but the decision to take action without Smart Start funding set an important precedent for the DEPC. Although the annual budget increases from $1,673,503 in 1995 to more than $4 million in subsequent years, the DEPC never relies upon a single funding source. Additional funds are obtained through varied state and federal grants, grants from private foundations, and business contributors. As the auditors note:

> The Down East Partnership is an example of a non-profit business that incorporates several funding streams, including Smart Start. Because of the additional funding, the Partnership has the flexibility to offer services, which do not necessarily fit under Smart Start criteria. This enables them to be less dependent on one funding source and to implement programs that will have a long-term impact on the community. (Coopers & Lybrand, 1996, p. 25)

The Child Care Scholarship program is conducted on-site in collabo-ration with Social Services, but the partnership is able to use multiple funding streams to establish graduated eligibility criteria that allows parents to wean off the subsidy as their income increases. The DEPC scholarship program continues to support families who reach an in-come level that exceeds the Department of Social Services eligibility level of $13,000. Close attention to costs has made the grants from business and foundations go further (Coopers & Lybrand, 1996).

One board member cautioned that all members of the board must understand the financial picture and be trained in fiscal management. They have considered establishing their own foundation and obtaining outside assistance. External assistance may be required to monitor and reevaluate administrative structures to be sure that they support both the day-to-day operations and the long-term goals of the partnership.

In structuring a collaborative effort, there is always a danger that the new collaborative effort takes on some of the bureaucratic characteristics of the unresponsive organizations it was designed to replace. Although DEPC programs are grouped loosely in three areas (Child Care Resource and Referral, Family Resource, and Information and Exchange), many initiatives are interrelated, and members of the staff "regroup" to work on projects as needed. Staff members are able to articulate the relationship between their specific job descriptions and the four DEPC goals. Links to multiple goals complicated efforts to restructure the administrative groupings. Specific activities support multiple goals that are consistent with the vision of integrated services, as shown in Table 9.1 (page 165).

Though there are stages of collaboration (Gray, 1985; Reed & Cedja, 1987), not all events are sequential, which demonstrates the need to cycle back through earlier stages before moving ahead (Melaville & Blank, 1993). As late as 1999, severe flooding in the two-county area causes the DEPC to return to the problem-setting stage. Following the urgency of disaster relief efforts, the partnership reaffirms its commitment to the original goals but does not take the lead in long-term recovery efforts.

During the life of the DEPC, positive results multiply. As a result of the Child Care Resource and Referral Program, resource and referral services for parents and technical assistance and training for child care providers are in place. The quality of childcare improves as more facilities become accredited. Through the efforts of the DEPC stakeholder groups, the network of family resource centers in schools and communities grows. Millions of dollars from grants and other outside sources benefit residents of the two-county area, and the partnership and its funded programs serve approximately 12,000 children and families annually.

As the DEPC becomes a more structured organization, there are more conflicts among stakeholder groups over differences in procedures and issues of control. The boundaries of the DEPC and partnering organizations are more likely to overlap when new programs are implemented, and boundary-spanning activities become more uncertain and sometimes threatening. At the same time, the strong, early interest of school district leaders becomes less consistent. As the early school district boundary spanners move to new positions in other counties, superintendents changed, and as the DEPC moved toward increased involvement in education issues in the two-county area, the relationships with the two school districts are less collaborative.

## THE ROLES OF TWO SCHOOL DISTRICTS

From the beginning, representatives of the school districts participate in efforts to assess community needs and develop long-term plans to address them. Just as the DEPC includes representatives of comparable agencies in both counties on its board of directors, the superintendents of both districts serve as board members, and a variety of the superintendents' designees attend meetings and are involved in formal positions on the board and in committee work. Both districts submit proposals for DEPC funding. A number of incidents shift the relationships between the DEPC and the school districts, and three themes emerge in the search for collaboration between these schools and community agencies.

## Relationship-Defining Incidents

Each school district's relationship with the DEPC is unique, but critical incidents define them. Just as shared successes strengthen the partnership, negative incidents challenge the relationship with the DEPC, and some have been difficult to overcome. In the beginning, representatives participate in early needs assessment and planning. Over time, school district involvement becomes more reactive, and district representatives seldom initiate joint efforts. One district unilaterally establishes its own early childhood center in direct competition with DEPC.

A representative of the other school district consistently works with DEPC because her early roles made the project salient. She was principal of a school with a preschool center and, later, director of a federal program. Events in her life lead her to be a boundary spanner. Currently, neither school system is looking outside of its own limits. Both school systems are participating in planning a major conference on "transition to school." They are searching for answers and respond to invitations for cooperation when situations are very public.

## Needs Assessment and Planning

Representatives of both districts participated in the pre-DEPC needs assessment efforts of Project Uplift, Visions 2000, and Common Ground. Edgecombe County has a longer history of collaboration around the efforts to understand the problems of children and their families, and the security needs in Edgecombe County are recognized to be more serious than those in Nash County.

Health and education measures are more similar. Edgecombe, the more secure county, has an infant mortality rate twice as high as Nash and the state. Though other health measures favor Edgecombe, Nash does better with respect to dropout rates, college entrance board results, and high school graduation. For various education measures, both counties are lower than the average for the state (North Carolina Advocacy Institute, 1995).

Quality of education and related health issues are important concerns of the community for the two-county area and their stakeholder groups. The school districts are needed at the discussion table, and they want to be there. Funding agencies, including Smart Start, expect evidence that the school districts were significantly involved in the proposed collaborative programs. The school districts recognize the need to participate, to monitor the discussion, and to be aware of, and possibly prevent, any "threats" to their own organizations and programs.

For the districts, the partnership is an "unknown" group. When DEPC delves into education, health, and social issues, empowers parents and community groups, provides information, and encourages people to ask questions, school districts are threatened, particularly when their boundaries become an issue. School leaders' interest and involvement in DEPC tended to vary over time, depending on the current focus of the partnership, the specific project under discussion, and other demands facing the school districts.

### Incubation Space

The first office space for the DEPC, provided by the Nash-Rocky Mount Schools in their Teacher Resource Center, was a major boost. The district's visible support helped enhance visibility and increased the number of services that could be provided. The later withdrawal of this space becomes a problem, which is overcome, but there are other problems emerging with this district.

### Funding for Special Projects

Along with other groups in the two-county area, both school districts could submit grants to support special programs in the schools that are aligned with DEPC goals. In the early years of the DEPC, the partnership supports initial and follow-up training for schools in both districts to establish peer mediation programs. Although remnants of those programs remain, changes in district priorities and the availability of district financial support limit the ability of individual schools to sustain the programs with support of the DEPC. Other school projects funded by the DEPC include parent education, preschool programs, developmentally appropriate playgrounds, and school transition programs. As the DEPC matures, the board becomes more interested in grants that are aligned with the shared goals of the DEPC.

### Conditions Placed on Grants to the School Districts

As the expectation becomes more explicit that DEPC funding should support programs related to the strategic plan rather than isolated, single-shot initiatives, some school district proposals are returned for revision. While one district is able to weave its initiatives into a strategic effort that includes Title I and Even Start funding streams, the other district continues to struggle to articulate long-term goals and frame "acceptable" proposals. School district personnel in the second district express concern that they didn't know "what the DEPC wants" and questioned the value of continuing attempts to submit proposals. In one instance, this system returns funds because they do not want to do things DEPC's way. To them the proposed projects are not essential and they are plenty of other responsibilities that demand their attention.

## Aborted Pre-Kindergarten Programs

DEPC grants support pre-kindergarten programs in schools in both districts. While the DEPC is interested in creating new programs in areas where child care spaces are needed, classroom space is not always available in underserved areas, and principals are not always willing or able to collaborate with the DEPC. When two pre-K programs in one district are "closed" by the principals because they are "too much trouble," the relationship between the district and the DEPC suffers.

## Returned Funds

DEPC staff takes pride in the responsible management of their financial resources. They are sensitive to funding deadlines and meticulous about using all available resources to benefit the communities. When the same district that closed the pre-K programs fails to spend all their allocated funds within the fiscal year, $35,000 reverts to the state. Although this is not a large amount of money compared to the school district budget, it is a significant portion of the DEPC budget. The DEPC staff and board takes the loss seriously and resents the damage done to their own credibility as a result of the school district's mistake.

## Successful Family Resource Centers

Both school districts and the DEPC are proud of the growing network of family resource centers, which provide social services and crisis assistance to families and their children. The centers benefit from the support of various agencies. The local Communities in Schools organization is an active partner in two family resource centers. One is located in an urban elementary school, and the other is housed in a surplus school building. Additional services are provided by businesses, community colleges, health departments, and the departments of social services. When family resource centers are located on school grounds, the role of the principal and the teachers and their commitment to the community are key factors influencing success. The principals do not always see the centers as an important responsibility.

### Competition for Day Care Providers

A new Early Childhood Center, built by one of the districts, alarms the child care community. In both counties, child care providers fear they will lose clients if school districts begin to serve younger children. District representatives point out their programs are supported by categorical funding and are to serve children with specific needs. These are not the children being reached by private child care facilities. As the new facility grows, private providers continue to look to the DEPC for support and "protection."

### Changes in Leadership

Building positive collaborative relationships is more difficult if the school district representatives or boundary spanners keep changing. Continuing turnover in superintendents, principals, and other district contacts requires all stakeholders to "spiral back through" the stages of collaboration (Melaville & Blank, 1993). At times, these changes delay forward progress. On the other side, the leadership of DEPC provides an anchor to seek new ways to cooperate.

## EMERGING THEMES

Three themes emerge in the search for components of successful collaboration between the DEPC and the partnering school districts. A clear understanding of and commitment to the shared vision of the partnership, the ability to resolve or accept differences in administrative procedures, and effective boundary spanning activity within and across organizational boundaries contribute to successful implementation of collaborative projects and activities.

Representatives of each school district reported that the district and the DEPC share a vision for their partnership, but the visions they describe are different—"doing what's best for children" versus "making access to all services available to everybody." The second interpretation aligns more closely with the vision and goals of the DEPC and implies more specific and systemic initiatives. The emphasis on access to services is articulated by the longest-serving school district representative who continuously developed goals with DEPC.

Visioning continues throughout the life of a collaborative effort. As the participants and the context for the partnership change, stakeholders continue to clarify and refine the vision. When new partners enter into a collaborative effort that is already underway, it is difficult to ensure that all partners achieve the same level of understanding of the conditions that led to the formation of the partnership.

The problem of renewing the original understanding is revealed by differences in viewing administrative procedures. School district representatives describe a variety of meetings, reports, and other requirements associated with DEPC grants and other joint activities, and the DEPC expresses frustration when school district contacts miss meetings and reporting deadlines. In one district, the problems with administrative procedures are potential deterrents to future collaborative projects. In the other district, the inconveniences are a "small price to pay for the benefits to children and their families." Differences in administrative procedures could lead to a better understanding of the needs and concerns of both school districts and the DEPC. In turn, efforts to simplify procedures could benefit relationships with other stakeholders as well.

Boundary-spanning activity leads to finding ways to synchronize administrative procedures with common goals. The district vision, which aligns with the DEPC vision and goals, continues to reach for understanding on operational measures. This alignment in one school district results from effective boundary spanning activity within and across the school district's organizational boundaries.

Effective boundary spanning requires consistency, communication, and coordination. Both districts experience changes in superintendents and in other leadership positions. In the district where shared vision is most evident, one key boundary spanner is an early childhood educator. As a teacher, principal, and Director of Federal Programs, she participated in the early needs assessment efforts. She continues to build support for early childhood education, planned parent education, and parent involvement.

In her role as Director of Federal Programs, she is able to access varied funding sources to put different "pieces" in place, including a Title One preschool program, Reading Recovery programs, and a major Even Start initiative. The systemic results demonstrates how personal linkages provide opportunities for unique and creative solutions (Eisenberg, 1995). At the same time, her ability to share information and maintain support within the school district assures success for the programs.

## CONCLUSIONS

While education partnerships often focus on bringing new material resources into schools, an increasing number of partnerships bring a variety of services into schools to help children and their families. These newer partnerships, including community and full-service schools, seek a broad understanding of the problems encountered by students and their families and the coordination of resources to meet those needs. Strategies aim to improve the delivery of education, health, and social services by linking programs and agencies, and they may place health and human service professionals in schools to work alongside teachers, principals, and other school personnel (Hooper-Briar & Lawson, 1996).

While there is some concern that such arrangements may interfere with the school's primary function of teaching and learning (Crow, 1998), others believe that teaching and learning will be ineffective if students are not physically, emotionally, and socially healthy and ready to learn. When schools and districts want to partner with parents and the community, they need to possess the knowledge, skills, and attitudes required for successful collaboration. They can find themselves stuck in a "rhetoric rut" (Epstein et al., 1997), talking about their need for partnerships and expressing their support for collaborative work, but not being able to demonstrate results.

Collaboration develops in a sequence for the DEPC cases. Early activities or "preconditions" appeared to be particularly significant, both for the development of the DEPC and for the quality of the relationships with the two partnering school districts. Both school districts are involved and supportive during the early stages of collaboration. Over time, key personnel change, and the districts' attention or initiatives compete with DEPC plans.

Collaborative efforts threaten school leaders who are used to being in control. Unfortunately, reversion to unilateral decisionmaking may result in missed opportunities to resolve issues to benefit students, their families, and the community. The challenges and opportunities for collaboration must be seized. When joint projects tended to be more successful, boundary-spanning activity is more consistent and programs between schools and social agencies are articulated toward a common goal. Key individuals at the boundaries link resources, craft solutions, and weave together available programs and resources into a long-term vision. They need fellows or compradors within and outside of their original organizations.

## EDITOR'S NOTE

Schools and social agencies are trying to cooperate. Both are being challenged to change their definitions of professional work. The problems of families and students are ones that teachers still want to transfer to social workers even when the social agency is located in schools. Social workers want educators to give priority to children's needs before they march ahead with their academic programs.

For social agencies human needs are the problems, while for educators they are the problems of a minority. The need is to show educators that academic progress frequently depends on early intervention and continuing communication between those in these different institutions.

In this chapter, Dr. Bradshaw argues boundaries between organizations are a means for engineering cooperation among them. The boundary roles cannot be expected to alter the core of the organization. For this reason, studies of integrated services have not found teachers to change their teaching (Mitchell, 1998). Nor can integration of services be expected to overcome the social inequality in the community. Edgecombe might benefit more from a work program than from social services and referrals.

Organizations remain unresponsive to new opportunities. The achievements of the community agencies in integrating services around the needs of a few clients, such as Home Builders, is seldom appreciated by school personnel (Schorr, 1988). Schools wrestle with far larger numbers, but ironically spend an inordinate amount of time on difficult children and their families.

To deal with this dilemma as well as others, the Down East Partnership finds different sources of income and sets its own agendas. The partnership unites two counties that differ enormously in terms of security and reported crime. They are able to go beyond the limitations of Smart Start and may be able to find more opportunities in the future as they develop their bonding skills.

These two partnerships are focusing on the dismal educational achievement of children in both school districts. The districts face a similar problem that is greater than their differences. The districts need the agencies to help them to move beyond protecting their turf. They need to reach for a new vision of what is possible for poor families. Poor students benefit from enriched programs, as shown by the Accelerated School Project (Mitchell, 1998). The poor need the richest education if the cycle of failure is to be reversed.

The problems with the schools lead Dr. Bradshaw to overlook the possibilities of empowering people further through community organization. The director of the DEPC is "quite a visionary" and the DEPC is "an interesting organization that continues to evolve" (L. Bradshaw, personal communication, December 14, 2000). The community organizations, together with the DEPC director, need to appeal directly to parents and community members to influence school districts. Stronger advocacy can persuade the parents and community members to demand that schools join community plans as team members rather than as spectators.

In spite of their concern for people, this partnership is based more on expertise than it is on grassroots support. Compared to the Neighbors Project or the Symphony Partnership, there is less involvement and no celebrations or festivals are featured. Integrated services expands the groups involved for these North Carolina schools. Boundary-spanning suggests a process that many more people than a few experts may assume. Democratic process must supplement expertise and calculation for community improvement.

# 10

# Bridging the Rural Divide through Distance Education

## Michael Barbour

Newfoundland is an isolated and sparsely populated province located on the far eastern coast of Canada. Schools and communities within this underdeveloped province are affected by the rural divide. The old adage "Opportunity awaits on the other side of the overpass" is a common belief in Newfoundland. Those living inside the overpass are "townies," while those who are outside are "baymen."

The rural inequality in education was primarily approached through school consolidation. As a result of rural differences compounded with a province-wide decline in student performance and battles over religious administration of schools, the Royal Commission on Education was appointed in 1990 to rationalize or modernize education into a public, nondenominational system. Rural areas were offered distance education through technology. For this economically disadvantaged province the resources and skills for distance technology made partnerships essential.

Prior to 1993 commission, Frank Riggs conducted a survey of rural education in the province. In 1987, the *Report of the Small Schools Study Project* stated that "The delivery of course correspondence, computers, videotapes or a combination of these appears to be a most desirable way of ensuring that a greater variety of subjects are available to those who attend the small high schools." Building on this idea, the Royal Commission recommended creation of a School of Distance Education and

Technology that would "seek to deliver full credit senior high courses that meet provincial learning objectives" (Government of Newfoundland, 1993b, p. 321).

In 2000, a Ministerial Panel on Educational Delivery in the Classroom made the same recommendation when it called upon the government to create a Centre for Distance Learning and Innovation. Until 2000, the Department of Education offered most of the high school French, mathematics, and science courses through distance education. Responding to similar government directives, new organizations, school districts, and individual schools made significant advances in distance education. In most cases, these advances were based on technology and partnerships between private-sector and public-sector groups.

Two of these initiatives involved advanced placement (AP) courses in the province's smallest and most rural school district. In 1999 and 2000, the Vista School District Digital Intranet was developed by the Centre for TeleLearning and Rural Education at Memorial University of Newfoundland. The second project in the Vista School District is the CAPE Bonavista Initiative, a project of the local Discovery Collegiate School in Bonavista.

The Vista School District covers 7,000 square kilometers. The region has a population of about 35,000, located in 24 municipalities and about 80 unincorporated communities (Vista School District, 1999b). In 1999–2000, the district had 4,744 students, taught by 350 teachers in 18 schools (Vista School District, 1999a).

The Vista School District and its predecessor authorities try to do more with less. This is the aim of the rural educational authorities in the province. The problem of how to offer the same level of education to its students as urban authorities remains. Before the technological thrust, amalgamation of smaller schools was the solution to the problem. Consolidation meant students spend an hour or more each way on the school bus every day, while community and school links were broken.

In the late 1990s, the Vista School District tried a new approach to bridge the gap between the rural and urban schools. The District Digital Intranet resulted from central government policies, which created a favorable climate for an on-line initiative in mathematics and science disciplines, and distance education itself. The CAPE Bonavista Initiative is started by individual teachers, who saw the need for social studies at the local level.

## VISTA RECOMMENDATIONS

In the late 1980s, it was recognized that all students should have access to more advanced level courses in mathematics and science.

After the *Small Schools Report* (Riggs, 1987), the Department of Education, via distance education, undertook to offer the more advanced mathematics courses at the senior high level beginning with Advanced Math 1201. This form of distance education consists of audio-teleconferencing, a telewriter, and a fax machine.

In May 1989, the Task Force Report on Mathematics and Science Education, *Towards an Achieving Society*, recommended that "some courses be at a more advanced level than typically found in high schools, and that there be some provision for advanced credit at the post-secondary level for such courses" (Government of Newfoundland, 1989, p. 170) The Task Force had a preference:

> **Recommendation 8.8**: That a package of advanced courses in science and mathematics be developed, to allow greater specialization by students who show exceptional promise in these areas. (Ibid)

This push toward mathematics and science courses continued in the 1993 Royal Commission which stated that "certain areas such as language, mathematics, and science are essential to further advancement and therefore must take precedence over others" (Ibid, p. 299). Six years later, *Directions for Change: A Consultation Paper on the Senior High School Program* made similar suggestions:

> **Recommendation 31**: That distance delivery of specialized programming such as AP be explored to determine the range and feasibility of alternative distance delivery models. This should not be limited to schools currently identified as small schools. (Government of Newfoundland, 1995, p. 52)

It was from these consistent policies that the Vista School District Digital Intranet was created.

In 1997, the Vista School District released the *Strategic Education Plan*, which included the statement, "We will work with the Department of Education and other school districts to coordinate provincial and local initiatives, determine priorities, and establish partnerships" (Vista School District, 2000). Prior to the creation of the Vista School District Digital Intranet, the main parties entered into an agreement in Summer 1997 known as the Clarenville-Memorial University of Newfoundland (MUN) Partnership.

This partnership was initiated by the administration at Clarenville High School and at the Faculty of Education (MUN) to provide a research initiative for the faculty. This research places Clarenville High at the cutting edge of educational technology and practice. The specific research initiative of the faculty connectsd a Canada-wide effort to the

National Centres of Excellence (NCE), specifically Theme 4 of the TeleLearning NCE.

The prime focus of Theme 4 "is to develop effective technology-based approaches to the major educational challenges facing Canadian schools" (TeleLearning NCE, 2000). Through a series of partnerships with the Vista School District, the Faculty of Education at MUN, and IBM, Clarenville High creates a Mathematics Laboratory for integrating technology into the mathematics curriculum.

There are research projects to consider differences in achievement between two different groups of biology students: some have technology integrated into their classroom and the others are taught in the traditional way. This initial partnership include many of the same people who began the Vista School District Digital Intranet project (Memorial University of Newfoundland, 2000).

In order to conduct further research on a subtheme, Theme 4.3 considers the use of "interactive computer-based laboratories in science, technology and mathematics" (Center for TeleLearning and Rural Education, 2000). The Centre proposed an extension of the Clarenville–MUN Partnership, which became the Vista School District Digital Intranet.

This new project would develop a district-wide intranet to offer university-level mathematics and science courses to all schools within the Vista School District. It permitted the Vista School District to fulfill its mandate to provide "access to more advanced level courses in mathematics and science." At the same time, the Vista School District is able to fulfill one of the objectives listed in the section to "increase student and staff understanding in the use of technology" of its *Strategic Education Plan*. This section says a "district intranet that will be used to support staff development and other activities." The Centre for TeleLearning and Rural Education and the TeleLearning NCE provides interactive computer-based laboratories in science, technology, and mathematics.

The Vista School District Digital Intranet is funded through a grant from Industry Canada in 1998 in order to develop four AP courses throughout the entire school district. The AP curriculum, offered by the College Entrance Examination Board in the United States, includes university-level courses. These senior high school courses require students to take a standardized exam in May to determine their ranking on a scale of 1 to 5. The vast majority of universities across Canada and the United States will offer university credit to students who receive a level 3 or higher.

During the creation of this intranet, the Centre for TeleLearning and Rural Education undertook to create a number of partnerships to ensure the successful completion of this project. The first of these partnerships involved select staff and students at the Vista School District. The Vista School District provides the equivalent of one teacher for the project.

Another essential partnership is with the Student Teacher Educational Multimedia Network (STEM~Net). STEM~Net provides Internet access to students and teachers all across Newfoundland since September 1993. STEM~Net aims to encourage participants to contribute to the development and sharing of on-line educational resources and content; enhance the distance education opportunities for K–12 students; assist schools, districts, and the Department of Education in pilot projects and innovative practices in education; and, finally, promote educational networking as a communication tool for the K–12 educational community in Newfoundland and Labrador (STEM~Net, 1999). As a partner in the Vista School District Digital Intranet, STEM~Net provides access to e-learning software: Web course tools (WCT), Microsoft Netmeeting and MeetingPoint, and technical support for both the software and hardware.

With these two partnerships established, the Centre for TeleLearning and Rural Education submits a proposal to the Information Highway Branch of Industry Canada and receives the necessary funding. The Vista School District approves the leave of four teachers in April 1998 to begin to develop these courses. These four teachers work with four university students to design and construct four on-line AP courses.

These individuals work in a Multimedia Research and Development Laboratory. After selecting course textbooks, the Centre enters into a partnership with Addison Wesley Longman, ITP Nelson, and Prentice Hall Ginn Canada to purchase one multimedia workstation with all the necessary hardware and software. Through a partnership with the Canada-Newfoundland Cooperation Agreement on Human Resource Development (a fund administered by the Atlantic Canada Opportunities Agency), the Centre for TeleLearning and Rural Education purchases four additional multimedia workstations (W. Boone, personal communication, June 28, 2000).

The Centre for TeleLearning and Rural Education needs to ensure each high school in the district had the necessary technology to access these on-line AP courses. Through partnerships with STEM~Net/SchoolNet/Industry Canada, NewTel Communications Inc., and Canada-Newfoundland COOPERATION Agreement on Human Resource Development, each school is provided with a satellite dish for the school (David Power, et al., 2000). Each AP student has access to a computer.

At the school level, Digital Intranet is greeted warmly. Administrators at schools involved commented:

We were able to offer courses that otherwise were not possible because of small student numbers;

AP got the internet for this school and the rest of the school has "piggy-backed" on this development;

AP has provided more choice and opportunity for senior students; [and]

It has been a very positive experience for the school and provided us with an enhanced service (Stevens, 1999, p. 9)

These positive responses by administrators are largely due to the initial planning and resources, the four teleteachers, and continuing technical support. The overall success of this project is best described by Dr. Ken Stevens:

The Vista [School] District Digital Intranet has attracted a considerable amount of attention within the province and beyond. Since overcoming early technical difficulties, many educators in the district became increasingly positive about the long-term benefits of this way of delivering teaching and encouraging learning. There is a sense that the district is at the forefront of developments in the application of telecommunications to education in Newfoundland and Labrador and that important steps have been taken in overcoming geographic isolation as a barrier to educational opportunities. (1999, p. 16)

The Vista [School] District Digital Intranet is a model for other districts, but other districts may not want AP courses. One teacher in the district who was not a project participant thought the intranet would be an effective way of delivering technical and vocational subjects in the future.

## THE CAPE BONAVISTA INITIATIVE

While the Vista School District continues to place an emphasis on advanced level mathematics and science courses, other subjects are ignored. During the 1998–99 school year, many small schools were able to offer only history or geography. The single AP social studies course offered in the entire province is in two large urban high schools.

In addition to the establishment of a district-wide intranet in 2000, the Vista School District promises to evaluate the effectiveness of current distance education activities, to explore new models for all students, and to develop independent study activities for students. This district pursues these goals through an AP social studies course with the CAPE Bonavista Initiative.

In 1993, the Department of Education released *A Curriculum Framework for Social Studies: Navigating the Future*. This document outlines the future of social studies within the Newfoundland and Labrador school culture. At the high school level, the courses are:

**First Level**: Courses are offered in Canadian History and Canadian Geography. These are foundational courses and provide a springboard for other program options;

**Second Level**: Courses in Canadian Studies consist of Canadian Law, Canadian Economy, and Canadian Issues. A pre-20th century World History course is also offered at the second level;

**Third Level**: Courses in World Studies represents the capstone of the Social studies program. History, Geography, Global Economics, and Global Issues offer the learner a comprehensive examination of 20th century events, issues, and social and physical phenomena; and, finally,

**Fourth Level**: Advanced Placement courses in Microeconomics, Macroeconomics, European History, and Government and Politics are available for senior graduation credit. These local courses offer further challenge and greater depth of analysis. (Government of Newfoundland, 1993b, pp. 46–47)

While there is a provision for AP courses to be offered at the high school level, few schools in the province have the enrollment for these courses. In the 1999–2000 school year, there are six AP courses listed under social studies: art history, comparative government and politics; European history; macroeconomics; United States government and politics; and, finally, United States history. In 2001–02, human geography and world history were added (College Board, 2000). Several of the teachers thought these are the limit of possible courses that could be offered in the sparsely populated province.

Initially, only the European history course is offered in two urban schools, unlike the more numerous science and mathematics courses provided. There were four different mathematics and science courses offered in 32 different schools (B. Wheeler, personal communication, August 28, 1999). In April 2000, the Ministerial Panel on Educational Delivery in the Classroom submitted its report, *Supporting Learning*, to the provincial Government. The report discusses the evolution of distance education in the province of Newfoundland and Labrador, including a recommendation for the establishment of a Centre for Distance Learning and Innovation. This centre would focus on secondary-level mathematics and science courses (Government of Newfoundland, 2000). Action on any courses is left to individual schools and school districts.

The decision to offer AP social studies courses originates at the school level, Cape Bonavista's Discovery Collegiate. During Summer 1999, as a teacher and administrator in that school, I propose offering the AP European History course on the Internet. This course would become a pilot to a larger proposal to offer all eight of the AP social studies courses over a three year period.

In Fall 1999, the CAPE Bonavista Initiative receives developmental funding from the Office of Learning Technologies (a division of Human Resources Development Canada). This funding is to develop partnerships, a business plan, and an evaluation plan. The CAPE Bonavista Initiative secures the support of the Vista School District, which allowed it to offer its AP courses to high school students within the Vista School District. The district provides some administrative and technical support, since this project would be housed at Discovery Collegiate—the largest school in the Vista School District.

AP social studies courses does not have the same support as the AP mathematics and science courses. Since the early 1990s, AP mathematics and science courses are accepted for university credit by Memorial University (MUN). The only AP social studies course that had been recognized by MUN for university credit is the AP European History course.

Since MUN is the only university within the province, its support was essential. The CAPE Bonavista Initiative and the College Entrance Exam Board (through their Canadian coordinator), creates partnerships with the departments of Economics, Geography, History, and Political Science at MUN. Three departments recognize related AP courses for university credit, but the Department of Political Science only agree to take the issue under advisement.

Advanced standing means students could use AP courses toward a university major or minor, or simply as an elective. It allows these students to register before other prospective first-year students. All four departments want students to read in their subjects during high school. They donate approximately $5,000 worth of textbooks and other print resources toward the creation of an AP Resource Centre at Discovery Collegiate.

The Vista School District Digital Intranet is a constant model and support from similar partners is sought. The Centre for TeleLearning and Rural Education becomes a partner for the delivery of on-line courses. When the pilot AP European History course begins well in the 1999–2000 school year, STEM~Net provides use of the e-learning software WebCT for this course. STEM~Net's Netmeeting and MeetingPoint software were also made available, together with technical support.

The CAPE Bonavista Initiative is able to establish a partnership with Merrill Lynch Canada. Merrill Lynch Canada agrees to donate computer equipment for the purposes of establishing a distance education computer lab at Discovery Collegiate. In total, Merrill Lynch Canada provides 21 Pentium-level computers for the CAPE Bonavista Initiative to use. This lab, for which the Vista School District provides the necessary network support, allows the students at Discovery Collegiate to take advantage of the courses offered through the CAPE Bonavista Initiative. This lab is the centre of the CAPE Bonavista Initiative.

CAPE Bonavista Initiative's original intent is to expand the project beyond high school students to include adult learners. I contacted two

Discovery Learning Centres (institutions for basic adult education) on the Bonavista peninsula; the public college (College of the North Atlantic), which has two campuses on the peninsula; the nine Community Access Programme sites; and the local and provincial development associations. I want adult learners to enroll in the courses offered by the CAPE Bonavista Initiative through our Internet access.

In June 2000, the Office of Learning Technologies chooses not to fund the CAPE Bonavista Initiative for adult learners. The Community Learning Networks Initiative funds projects that create a network of learning sites to provide training programs for adult learners. Hugett Richard, Senior Program Officer, Office of Learning Technologies, says the CAPE Bonavista Initiative promotes formal courses in a limited and specific field, as opposed to lifelong learning (Letter, June 20, 2000). CAPE Bonavista Initiative is seen as an information learning environment, not a network of learning sites. The Office of Learning Technologies no longer targets adults in formal schools.

Though it is not possible to expand the program, CAPE Bonavista is able to offer four of the five courses in high schools that had been planned for the 2000–01 school year. AP European History and AP Human Geography courses are offered to high school students within the Vista School District and AP Comparative Government and Politics and AP United States History were offered locally at Discovery Collegiate. The plan is to offer these courses district-wide the following school year.

Neither of these Internet initiatives is a reaction to a crisis in education. Both projects address a problem discussed by the government for over a decade that was born out of a need to balance rural inequity as seen by teachers. The teachers for the Vista School District Digital Intranet are selected by the Vista School District. They are released from their teaching duties for a two-month period to design the courses, and for a two-year period, teaching these on-line courses is one quarter of their load.

In contrast, the teachers and administrators in the CAPE Bonavista Initiative volunteer to pursue this initiative. In addition to their regular teaching duties, these teachers and administrators are involved in partnership development and in writing the group's developmental proposal and business plan. The pilot course is taught by a first-year teacher in addition to a full-time teaching load.

## CONTINUING ISSUES

While both initiatives meet with a fair measure of success, Vista School District Digital Intranet is far more successful in securing government funding and being able to implement its entire project. During the 1999–2000 school year 2.5 percent of all students in the Vista District are taking at least one AP course. This figure equals the number of students who are taking AP courses in the Avalon East School District, which has the highest concentration of large urban schools in the province. Some measure of equity between the large urban schools and the small rural schools for the AP initiative exists.

The success of these AP initiatives in the Vista School District leads to the creation of similar projects and courses in other predominately rural school districts. At present, STEM~Net hosts three other district-wide AP Mathematics and AP Physics courses, along with one other district-wide AP Biology and AP Chemistry course. There are a total of 32 different on-line courses hosted by STEM~Net, aside from the Vista School District Digital Intranet and the CAPE Bonavista initiatives (STEM~Net, 2000b).

Both of these latter initiatives are made possible through the work of the Centre for TeleLearning and Rural Education. Initially, it developed the approach with the Vista School District Digital Intranet. Later, it incorporates the lessons that they had learned in a program for other districts. The most important continuing problem is to prevent student withdrawal.

In its first year, the Vista School District Digital Intranet had high student attrition rates from the course throughout the year—a number of students, who remained in the course, declined to take the AP exam. Since its inception, there is only one student from Cape Bonvista who drops out of the course. The remaining students elect to take the exam for university credit. In their second year, the CAPE Bonavista Initiative grows, while the Vista School District Digital Intranet declines.

The level of withdrawal from AP programs is significant because of the constant criticisms made by outside administrators of the AP program. A lot of resources are said by them to be put into this program with few returns. Other educators object to the AP because they target high-ability students. The high dropout rate suggests the program may be too difficult for those involved as well as a wasteful use of scarce resources for a small number of students.

The Vista School District Digital Intranet is the first initiative of its kind and its successes and failures are a benchmark for other distance education initiatives. The result is greater equity between rural and urban schools in the Vista project. The Centre for TeleLearning and Rural Education, through their research, is a catalyst for other Internet projects. None of these efforts would occur without the resources and support provided by public and private partnerships.

## EDITOR'S NOTE

This chapter is a limited contribution to a very significant problem: equality for rural education. The author, who is involved in these innovations as a principal and teacher, does not accept the limitations of advanced placement courses. The attempt to acquire additional funding as an adult education project shows a failure to rethink the format of specialized courses through distance education. Though aware of the unique society of Newfoundland, the author does not include its society or culture in his innovation. The evidence that the local project is more successful could be generalized to community involvement.

The accomplishment of the two initiatives is substantial. Rural society continues to reproduce the greatest inequalities in Canadian society (Bollman, 1992). To raise the achievement levels in AP subjects of the smallest district to that of the largest city in Newfoundland, St. John, is important. The program needs to be rethought in terms of links among people if it is to obtain grants for adult education, and if it is to make a greater contribution to rural society.

Rural society constantly falls further behind urban centers in terms of technology. To fall behind in Internet use is curious because such technology makes it possible for talented professionals to live and work in the most remote areas (Mitchell, 2000). People in smaller areas have been sources for many traditional trades. The schools could serve as a mentor for the new technology as well as a link to these traditional achievements.

The school is not expected to lead the rural revolution alone. Many of the partners who have entered into "partnerships" with these two AP initiatives need to help the communities, while the school becomes a resource for them. As Chapter 11 makes clear, government is a significant source for a broader development which also has a deeper meaning for rural partnerships.

In this chapter, partnership seems to involve mainly approval by university departments, acceptance by the school, and provision of resources by businesses and government. None of these agents has gone very far beyond its own immediate interests and usual ways of conducting business. Significantly, in spite of the telling meaning attached to being a "bay man," no attention is paid to bay leaders. They are not involved in these projects. Informal contact and discussion is the basis for garnering support for innovations to spread beyond school walls into rural communities.

The Internet innovation for social studies only breaks the mold when the largest school in the smallest district leads the way. Small rural efforts leading to partnerships with urban schools and organizations are needed. It is important that the "place" values of rural areas be developed in any partnership. This international AP set of courses does not relate to the communities from which its students come.

# 11

# Following Your Star: Teachers, Communities, and Countries

## Ann Jones

Everyone who talks about partnerships believes they are important and that they make many general contributions to students and schools. Successful partnerships change the learning environment and opportunities for students. Communities offer students authentic experiences that help develop civic pride, a sense of how business interests are important to community development, and how agencies support the population. School boards and individual schools seek partnerships to support students, provide students with interesting and authentic activities, and allow young people to serve their communities. In this way, our students and schools are connected to community interests and needs. Students also learn the rewards of service.

To contribute to learning, education/community/business partnerships must develop a joint approach that is measurable, subject to change, and provided with additional financial support. All partnerships must:

- Have a reason to build an education partnership with clear objectives that focus on the student;
- Have specific objectives that can be achieved, at least initially, in a reasonable amount of time;
- Be innovative, relevant, and socially responsible;

- Provide a positive outcome for all partners;
- Be championed by individuals at the school board and the community or business that are at the decision-making level;
- Have access to direct support through funding, resources, and time allocation;
- Have a method to evaluate success that is linked to the objectives but is not so restrictive that it gets in the way; and
- Be flexible enough to evolve and to change strategically.

Generic partnerships need to be considered in specific contexts that allow communities to contribute in different ways to students' learning. Since partnerships connect communities of interest with school systems, they are by definition situational. Education must reflect community norms and assist in economic support and renewal in communities. When students are active partners in their cities, towns and villages, rural areas, and the suburbs, they respect the context in which they live and they are appreciated and better understood.

Building partnerships in a rural area has a different set of dynamics than in an urban area. As a senior administrator in both urban and rural areas, I experienced specific lessons about the approach to take, what people or organizations to include in the partnership, longevity, focus, and how to influence the expected outcome in these very different situations.

## AN URBAN PARTNERSHIP IN OTTAWA, CANADA

Partnerships in urban areas tend to be with businesses, governmental organizations, or nongovernmental organizations that are able to make decisions locally. Discussions are held face to face, meetings can be scheduled quickly, and traveling to meetings and finding a suitable meeting location are not difficult. Urban partnerships have more direct access to decision making. Those working on partnerships at the table have the power to move the partnership forward.

In 1996, in my position as assistant director with the Ottawa Board of Education, I was working to link our schools in a wide area network. The Ottawa Board of Education has amalgamated with the Carleton Board of Education into the Ottawa-Carleton District School Board (OCDSB), with over 70,000 students located in an urban center of almost one million people. Ottawa, a center for high technology, has colleges, universities, a well-developed community infrastructure, and a high interest in education. It is small enough for the education, business, and government communities to know who the decision makers are. Ottawa being the national capital of Canada, there is direct access to federal government and national headquarters of nongovernmental agencies.

With all of these advantages, a natural outcome is the building of significant education/business/community partnerships. During a meeting at the Ottawa-Carleton Media Centre shared by all boards of education in the area, we identified the need to link all of our schools. Since the infrastructure of the Media Centre existed, senior decision makers worked with each other. In this context, the partnership had an easy and a natural beginning. The next step was a search for partners who would supplement their efforts.

This partnership did not try to be a large and complicated project. As many good things do, it started with a casual conversation about mutual interests and some good ideas. This was followed by the most important statement needed for any successful venture, "Why don't we . . .?" The idea was to connect all of our schools in the Ottawa Board and to automate the libraries.

In the City of Ottawa and Carleton County, public and separate schools have either French or English as the language of instruction. There is a well-developed library system that connects the public library with the libraries of the University of Ottawa and Carleton University. There are high-technology firms that need a venue to see if their products can support community and educational needs. The result is the Ottawa/Carleton Network for Education: World Consortium Project (ONEWorld).

Unique to an urban area, there already existed the Ottawa-Carleton Learning Foundation (OCLF), established to assist partnerships. The existence of the foundation made finding the partners easy, gave us a neutral venue for meeting, and provide facility for telephone and video conferencing. The foundation provided us with leadership. By assigning time of the executive director of the OCLF to ONEWorld, the partnership could maintain minutes, and access to public relations professionals and writers. This infrastructure is essential to facilitating and maintaining the partnership.

ONEWorld partners include the two French language school boards, two Roman Catholic separate school boards, and two public boards of education, Bell Canada, TV Ontario, Apple Canada, Ottawa/Carleton Media Centre, Exocom, Napean and Ottawa Public Libraries, Dymaxion Ltd., SchoolNet, and Knet First Nations. Each joins the partnership to enable schools to connect to each other, to the library, and to outside resources, in order to test the application of products to education, and to generally "push the envelope" of network technology applications to education. ONEWorld connects all six boards to curriculum materials, student information systems, student/teacher networks, administrative networks, and Multi-media on Demand.

The project did have a clear objective and as partners were added, the objective took on a broader context but always had the focus of connecting the student with resources that are beyond what a single school board could provide that did not have access to the wider community. Another important element of the urban context of this partnership is access to decision makers who champion this project and who take part in its planning and implementation. These leaders make quick decisions and provide resources. Those involve take risks.

Since the beginning of the project the overall objective did not change, but the players are different. Successful partnerships need time to plan and even more time to implement their plans, which changes in education make diffiicult. Education in the last decade has become highly politicized. The result is changes in governance of education, reduction in funding, and amalgamation of boards and administration. These changes create an atmosphere that is not fertile ground for innovation or risk taking.

With the instability of the leadership and structure of educational institutions, the necessary time and commitment is difficult to maintain. More time is required to implement and evaluate the changes in them. This is frustrating to educators and to their potential partners. Each partner needs to be able to trust the commitment of others in the project. This is very difficult if the educational partners are operating in an area of uncertainty.

For ONEWorld, the uncertainty about funding, the loss of key players, and the disruption due to the amalgamation of the school boards, caused the partnership to be suspended. During this time the overall objective, the connection of students to resources via technology, continues, but at a much slower pace, and without being able to take advantage of opportunities offered by the partners.

Partnerships in urban areas can be started because the resources are available, but like all partnerships, once established, they need continued support to prosper. Changes in urban environment make partnerships difficult to direct.

## RURAL PARTNERSHIPS IN NOVA SCOTIA

In rural areas, building partnerships between education and the community takes on a very different dynamic. In small communities and towns, schools are a focal point. There is a great deal of support for education, including trust and respect for educators. Administrators and teachers are leaders in the community and in many cases, hold political office at the municipal or provincial level. In Nova Scotia particularly, school board members are known, they know their communities, and most believe that their board members act in the best interest of their communities. The leadership for building partnerships comes more from within the educational system, administrators, teachers, and board members than in urban areas.

Although large businesses impact on rural areas, the decision makers are more remote. Partnerships must be built with local or regional managers who are very willing but are not given direct authority to act. This slows down the process and requires commitment to the project to move it forward.

Local business owners are an important part of the rural community and are essential partners. In small towns, there are so many small businesses and entrepreneurs they are difficult to contact. They are very diverse and are busy with their businesses, which are more "hands on." Local service organizations such as Rotary, Lions, Women's Institutes, churches, garden clubs and exhibition societies play an important role in communities. As a source of support in time, money, and planning, they supplement small businesses.

Augmenting schools, businesses, and service clubs, in rural areas governmental agencies at all levels provide a great deal of the infrastructure for rural areas and are an important source of allies. Provincial hospital boards and health authorities; housing authorities; family and children's services; justice, sport and recreation, town and municipal councils; and public libraries are natural partners to education. Since all have limited funding and large responsibilities, they are receptive to cooperation with education. It may be a case of "misery loves company" or "absolute necessity."

At the federal level, particularly in rural areas, Human Resources Development Canada (HRDC) is a most important source of support, direct funding, and personnel resources. Their mandate is human and community development and they are linked to education through many federal programs. HRDC wants to ensure that its monies buy results. They have local expertise and are able to access resources to help with the structure of a partnership.

Aside from all the formal organizations, rural partnerships are different. A partnership in a rural area depends on the informal leadership in the community. There are leaders in communities that hold no elected office, neither municipal councilors or business leaders, but are people who get things done. These individuals are essential to a good educational partnership. They know how to make the necessary connections with service organizations, small and large businesses, with other community leaders and the community in general.

When I moved from Ottawa to Nova Scotia in 1996, partnerships were developed in every possible rural community. As the first superintendent (CEO) of the Southwest Regional School Board (SWRSB), I was able to pursue these opportunities. The SWRSB is fairly typical of a large rural board with many diverse communities. The SWRSB was established in 1996 as an amalgamation of county school boards serving Digby, Yarmouth, Shelburne, Queens, and Lunenburg counties. The board has 19,000 students spread over 5,500 square kilometers, with 65 schools that range from 10 students, K–5, on Big Tancook Island, accessible only by ferry, to a high school of 900 students in the Town of Bridgewater.

Students come to SWRSB from rural and small towns with diverse economies along the shore of the Gulf of Maine, the Bay of Fundy, and the Atlantic Ocean. The area is supported by lobster, scallop, and ground fishing and by inland areas where small farms and logging are the main occupations. The five counties that make up the SWRSB have a $450 million fishing industry. This represents 70 percent of the total fishing income in Nova Scotia that in turn is economically the most lucrative fishing industry of any province in Canada (ITG Information Management, 2000).

Because the school board amalgamation causes disruption in the web of informal contacts so important in these places, SWRSB is seen as very remote from the communities and their individual schools. Links between the new board and the separate schools are essential. The SWRSB worked with communities and schools to be the first school board in Nova Scotia to fully implement and support school advisory committees (SACs). These SACs link school administration, teachers, parents, and the community and are charged with the task of school improvement. Establishing SACs were essential to the building and maintaining of partnerships.

After establishing SACs, a series of partnerships or groups of partnerships were established. An initial project included community literacy and encouraging school competition. A significant group, Blacks in Nova Scotia, was the concern of a community. Community services for children and youths are integrated. Individual teachers have organized projects, such as respect for war veterans. A huge partnership has been organized with three American states and another Canadian province for environmental education.

Each of these partnerships grows from the identification of a community need, and connecting a group of dedicated students, educators, parents, and community members who work toward a goal that matters to them. Partnerships are human endeavors that connect people. My own personal interest in partnerships was nourished in Ottawa. Community needs and my interests were cast into a shared set of goals. Rural partnerships become easier to maintain because their returns are more tangible and the program areas more localized. People, resources, and the environment are welded.

## LEARNING COMMUNITY PILOT PROJECT

In 1998, a series of projects began in one of the communities in SWRSB. This community is on the Atlantic coast: Barrington, Barrington Passage, and Clarks Harbour, including Cape Sable Island. This is an area with two industries, lobster and ground fishing, and tourism. It is a place with an active and innovative Municipal and Town Council with strong leadership.

One of the informal and important connections in this community is the warden of the municipality. He is the husband of the first Vice-Chair of the board and former Chair of the Shelburne County Board. When the SWRSB first amalgamated, all board members in the six former boards remained on the board until the next election, October 1997. For a full 16 months between the amalgamation and the next election, there were 52 board members. As the board moved to 18 members, many of the former board members either did not run or were defeated. These former board members were leaders in their community who knew the school system and their communities and wanted to continue to be of service to students. The former Vice-Chair, Linda Stoddart, was one of these people.

A talk over coffee at Tim Horton's between Linda and her husband, Warden Steven Stoddart, turned into a "Why don't we?," which became the Learning Community Pilot Project (LCPP) in Barrington, Barrington Passage, and Clark's Harbour. Included in this conversation was Don Glover, the former superintendent of the Shelburne Board and current Director of Learning Services with the SWRSB, who is a long-time resident in the area. This is a pattern that has repeated itself as partnerships with literacy groups in Yarmouth and antipoverty groups in Bridgewater were built.

In these settings, what is important is the attitude. When a person says, "Why don't we?," others have to say "Why not?" and "How can I help?" In a rural setting, over coffee, in a person's kitchen or board room, these confirming conversations are more likely to happen. The focus of the LCPP was very tangible. They were to make sure that students graduate from high school with a high level of literacy and numeracy, including computer literacy. These new skills are to benefit the community, not just the individuals.

The next step for our informal group was to meet with the Principals of the local junior high/secondary school and the four elementary schools in a planning session. Principals in rural communities are very important. They have deep roots in their communities, they are community leaders. Because the schools are small compared to urban centers, they know the families of their students. We spoke to current local school board members, teachers, school secretaries, bus drivers, and, with the help of Warden Stoddart, with municipal and town councils.

Some of those identified are formal leaders with titles, others are identified as people who are influential and respected by the community. Since we wanted those who make the program work, we invited students. Not just those who are part of student government, but those who are identified by their peers and by their teachers as students who influence their peers. We had a list of over 50 people from all age groups and all occupations.

At the suggestion of one of the principals who said that the best work gets done in the kitchen, we invited them to a dinner cooked by the cafeteria workers in one of our schools. Over 30 local leaders attend the dinner and those that couldn't, let us know that they supported this effort. The LCPP is established from this meeting.

We are able to focus on influential members of the community, families, businesses, municipal, provincial, and federal government agencies and educational institutions on the importance of learning. Because literacy and numeracy are critical for the success of the individual and the prosperity of the community, three committees are established: School-to-Work, Community Literacy and Support Services (CLASS), and Stay-In-School.

Each of these three committees sets clear and realistic goals. I find that people in rural communities are very realistic and pragmatic. While they have an overall vision of where they want to go, the steps needed to accomplish the goal need to be very concrete. They want their children to stay in their communities, to be able to make a living at home. The students share this view. While urban parents and families are focused on the job or profession, rural students and their parents focus on what they can do at home, in their communities. Moving away to Halifax is seen as going away from home.

The School-to-Work Subcommittee offered annual job fairs to assist students in course selection. They are working to produce a database of credentials required for certain professions for student use. Human Resources Development Canada (HRDC) and Access Nova Scotia partner to place a a job/career computer terminal at Barrington Municipal High School (BMHS); the terminal is replaced by Internet access once the school was connected. The students appear before the municipal councils of Barrington and Clark's Harbour to express their view about the need for diversification in employment in the area.

Activities of the School-to-Work Committee focus on local issues that affect their communities. Students working with the subcommittee approach Basin Productions to mount a theatrical production around issues raised by the Supreme Court decision on Native treaty rights for access to fish and forests. This is an important decision since lobster fishing is a million-dollar industry in this community. This project is being discussed with the Shelbourne Campus of Nova Scotia Community College as a partnership to produce a video.

Differences among students themselves are the focus of a partnership with Mental Health Services. This school-based project offers adolescent self-referral counseling services. This partnership works with the school board Coordinator of Race Relations, Cross Cultural Understanding and Human Rights (RCH) to organize classroom visits/student workshops to address diversity (gender, socioeconomic status, beliefs, etc.). The school and Nova Scotia Community College are jointly implementing courses in Mi'kmaq Studies 10, Oceans 11, and Personal Development and Relationship 7/8.

The second committee, CLASS, works with parents and community members as well as students. The board uses partnerships with Human Resources, Children's Aid Society, Mental Health, and Nova Scotia Housing Authority (NSHA) to establish locations for Family Community Support Centres within the community. One location is in a former school board office, in a newly renovated facility owned by the housing authority; later, it approached the board to use the former Barrington Elementary School. For ease of access to the community, these facilities are located across this coastal area, including Cape Sable Island. These centers offer parenting support classes, a preschool parent–child learning centre, homework clubs, anger management programs, adult upgrading, family literacy programs, Special Olympics programs, subsidized child care and school-based school age care, seniors programs, drug and alcohol dependency support, and a Community Access Project.

The Stay-in-School committee implements programs and courses at BMHS, including career programs, cooperative education, and work experience. Working with the Coordinator of Junior and Senior High Programs, it offers courses through Nova Scotia Community College, Shelburne Campus. This third committee, joining with the Stay-In-School Committee, links with the Open for Business Centre and entrepreneurial support service, will have a job terminal, with the support of HRDC in the school.

The Stay-in-School Committee is in discussion with fisheries groups to keep students in school. With a winter lobster season from November to May, students in the senior grades are attracted to the fishery, where they can make upwards of $30,000 for the season. Parents are concerned that their children will give up their education for the money in the fishery. Because of their lack of a high school diploma and academic skills, these young adults are not going to be able to advance in the fishery. With high tech equipment on boats and the entrepreneurial nature of being a captain of your own boat, the lack of formal education is a limitation.

This project is developing a half and half program, which allows students to start four semestered courses in the Fall, leave school in November to fish on a lobster boat during the season, and return to school in May to complete the four courses. Student time on a lobster boat could be given credit through cooperative education. We are working with the general fishing community to establish courses at Nova Scotia Community College to train for Master, Mate, and Mechanics papers for the industry. Having this program in the community will show students that just "hauling rope" on a lobster boat, while attractive when you are young, leaves you with little future in the industry.

The Learning Community Pilot Project is successful because it is grounded in the community. It has empowered community members and students to take an active role in the projects. They are supported by federal and provincial government agencies such as Human Resources and the Housing Authority. Because of these connections, this project is not affected by changes in leadership at the board level or funding issues. It continues because the community owns these programs and believes "we're OK." This project receives a grant from the Walter and Duncan Gordon Foundation to determine the reasons for its success, which might lead to replication in other rural communities.

## SUPPORT FOR BLACK NOVA SCOTIANS

This partnership in Digby County is unique because it is not the creation of a new partnership, but a revitalization of one that was established over 20 years ago. In 1978, human rights judgment, the Green Report, recommended conditions of settlement for discrimination African Nova Scotian students were facing at their high school. The total community felt that the conditions of settlement of the complaints had not been fully implemented. One of the key conditions is the need for active cooperation between the school and the African Nova Scotian community, formally known as the Permanent Liaison Committee.

This issue came back to the school board because of racial incidents at Digby Regional High School in 1998. These tensions were an indicator that integration, understanding, and acceptance of black Nova Scotian students was lacking in spite of the Green Report's terms of settlement. Families of today's students lived and worked in the communities for generations and are frustrated that their children face the same racial tensions and discriminations that they faced when they were students.

The newly amalgamated Southwest Regional school board commissioned Dr. Blye Frank, Associate Professor, Department of Education, Mount Saint Vincent University, to conduct the external review and report to the board. The report recommends a comprehensive historical overview of significant documents and policies, an evaluation of present state-of-affairs in light of those documents and policies, and specific actions.

The recommendations were not easy for the board to implement. Because the board is large, taking in five counties, many of the board members could avoid relating to the issues in Digby. Members of the board from the Digby, Yarmouth, and Shelburne area understood the issues because they are confronted with a significant African population in these counties. One board member from Digby is a former teacher and the other one was a student at Digby Regional High School during the time of the Green Report. The two board members persuade other school board members.

Although the board had no black member during these discussions, a former member of the board when it was larger is a well-respected leader in the black communities in the area. Her presence at meetings influences the board to act. The issue is emotional and highly public, and the indigenous Black population across Nova Scotia is waiting for results.

As said about previous partnerships, rural communities depend on individuals who have the respect of their peers. These individuals are easily identified when you ask. In this case, I found out about factions within the communities, as well as which groups cooperate in each community. In rural communities, everyone knows everyone else, even if they disagree.

Building a partnership through the selection of respected individuals is fundamental to the success of the new efforts by SWRSB. A second report is commissioned to look specifically at the evolution of the Permanent Liaison Committee. This report is written by Dr. Harriet Edwards, who was, as they say in Nova Scotia, a "come from away," or CFA, from Jamaica. Although she is a Black woman, there is distrust because she is not a member of the African Nova Scotia Community. She met with all the parties, is open and honest about the issues, and her report outlines concrete actions to be taken. These research activities bring Dr. Edwards into direct contact with community members and she gains the trust of all the parties (Edwards, 1999).

The issues addressed in the report are long standing. Actions to solve the problems over the last 20 years were failures. All parties meet new initiative with skepticism and distrust. What the Edwards Report captures in conjunction with the Frank Report are ways to proceed in measured steps. What is needed to take these steps is a dedicated staff.

With the two reports in hand, SWRSB approaches the provincial Department of Education and received special funding to hire a coordinator for the Permanent Liaison Committee. The board hires a project coordinator to build an active partnership with the schools, the communities, the Department of Education black educators, and the board through the Coordinator of Race Relations, Cross Cultural Understanding and Human Rights. The selection of the person for this new leader is critical.

Since there are factions within the community and a distrust of CFA's, the person chosen is an African Nova Scotian who worked away, but was returning home to assume this position. We have the best of both worlds. Someone rooted in the community, but not directly involved in the issues over the last 20 years.

Community Liaison committees, established under the Green Report in 1978, became integral to the work of the project coordinator. A monitoring committee, chaired by the project coordinator, is also established, consisting of the high school principal, the board RCH coordinator, Chair of the Liaison Committee, a parent representing the African Nova Scotian community, and a member of the SWRSB. School-based student support workers are hired to work with students in the schools.

For the people involved, this project is successful. The project coordinator and the student support workers, the board RCH coordinator, and all African Nova Scotians, have brought the communities together in projects. There are now clear lines of communication with the African Nova Scotian Community, the staff, administration, and the school advisory committees. All gained insight into the needs and concerns of African Nova Scotian students. The programs in the schools have been enhanced by resources, special programs, support for "at risk" students, homework and study skill support, presentation of positive role models, and presentation of programs that enhance student self-esteem. The students establish an African Nova Scotian Student web site. The overall result is better and positive communication between and among all parties.

The project completed the first year very successfully. It was successful because the Frank and Edwards reports gave concrete direction developed with input from the community groups. It is significant that their efforts are supported by the school board, Project Coordinator, Coordinator of RCH, board senior administration and by the Department of Education who provided the funding. Progress is made by improved communications. Issues of race relations and emotion are approached positively and with an open mind. The first step is understanding, the second, acting on that understanding. This project has both elements and is successful.

In spite of this partnership's success, the program is now in jeopardy because of reduced provincial funding. The province does not fund the project in the second year and the respected Project Coordinator is lost.

The structure of the board changes and some of people who supported the efforts at the board and administrative level move to new responsibilities or leave the board, including the Project Coordinator, Coordinator of RCH and the Director of Learning Services. The infrastructure for the project is lost.

While it is hoped that the school and community will sustain the work done to date with volunteers, the reduction of direct support has brought back the original concerns of support and commitment to implement the conditions of settlement of the Green Report. There is concern from the Black community that the mainstream majority is again showing that it does not support or even recognize the seriousness of the issues for their children. Having spoken with leaders of the African Nova Scotian community, I am concerned we may fall back once again into the distrust of the past. Money does equate to commitment.

## INTEGRATED SERVICES

Children and Youth Intersectoral Working Group (CYIWG) tries to connect all the helping agencies in health, education, and social services, which is not easy. The frustration of all parties leads to a partnership of provincial and federal governmental and non-governmental agencies: Mental Health Authority, HRDC, Family and Children's Services, Children's Aid Society, Housing, Sport and Recreation, and Justice, SWRSB and the Annapolis Valley Regional School Board.

The initial meetings of this partnership are more a gathering of those executives responsible for children and youth than a formal group. These executives could commit their organization to group activities. Though this might sound like an urban partnership, these leaders were coming together over a large distance, 7,000 square kilometers. Since traveling time is up to 2 hours, members of the group want value for a full day to attend the first meeting. It took many telephone calls to explain the benefits that would make meeting worth the time. That initial effort to hold the first meeting, the many calls, gave the group a feeling they knew each other. In fact, many of us did know and work with each other in the context of addressing individual issues for individual students. Planning together under such tight constraints result in all of us being more more efficient and economical.

After six months of planning, CYWIG becomes a formal group with established protocols for providing connected services for students and has become part of a larger network at the provincial level. This provincial group, Children and Youth Action Committee (CAYAC), is a committee of Ministers and Deputy Ministers from the Department of Education, Justice, Health, Community and Social Services, Sport and

Recreation. Although CAYAC has been a provincial committee for over five years, the results "on the ground" at the regional level are not evident. CYWIG gives voice and action to the vision of CAYAC.

The work of CYWIG in the first year focuses on shared values and understanding members' mandates. By the end of the first year members are becoming quite tired of the discussions and process-oriented work to the exclusion of concrete action. Since there are impending provincial budget cuts and reorganization of school boards and health authorities, the group feels there is a serious threat to the well being of children and youth.

Responding to these changes and budget pressures takes up the time and energy of the group. Restructuring impacts on the membership at the table. The group finds that it is using energy and resources to communicate their needs to government, to fight for stability, and not for the needs of the children they serve. They are developing a paper on concerns regarding the impact of budget cuts and reorganization. Cuts to one organization will impact the services provided by others so that there are multiple negative effects on the well being of the client. The paper points out CYWIG's willingness and potential to help create solutions to the problems government is trying to address in a way that is least harmful to the clients.

The ability to react to change collectively is a strength of a partnership like CYWIG. Regional authorities support rural areas where people feel remote from the central decision makers and the provincial or federal level. This partnership empowers the members of the group to act collectively to support their rural towns and communities. There are real savings and efficiencies that result when all agencies work together. This is what CAYAC at the ministerial level talk about, and what CYIWIG is implementing.


## INDIVIDUAL POWERS

In just a few years, individual teachers develop their own partnerships to reflect their visions and beliefs. Key people, such as principals or superintendents, encourage these teachers. Separate individuals bring an idea to their schools and communities, build partnerships and earn the respect and support of the community.

Individual "people" are very important in Nova Scotia. Family names like Stoddart, D'Entremont, Nickerson, Leblanc are common names. My name, Jones, is not. For the first time, when I introduced myself, I was told, "Jones, that is not a name from around here." How many generations your family has been in Nova Scotia and the South Shore is important to your identity. "Who is your father?" or "Who is your mother?" are common questions. People search for a connection, your roots. As a "Come from Away (CFA)" or an NFH (Not from Here), getting to know me and me getting to know them, was a major responsibility. I had no reference or compass point for the community.

People are not just individuals but are extensions of their ancestors. Who you are, how you connect defines you in rural communities. For this reason, partnerships that are started by individuals are defined not just by the person, but by how they operate and connect to their communities. These three partnerships that are successful represent many others that can be developed. Success means a connection with the unique environment and needs of their rural community.

### Oral Histories In Petite Riveria

"This is the best way to learn about history." "It's much easier to write the next chapter of our Dr. Cameron story now that we have been to the house where he used to live." "The best part of the project was the presentation in the community hall." "It didn't seem like school work at all" (Mary Jane Harkin, personal communication, June, 1999). These are some of the comments from students in Jessie Haché's elementary class.

In these rural areas, families have strong ties to their communities going back generations. Most live in the same area and live in a home that their parents, grandparents, great grandparents or even great great grandparents built. Rural communities are natural partners for student activities that focus on the history and cultural development of the community.

Each year students in Jessie Haché's class at Petite Riviere School participate in an oral history project. They decide on a project, gather data from a variety of sources including research at the provincial archives, conduct interviews with local seniors, and create a classroom museum where community members can bring information and artifacts into the school.

The project started in 1989 when Haché read from a diary of a former Petite Riviere teacher, Inga Volger. The diary talked about life in the community in 1916 when she was 10 years old. This inspires the students to begin to tell their own family stories. They found out that Inga Volger was still alive with family members still in the community. The students wrote to her and her recollections became the first edition. Over the years, with direct support from the principal, school board and superintendent, the work of the grade 6 students continues. They are writing a series of history books and companion storybooks about their local communities. The books are a part of National Library of Canada's Canadianna Collection and Provincial Archives Collection.

These oral histories are a writing process for children. They spend many weeks writing interview questions and taping interviews with community members, as well as writing and editing the manuscripts. They make decisions about what to include in the writing and what artwork to use.

Once the publication is complete, they have a community celebration. The night before, the children and their parents prepare an "old meal" of local traditional foods, during which the children and the community members discuss the collected information. The final celebration is a public presentation in the community hall. The children engage in readings, plays, dances, and a presentation of their books to the community members who have been involved in their project.

This project illustrates what one person can do. Jessie Haché responds to the interest of her students in a unique teachable time. Like many rural teachers she comes from the community where she teaches, she has a strong connection with the community. Haché comments, "Students discover the richness of their culture, their community, and their experiences through their writing. They feel special and they think of themselves as writers. They have goals and aspirations and they see themselves as successful" (Mary Jane Harkin, personal communication, June, 1999)

### Good Citizenship in Yarmouth County

In November of 1984, a teenager took off his poppy and squashed it in the ground in front of several veterans, bringing tears to their eyes. Joe Bishara, junior high teacher at Maple Grove Education Centre in Yarmouth, witnesses this incident and decides to work with junior high students to establish the Maple Grove Memorial Club. The purpose of the club is to connect youth volunteers with veterans and senior citizens in their communities so they can learn the importance of being Canadian and to appreciate the contributions made by those who fought and died in war.

In recent years, the Club expands into the local high school and numbers increase to over 200. What started as The Maple Grove Memorial Club is now The Maple Grove/Yarmouth County Memorial Club. Bishara stresses that the Club is successful because the kids make the decisions about the partnerships they form and the activities they undertake. They have strong leadership in Bishara.

In the Spring of 2000, I witnessed students in The Memorial Club, in the cold, pouring rain standing in front of Camp Hill Veterans Hospital, presenting a salute to veterans and then marching in a veterans parade. All without lunch. But when Bishara shouts, "Respect!" all activity and chatter stops and the students focus on their objective.

The students decide on the activities in which they will participate and the organizations for which they will fundraise. Activities include performances in marching parades, playing the "Last Post" at veterans' funerals, and fundraising for a local hospital and health organization, as well as children with special needs. In 1997, provincial and local papers carry the story of one student's meeting with a veteran, with whom she is corresponding. A wonderful friendship, which was valued by both families, crosses all generation boundaries.

How do you get teenagers to demonstrate such pride, respect, compassion, responsibility, and a willingness to help each other? It takes a special individual. Joe Bishara acts on his vision of what the community would support. The community has a group of teenagers with positive, caring attitudes about themselves, their school and the community.

Angus MacIssac wrote in his "Voice of the People" column in the *Halifax Sunday Herald*, June, 1999: "For those who missed the program at the Grand Parade on June 6, all I can say is that you missed one of the finest displays of dedication, love and friendship that one group could show for another. . . . A group of students from Yarmouth County spent their Sunday entertaining veterans and seniors, by paying tribute to the wartime merchant navy members. These young folk are an inspiration and a role model for other youngsters in the country to follow."

The Bishara family is two generations old in the Maritimes, one in Yarmouth County. Compared to some, he is a relative new comer. What he brings to this partnership is a history of a father and grandfather and uncles who are veterans. This history is known in the community and provides a context for his passion for assuring that students have an understanding and a respect for the sacrifices made for our freedom. Like Jessie Haché, his interest is real and everyone in the community knows it.

### An Institute without Walls

A very large project happened because one individual, John Terry, had an interesting ideas about the environment in this part of the Atlantic Ocean. Unlike Haché and Bishara, Terry is a newcomer to the area, another CFA. He is an educator and a former professor at the Massachusetts Institute of Technology in the United States. He is also the editor of *New Designs for Youth Development*, an American publication. When Terry walked into the school board office, he had the idea of a service learning projects focusing on the Gulf of Maine watershed. He is familiar with projects in Massachusetts and New Hampshire and believes that these projects could be linked with similar efforts in the Southwest of Nova Scotia.

The Gulf of Maine is essential to the economic, physical and social well being of the population in Digby, Yarmouth and Shelburne Counties of the Southwest. The Gulf of Maine and its watershed, shared by Canada and the U.S., is one of the richest regions in terms of biomass in the world. To focus students on the importance of this area, boards and community groups in Nova Scotia, Maine, New Hampshire, New Brunswick and Massachusetts formed a partnership around the common interest of living around, and being supported by the ecosystem of the Gulf of Maine called the Gulf of Maine Institute Without Walls (GMIWW).

The credo of the GMIWW is: Youth are our most Valuable Resource. They are the citizens, scientists, decision-makers and cultural transmitters of tomorrow. If we are to ensure a sustainable future for the Gulf of Maine region, we must engage in actions today that create and support networks of people who care about it as a rich and varied resource in perpetuity. Learning through doing, in apprenticeship and partnership with adults, is the most effective way to prepare youth to secure this future (John Terry, email, December 12, 2000).

The GMIWW now has five major projects, one in each of the three states and two provinces. The projects are divided: Nova Scotia does environmental research on the Tusket River, Yarmouth shore and Cape Forchu; New Hampshire has the Cocheco River Watch Project; Maine organizes the Official KIDS Guide to the Marginal Way; Massachusetts' project involves the effects of acid rain on salt and plant life in the Muddy River system; and students in New Brunswick act as the official masters of the BMIWW website.

These projects require fundraising. After much work, many disappointments, the formal funding partners are: Tusket River Environmental Protection Agency (TREPA), Gulf of Maine Council, United States Environmental Protection Agency, Southwest Regional School Board, Canadian Maritime Millennium Initiative, community businesses and agencies. The total budget for the 5 projects is almost $500,000. The Gulf of Maine Council, an international body of governmental and business interests, which is supported by the governments of Canada and the United States, sponsors this institute.

Assistance is provided by local service clubs such as Rotary and Lions and by small businesses who donate everything from hotdogs and milk to canoes. Though initially welcomed and encouraged by educators at the board level, the project captures the imagination of the entire community. Family members join with members of the school board, municipal council, senior citizens, garden clubs, university departments and environmental groups.

The GMIWW receives a $108,000 millennium grant from the Government of Canada to have the first Summer Institute Without Walls. In

July 2000, the Institute is held in Yarmouth, Nova Scotia. This is the first time students, teachers, university and community supporters, for all five jurisdictions could meet and share their work and findings. The institute allows students to present their projects and to take part in cultural and environmental activities in the Yarmouth area.

Students from Nova Scotia are on their land with those from another province and another country, taking part in a project that connects their individual interests with those who live with them in a common environment. They ride in canoes in the Tusket River watershed, slog through marches, clamber over the rock of Cape Forchu, and take part in a Sweet Grass Ceremony lead by an Acadia Band First Nations elder. One student from inner-city Boston, lying on the wet grass feeding a mallard duck from his hand says, "I didn't think these ducks actually existed." The Summer Institute includes a trip to New Hampshire for students to be part of the Gulf of Maine Council's tenth anniversary celebration.

This project is successful because an individual brought an idea and the small communities, provincial and state governments, federal governments and non-governmental agencies saw the potential. There is a direct connection to the community. There are so many activities of this type in an urban area that it is hard to have one focus for all agencies and levels of government. Because it happened in a rural area, it is unique and exciting. It would not have happened anywhere without a person with a vision. When people see the value of the idea for their place and lives. Being a CFA or NFH is an obstacle that could be overcome with perseverance and the support of key people.

## CONCLUSION

These group and individual partnerships represent the variety of activities that link students with their rural communities. These projects are encouraged and supported by the board and administration at all levels. They are successful because they meet needs. The communities in the areas around South West Nova Scotia value these projects and, are willing to support them.

Would these partnerships be the same in an urban setting? Would they even be possible outside a rural context? I believe they are successful because they are rooted in directly lived culture of rural people. Evaluation of the projects is very personal, direct and honest. If a partnership does not directly impact the community and is not relevant and socially responsible, there will not be community support. Successes in rural partnerships depend on individuals. People will tell you what they believe is working and what is not working, if the project is going in the right direction, and what needs to be done to improve it. What rural supporters respect is openness and honesty in return.

Though rural partnerships follow a different route, all partnerships need an infrastucture of support from organizations and individuals. Partnerships develop in a stable political environment. Leaders of communities, school boards, small and large businesses and governmental and non-governmental agencies must be free to take risks, work with secure sources of funding, and be allowed to make decisions. With these elements, partnerships in either rural or urban areas flourish.

## EDITOR'S NOTE

Partnerships all require financial support and social recognition. ONEWorld in Ottawa, the liason work with Black Nova Scotians, and the integrated social services were all restricted by governments that reduced funds and increased restrictions on partnerships. Individuals, such as the founder of the Memorial Club, do not need extensive supports, but social support is required for the program to expand. The Gulf of Maine Institute is able to leap over state and provincial restrictions so that it is not dependent on one province limiting its vision. Partnerships require more than a cooperative attitude. They need financial support, social recognition, and political influence. They need a place to meet and organize. Because schools or other institutions give their structures over to the partnership, the necessity for facilities is not recognized. Chapter 9 and this chapter discuss how space is needed as an incubator for any partnership.

The lack of other places and resources is what makes schools so critical for rural areas. There is no debate where integrated services, which are discussed in Chapter 9 and this chapter, will be; they must be based in the school. Urban areas have community resources that provide alternative sites. Rural areas welcome new facilities, but do not count on them. The school is understood as their central institution. Urban areas have to develop a parallel to this central focus. As all partnerships develop, they need facilities of their own where individual partnerships are presented and where political and business support is focused.

Knowledge and politics merge as the resources for partnerships are considered. Though technology is an important link for expanding new school operations, it is not enough, as the author of chapter 10 discovers when he tries to expand into adult education. Social capital includes understanding of different structures. The total infrastructure for partnerships must grow as the size of the problems or undertakings increases. Chapter 12 shows how critical all resources are in overcoming racial divisions in South Africa.

The racial differences in Nova Scotia are difficult to overcome. Financial resources and social capital are needed for the Permanent Liaison Committee. Rural leaders are not prepared to abandon their world in pursuit of unrealistic ideas. They want practical ideas that will enhance the value of the places where they and their relatives live or have lived. Not all rural communities and schools in these communities are as closed to outsiders as those in Nova Scotia. All rural communities feel they are expected to emulate urban values and customs while the experts from urban center look down on the "country mouse." CFA is a response to the marginality that those in the closed communities feel to invidious comparisons. Rural areas need projects made in their own images.

# 12

# Community Development and Professional Education in South Africa

## Walid El Ansari

Health care reforms based on joint working principles are debated globally. A variety of partnership efforts are being employed as multidisciplinary approaches to interrelated problems in health, social care, and educational reform (Statham, 2000; Zuckerman et al., 1995). Coalitions between academic institutions, health agencies, lay organizations, client groups, and health service providers emmerge in local communities (El Ansari, 1998a). Such synergistic groups meet with increasing enthusiasm among grassroots and government organizations in many nations (Butterfoss et al., 1996; Kreuter & Lenzin 1998).

Five South African community partnerships (CPs) are particularly challenging, because of the racial and historical context of that country. As part of a wider community health care movement, CPs call for a change in the roles of health professionals as part of a collaborative effort to enable health professionals' education (HPE) to be community-sensitive. These efforts at change in CPs–HPE collaboration are sponsored by the W.K. Kellogg Foundation.

Collaborative planning is implemented through alliance building to foster community development and facilitate social capital. The aim is to create and maintain partnerships. A general understanding of partnership fostering requires stakeholders' perceptions of their power and opportunities for consultation and involvement. If stakeholder participation in collaborative initiatives is to succeed, an atmosphere of tolerance, shared vision in the governance and mechanisms for decision making, and conflict resolution need to be established.


## PRIMARY HEALTH CARE

In 1978, the over 150-plus members of the World Health Organization (WHO) endorsed the Alma Ata declaration, making primary health care (PHC) the focus of their national health policy (WHO, 1978). PHC, as an approach to health development, involves the total reorientation of the health system. Its characteristics are: (a) reorientation of the health services to enable secondary and tertiary care to support care at the primary care level; (b) a more even distribution of health resources, with more allocated to promote preventive and rehabilitative care; (c) coordination of related institutions; and (d) the active participation of the community (WHO, 1987).

Primary care is conceptualized in both narrow and broad terms. Narrow definitions include those that consider PHC to be a first-contact medical practice. Those more encompassing definitions reflect involvement of a variety of practitioners, including nurses, nurse practitioners, physician assistants, dentists, managers, and others. Community-oriented primary care is part of an orientation toward the involvement of communities in the development of services for their populations (Deushle, 1982c; Mullan, 1982). PHC strives to ensure a continuum of preventive and caring service for the community involved (Eng et al., 1992).

Interest for involving nonprofessionals in health care activities developed over the last decade or so. Public involvement is the key to radical health improvement for the majority of the world's people, especially the poor. There is a growing recognition and belief in realizing healthier lifestyles through citizen participation and community development (Howard-Pitney, 1990). Heller (1990) calls for a return to community and increased citizen empowerment to counteract observations that local groups are less powerful, while decisions and resources flow downward from the federal level.

Maintaining attempts to define health promotion, Watt and Rodmell (1988) highlight the need for community engagement. Hildebrandt (1994) argues that community involvement in health care needs to be organized from the perspective of the recipient, while the notion of community involvement in health finds wide acceptance in all kinds of political regimes (Madan, 1987). Involvement is the best way of providing comprehensive solutions to public health problems.

This enthusiasm for public involvement in health gained great popularity over the last decade. Initially, it was a panacea for the ailing health care systems in most countries. Rifkin (1987) asserts the involvement of communities in decisions about health and health services is difficult and is not understood.

Eng and colleagues (1992) argue that primary health providers and managers should engage in the dynamics of community empowerment; for this to happen, change is needed in the usual patterns of education and practice, including: (1) paradigm shifts to include the community in the vision; (2) engagement of the 'clinical' perspective to serve the cause of community organization and empowerment; (3) inclusion of other providers in the PHC network, for example, pharmacists, laypeople, alternative and faith healers, acupuncturists, and informal caregivers; (4) learning new skills in order to empower communities; (5) remaking institutions to respond to community needs and desires; and (6) removing barriers between professionals and members of the community.

The same source asserts educators of health care professionals need to change. The well-guarded and isolated medical center rising out of a poverty-stricken community is often the location of professionals' education. The curriculum, which relies on hospital-based learning experiences, carries a message that community members are dependent, and have little in common with the provider. Each health care profession has its own unique mechanism for keeping common learning experiences to a minimum.

## "LAY" KNOWLEDGE

Taylor (1996) comments on the need for change in the culture and attitudes of the professional staff and their managers to enable them to work *with* as well as *for* people. They need to develop a partnership with the people receiving the services and to value their contributions, as well as those of other professional experts. Although the significance of lay knowledge is established within the social sciences, this knowledge is still inferior within scientific disciplines (Popay & Williams, 1996). Stacey (1994) reports that each health worker may be an expert in their own area, but faced with expertise of another kind, they are just one of the clients.

Appreciation of lay knowledge leads to a synthesis of partners' understandings, values, knowledge, and judgments. The contributions from the stakeholders are to be given equal weight in a holistic health promotion approach (Klein et al., 1999). People power, helped by professional authority, maximizes the impact of any collaborative undertaking. A combination of constant contact and numerous discussions during training are the horizontal connections through which social capital flows and provides the "glue" for alliances and partnerships (Harper & Carver, 1999; Putnam, 1993). Barriers between professionals and the community involve status and fear as well as occupational knowledge (Mackay et al., 1995). The long-term mechanisms for promoting alliances and partnerships include appreciation of each partner's resources and skills.

## THE CONTEXT OF SOUTH AFRICA

South Africa is a developed economy with underdevelopment problems. An estimate of the population is 39 million, 60 percent urban and almost 40 percent under age 15 (World Bank, 1993). About 300,000 illegal "back street" abortions are estimated to be carried out each year, roughly 40 percent of births are properly supervised, and 60 percent of children under age 2 are fully immunized (National Progressive Primary Health Care Network, circa 1994). About 16 percent of newborns have low birth weight and 30 percent of children are malnourished (Department of Health, 1995a, 1995b, 1996). Three quarters of the population is "Black", three quarters of whom live in rural areas. Basic health indices compare poorly with other similar countries.

Apartheid systematically "underdeveloped"—deprived—the disadvantaged people of this country and produced severe inequities. The health system is fragmented for ideological reasons, hierarchically among national, provincial, and local authorities. Until recently, there were 14 national departments of health and four provincial administrations, while there were departments of health for the four racial groups (National Progressive Primary Health Care Network, circa 1994). Kale (1995a, 1995b) asserts the artificial paradox of the best of First World medicine and the worst of Third World medicine are within a few miles of each other, producing extreme inequity in the health profile of the country. After the 1994 democratic elections, one unified Department of Health began to serve the whole nation.

Women, who are the poorer part of the nation, are still excluded from power; their health problems reflect educational discrimination, violence, and exclusion from decisionmaking (ANC Health Department, 1994). The maternal mortality rate varies from 8 to 58 per 100,000 live births (Department of National Health and Population Development, 1992); actual rates are probably higher. Most women are living below the poverty line (Patel, 1993), and male-controlled decisionmaking is the norm, ignoring the problems of women (National Progressive Primary Health Care Network, circa 1994).

South Africa spends around over 6 percent of its Gross Domestic Product on health, comparing favorably with WHO's 5 percent target.

Real public sector health expenditure on about 80 percent of the population is less than half the national expenditure (National Progressive Primary Health Care Network, circa 1994). Financial allocations skew against the poor majority because some provinces have higher per capita expenditure than others, and tertiary care receives more than primary (ANC Health Department, 1994).

## THE PROBLEM

The problems of powerless people condition the global movement to transform the education of health professionals (Kisil & Chaves, 1994). Developing countries realize that models of education based on industrialized countries are not producing trained professionals to meet their health care needs. In 1978, the Alma Ata Conference confirmed the need to reform health manpower development programs. The Edinburgh Declaration, adopted by the World Federation for Medical Education (WFME) and by many governments and regional medical education bodies, calls for a worldwide change in the education of health professions.

Graduates in the medical field could improve the country's health status. Some of the goals are an enlarged range of settings to conduct educational programs, inclusion of all health resources of the community, curriculum content to reflect national health priorities and resources, education throughout life, and a shifting emphasis in education to more active learning (Schmidt et al., 1991). Community-based education involves the integration of education and work, joining experiences in medicine with those of people in the community.

In South Africa, there are two critical problems. The first involves access to health care. Most of the world's population cannot consult a physician when needed (Schmidt, et al., 1991). Graduates of medical schools practice where opportunity for private practice exists, as well as in places with adequate technical resources and educational facilities for their children, the middle-class neighbourhoods of big cities or medium-sized towns. In South Africa, the problem is exaggerated by geographical and racial segregation once enforced under the "Groups Act." A multitier health care system is continued by the number of qualified and highly trained health professionals who migrate out of the country in recent years, and the number of graduates who pursue further studies overseas and who do not return to South Africia.

The second problem is that medical education students are typically trained within a hospital context (Schmidt et al., 1991). Clinical training takes place in tertiary care hospitals that have facilities, which are not available in work locations after graduation. Students experience serious trouble adapting to environments different from those in which they are trained. The case-mix of patients seen in an academic tertiary care setting is not similar to the populations normally seen by physicians.

Most of the medical schools in the developing world are modeled on their counterparts in industrialized countries. Their educational programs do not usually focus on the health problems of the poor in warm climates. Doctors have difficulty in assessing and evaluating the health care needs and priorities of their own people. They are ill prepared to provide effective health education, implement preventive programs, work in the slums of the cities, or manage rural health care teams. Education courses need to relate students to community health needs from the beginning of their careers, and to develop support for community health.

The learning process is facilitated by direct exposure to health problems. Students must have the opportunity to observe health and disease in their intricate relationship with the environment and with the habits and views of people. Medical education of the traditional kind implies that students are only shown the sick person who is admitted to the hospital. This may result in the students seeing their role as doctors to cure individual patients. A better philosophy of education focuses on populations, prevention of disease, and the promotion of health (Bollag et al., 1982).

## COMMUNITY–CAMPUS CONNECTIONS

The Network of Community-Oriented Educational Institutions for Health Sciences (NCOEIHS) represents a group of schools that pioneer in the area of HPE (1991). The Network was established in 1979 at the instigation of the World Health Organization to make medical education responsive to the health needs of large segments of the population, both in the industrialized and in the developing world.

Through NCOEIHS, new emphasis is put on partnerships between universities, governments, and communities to achieve the common goal of "Health for All by the Year 2000." Community-oriented education focuses on population groups and individual persons, taking into account the health needs of the community concerned. The basic principles for educational activities are determined by the local community.

Students need to be exposed to the realities of health care in the community as soon as they enter medical school and such postings in the community should not be brief, transient experiences, but an integral part of the curriculum (Schmidt et al., 1991). Programs need to adopt a comprehensive rather than a mainly curative approach to health promotion, thus indicating a commitment to the goal of Health For All. Community-based education is associated with efforts to involve students and educational institutions in national development and to combine theory with practice (WHO, 1987).

## W.K. KELLOGG CP-HPE INITIATIVES

The Kellogg Foundation made the Community Partnerships in Health Professions Education (CPs-HPE) a major priority by investing over $50 million in United States sites over a five-year period, and provide additional funds overseas. CPs-HPE are large-scale demonstration projects at seven sites around the United States and in several other locations in Latin America and Africa (W. K.Kellogg Foundation, 1992). These initiatives include three types of paired relationships (university–community, university–local health system, and local health system–community).

The goal of the community partnerships (CPs) is to provide undergraduate medical, nursing, and allied health students the opportunity to learn and experience team-based, nonhospital PHC in community settings. Community agencies and constituencies become part of the decision making for education, research and services, and policy. The Kellogg Foundation requires major matching funds from the participating universities and provides significant technical support, program leadership, and the dissemination of information about the program to the media and policymakers (Knott, 1995).

The Foundation's criteria provides:

- CPs are to demonstrate joint participation of communities and health professionals in determining priority health issues, planning educational bases, and in student selection.
- Community-based programs establish educational bases in communities to ensure the recognition of PHC practitioners, and their adequate socialization within communities. This requires sensitivity to the prevailing dynamics, strengths, and weaknesses within a given community and an awareness of available resources and shortcomings.
- A comprehensive PHC emphasizes attention to the needs of the underserved. A focus is on basic causes of ill health, which health professionals need to learn to address—the underlying socioeconomic determinants of health.
- Academic rigor in HPE ensures the education of health personnel within community bases can surpass that conducted within the confines of conventional teaching hospitals.

- Skill development includes an understanding of group dynamics, community decision-making processes, and leadership.
- Interdisciplinary learning emphasizes teams learning together in order to function efficiently.
- Student selection is based on potential, rather than achievement, and selection is from within the community served by CPs-HPE initiative.

For projects to achieve maximum potential during their implementation phase, the Foundation develops a supporting mechanism for the three project components (academic, local health system, and community), for leadership development at the project level, and for evaluation of each project and clusters of projects (Kisil & Chaves 1994). Support is provided for networking and dissemination, which encourages the sharing of experiences among the South African partnership projects and with other institutions (El Ansari, 1994, 1998a; El Ansari & Phillips, 1997).

## THE PROCESS

At the request of the W.K. Kellogg Foundation, universities in South Africia are invited to submit proposals aiming at reforming medicine, nursing, and allied health professions. From a large number of initial proposals, 7 were selected, but not all of them are immediately granted full funding. Although the selection of seven locations started as early as 1991–1992, several of the localities are given mini-grants as well as more time, support, and technical assistance from the Foundation to develop more comprehensive proposals. This process required an extra year.

The process of developing CPs involves the Foundation's principles, including the formation and establishment of work groups and task forces. Each CP has an executive board or steering committee comprising community members, academic institution representatives, and health service providers. Community members must be half of the board and the remaining positions are divided between representatives of the other two sectors.

Once the funding is granted, the process moves from exploration to building the partnership. One step is needs identification to prioritize problems of the catchment area. The establishment of the organizational structures is initiated (steering committee, coordinators, appointment of permanent staff). The partnership moves to embrace the involvement of the various agencies and organizations and to encourage the participation of stakeholders. Insuring the ownership and governance of the program by the partners is primary. When the operation of the programs begins, standards of evaluation are established.

The physical presence of a partnership in the community is important to maintain contact with the community, to remain sensitive to their needs, and to enhance their participation and involvement. The physical station is where each individual CP building is established and sometimes constructed from scratch. One is on the university campus proper with site offices established in the beneficiary locations. The second is on the university hospital grounds, but links to the communities through the support, upgrading, and enlargement of the health centers that are already established by the government. The third is close to the university, and again links to the beneficiary communities through government-established health centers. The final two are not on university campuses, but on separate "neutral" lands, situated in the actual catchment areas of the beneficiaries. In one location, the "tribal authorities" donated the land on which the partnership premises are built, a sign of goodwill toward collaboration.

To prepare selected sites, arrangements for the assignment of students is made together with the local authorities and community leaders. This involves explanations of the educational institution's philosophy and objectives, the criteria used in assigning students to segments of the community, and, most important, the community's role as a partner in health manpower training and its own health development. An essential component of the social preparation is the integration of the students within the community.

The role of community and its responsibility for involvement in health care must be understood before the establishment of partnerships. This process is slow and requires a spirit of mutual respect and sensitivity to the needs of the various partners in order to develop trust. The community cautiously responds to the idea of a partnership with the university. It is important to establish a commitment to a common task and sacrifice individual interests. The aim is to explore the ideals of the partners, to share a common vision leading to a contract, and to develop a common identity.

Several workshops are held, strengthened by consultations with university departments, community organizations, and healthcare providers. The process of building working relationships based on trust is evolutionary. New groups, representing different segments of the community, continue to approach the partnerships. Commitment is the major building block for involvement by the community.

The negotiating skills of the community and confidence in their own abilities develops. This is demonstrated when in one CP, community members insist on a logo for the program designed solely by the community and approved for implementation by the other partners. The robust element of community involvement comes from a strong sense that people are essential for the partnerships to succeed. This philosophy becomes the foundation pillar of the CPs.

The implementation of action plans commences but progresses slowly, handicapped by the amount of energy absorbed by the partnership process, as well as by the lack of infrastructure in the community. Once some infrastructure, like a health or community center, is erected, the partners are busy not only at the center, but also in the community, linking hands in order to stimulate the development process.

The processes involved in developing CPs includes several phases:

*Phase 1. Exploration:* submitting the proposals and their acceptance; agreeing on the protocols for community profiling and collection of data pertaining to the needs of the target populations; and establishing project committees and a trust deed.

*Phase 2. Building Partnership:* appointing project coordinator; collecting data compiled into community profile; visit other projects and attend Kellogg seminars; feedback to academic work groups and community representatives; awareness of partners' needs; lengthy discussions and consultations on empowerment and involvement; dissolving mistrust; and establishing organizational and liaison structures.

*Phase 3. Ensuring Ownership:* confirms identified needs; proposes concept plan for action; establishing community-based project committees; and establishes legal basis for the program to ensure autonomy, separate identity, and local ownership.

*Phase 4. Operationalization:* establishes staff and project committees; strategic planning and implementation; appoints health care and teaching and training coordinators and other permanent staff; monitors activities of committees; drafts final trust deed; and dissolves steering group.

*Phase 5. Building Infrastructure in the Community:* finds facilities, community hall, committee rooms, and temporary offices at the site; obtains food gardens at site; develops portfolios and activities; plans the permanent structures with building committee; starts outreach program in the communities; appoints the director; and implements the deed of trust.

*Phase 6. Refining the Health Center:* operates health center Phase 1 (150 patients per day); publishes newsletter; modifies activities; and celebrates successes.

Soon after the partnership is initiated, the South African Network of CPs seeks a representative from the HPE to network with sister CPs. The aim of the network is to share lessons and successes, to avoid pitfalls and to identify innovative ways of monitoring and evaluating the various facets of the CPs. The network investigates educational and service transformation at community-based academic centers and primary health care sites. A joint task force conducts a survey of the various evaluation activities within the sister partnerships. The task force generates information on national, regional, and local health policy and planning initiatives, as well as assisting in sustaining CPs.

## OUTCOMES

The target populations of CPs are the local communities in or near catchment areas, most of which were underserved before 1994. Fourteen geographically diverse communities, with populations ranging from 35,000–300,000, participate in these collaborative efforts. The common link between them is that they are the most disadvantaged communities in their respective areas.

When CP program begin, a gulf exists between the communities, the universities and the local health services. The programs are started by people from the communities and the universities who had a dream that the partnership would bridge this gulf. CPs aim to make both health services and the universities accessible to the disadvantaged majority. From an unlikely partnership, projects emerge that are influential in changing the way in which parties see each other. This creates the basis for many developmental projects in the community, health services, and universities.

CPs initiate a wide range of community development initiatives and educational workshops, including community gardening, welding and brick laying, coffin making, sewing and knitting, and car mechanics and other skills training. These development activities link the universities with projects in schools, teaching skills to unemployed youth so they can become entrepreneurs.

The educational programs range over vocational training, including community colleges, bursary assistance, training by health science students, staff education for health workers, and obtaining government supports. Affirmative action begins with student selection and continues with support systems for disadvantaged students. Existing health centers are upgraded and new academic community-based multipurpose PHC centers are started. CPs sponsor promotional activities, open days, health desks, clean-up campaigns, and awareness workshops. Table 12.1 shows the major CP activities.

**TABLE 12.1**
**Partnership Programs and Major Activities**

*Bridging programs:* In science and math, teacher training, and career guidance.

*Bursary assistance:* information and grants for students from participating committees.

*Health sciences stuents training programs:* formal and nonformal nursing and rehabilitation worker education programs.

*Vocational training program:* adult basic education, organization,and management skills.

*Local government facilitation program:* accountable government structures (health, environment, and education)

*Community college:* to fill gap between school and university/technical education

*Multi-purpose health center:* to increase community accessibility, various training undertaken in center.

*Community coordination programs:* entrepreneurial skills, businness, and economical development: coffin making, welding, chicken project, car service skills, food gardents, sewing, knitting, and cultural development.

*Sport and recreation program:* sport development and sport specialization at schools and in community.

*The aged:* day centers and rehabilitative services to improve mobility and self-esteem.

*Youth activities:* student representative leadership course, youth health desk, and youth development.

*Adult literacy program:* to combat the high illiteracy rates in South Africa. Health and development program for vulnerable groups: geriatrics and disabled children, crèche and stimulation, areas of play.

*Educare program:* training teachers, toy workshops, input from psychology department, nutrition working group, meals and food funding, involvement of community, networking, and parent meetings.

After-school program: education, meals, networking with school principals and parents, and training.

## CHALLENGES

Two broad challenges for South Africa relate to the past (Viljoen & Househam, circa 1995):

- *Lack of appropriate health care services, usually with lack of appropriate infrastructure.* Due to the lack of provision of adequate basic health and PHC services, a high percentage of patients use the services of tertiary referral teaching hospitals. Appropriate PHC facilities were not readily available, and the community is generally negative about the accessibility of services. Rapid urbanization is taking place after the removal of regulations restricting the free movement of "Black" people and contribute to population influxes which increase demand for health care services. Due to the inappropriate training of health care professionals in hospitals, students lack experience with PHC services or of meeting the total health care needs of patients.

- *Past discriminatory policies excluded "Black" students from most universities until the late 1980s.* In addition to this restriction, the language of tuition was Afrikaans, which in the case of "Black" students is their third language. Most of the "Black" children came from disadvantaged backgrounds and could not meet the selection criteria of universities. Apartheid policies created a situation in which mutual understanding between race groups. There was no communities among these groups.

Gray (1989) sheds light on some of the obstacles to collaboration. An important one is extent of institutional investment. Stakeholders are reluctant to abandon established ways in favor of the more uncertain outcomes of collaboration. Historical and ideological barriers are an obstacle, while relationships characterized by long-standing bitter conflicts are impediments to collaboration.

Power disparities and concerns about preserving an institutional power base pose difficulties, since parties will be reluctant to collaborate if they believe their interest will be deemed secondary. Certain societal-level beliefs restrain collaboration. For example, cultural norms in the United States are rooted in a strong sense of individualism (Hofstede, 1980). This orientation toward self rather than community encourages people to view collaboration with skepticism.

Limited resources are an issue for many public interest groups, since volunteers do much of their work at the local level. Participation in collaborative endeavors is viewed as a drain on time and financial resources. Gray (1989) maintains that budget cycles discourage the use of collaborative approaches because resources for colloboration need to be projected in advance. Other impediments are differing perceptions of risk and technical complexities.

Several issues are relevant to public involvement (Rifkin, 1981):

1. The issue of professional domination. To what extent is the public capable of understanding and implementing activities that traditionally are the purview of those trained in a highly specialized and technologically sophisticated field? In the past, the professional denied the nonprofessional access to the knowledge and practices, a denial that has social, political, and economic consequences (Freyens et al., 1993; Zwarenstein & Barron, 1993).
2. The issue of organizational management. How can suitable organizations be created and maintained to sustain the defined level

of participation in health activities? This reflects the tension between the need to institutionalize activities for endurance and
replicability, and the necessity to maintain flexibility in order to
meet the needs of individual communities and people (Butterfoss
et al., 1993; Gottlieb et al., 1993; Rogers et al., 1993).

3. The issue of how to get the public involved. How can the public
be motivated and mobilized to become involved in health activities? At the core of this question is the search for what motivates
individuals to participate and how can large numbers of people
can be mobilized (Prestby et al., 1990; Zimmerman, 1990).

The critical point is the extent of overlap among areas in the collaborative process (El Ansari 1998b, 1998c). These areas are formalized roles
and procedures, leadership and member characteristics, expectations
about outcomes, skills and training, benefits and costs, communication
patterns, and quality of the agencies' services. Organizational cultures
of the stakeholders and their demands for autonomy are barriers. Success partnerships involve satisfaction with services, resource allocations, understanding of operations, a continuing flow of information,
and democratic decision-making processes.

## INTERACTIONS AND DECISON MAKING

Some health coalitions are real while others are artificial (Lindsay &
Edwards, 1988). The artificial variety is formed when one agency, with
its own agenda, invites other groups to become part of 'their' coalition.
A coalition formed on this basis creates a temporary illusion of broad-
based interagency cooperation. Panet-Raymond (1992) identified two
models of collaboration on a continuum from real partnership
(*partenariat*) to paternalism (*paternariat*). Real partnerships are relationships, formal or informal, between equal but different partners.

Community-oriented partnerships should have their objectives defined autonomously, be rooted in the community, have strong credibility, and involve the board membership in a democratic structure. They
should have a strong power base that commands respect. The principle
of community involvement are sometimes a means of manipulating the
people (WHO, 1987). As Brownlea (1987) states:

> . . . participation may be seen as a way of broadening the range of inputs
> to a decision, but in fact may represent a kind of tokenism. The input is
> received, but very quickly discarded as of little or no consequence. The
> motions have been gone through. The democratic ideal has been observed,
> but there is little power behind the participants' input. (p. 605)

Collaboration involves a process of joint decision making among key stakeholders about the future (Gray, 1989). Dealing constructively with respect for differences is easy to champion verbally, but difficult to put into practice on a day-to-day basis. Collaboration involves joint ownership of decisions. It is a weaving together of diverse viewpoints into a mosaic, replete with new insights and directions for action, agreed on by all the stakeholders. When one party has unchallenged power to influence the domain, collaboration never occurs (Gray, 1989).

In order to investigate the decisionmaking climate across the South African CPs, I administered a questionnaire to respondents from each of the stakeholder groups (El Ansari, 1999c). Sixteen questions relating to the nature of interaction and input into decision making by the different stakeholders are analysed. The data collected from the CPs are pooled and the sample ($N$ = 668) is categorized into four groups, according to whether participants represent health services ($N$ = 111), academic training institutions ($N$ = 130), community members ($N$ = 367), and the partnerships' core staff ($N$ = 60).

In relation to partnership interaction, the questions query the extent of interaction, conflict resolution, differences, and disagreements, as well as control among the partners. In regard to decisionmaking, the questions measure the attitudes and beliefs relating to the opportunities for participation in decisionmaking in the CPs and the ease with which suggestions and ideas were welcomed by the project leadership.

The major findings are:

1. The four partners agree they have "a shared vision," "opportunities for participation," "are tolerant of one another" and "handle conflict effectively." Similarly, the stakeholders disagree that "professionals are too controlling" and that "decisions are made by a small group of leaders."

2. The community members are positive about the interactions between the partners. This group indicates a feeling of shared vision and togetherness, while disagreements are tolerated, conflict is handled reasonably, and there are established ways to settle differences. The community perceives that the academics and service providers are a significant influence in making decisions.

3. The academic institutions report it is easy to get their ideas across to the core leaders who encourage participation. The academics disagree about their exercising excessive control, and feel they and the service providers should contribute more to the decision-making process.

4. All stakeholders agree about the amount of participation and influence exercised by the community, but not by the other partners; significant differences exist among them.

5. The partnerships' core staff feel they participate because they are the full-time partnerships' champions and coordinators. They confirm that participation by the community is high. In some cases, they believe decisions are made by a small group of leaders.

No one person can stay in the forefront of knowledge (NICE, 1999), but there is much more to collaboration than simply working side by side (Davies, 2000a). The organizational climate of a coalition helps in assessing its "personality" (Giamartino & Wandersman, 1983). In relation to partnerships and alliances, the climate might be characterised by relationships among members, member–staff relationships, and a partnership's decision-making, problem-solving, and conflict resolution processes (Butterfoss et al., 1993).

Together, these findings suggest there is a friendly and democratic atmosphere in the CPs under investigation, where opinions were openly expressed. These findings support those of Zakus and Lysack (1998), who advise that one of the predisposing conditions for community participation in health is a political and administrative system that promotes local authority for decisionmaking, resource allocation, and programs. The skillful management of early interactions is often crucial to continued collaboration, since these informal interactions lay the groundwork for subsequent formal interactions (El Ansari & Phillips, 1997; Gray 1989).

## MORE FINDINGS

Specific findings involve student experiences, continuing the project after foundation funding, and disagreements among the partners concerning the effectiveness of the partnerships. For students' experiences, the questions measure the partners' perceived certainty that their CPs would be able to implement the planned multidisciplinary curricula, or if more medical, nursing, and other health professions' students enter primary care and practiced in underserved areas once they finished their training.

All groups believe more nursing students than other disciplines should "enter primary care" and "practice in underserved areas once they finish their training." They are not very sure their CPs will make the curriculum community relevant.

Second, in relation to the sustainability of the efforts, the partners are asked if their CPs would exist beyond Kellogg funding and if their organizations were ready to implement structural changes to sustain these coalitions. Although the partners express confidence in the continuation of the CPs as identifiable organizations and the readiness of their agencies to implement structural changes to sustain these efforts, they question whether it is possible to facilitate the CPs' existence beyond Kellogg funding.

Finally, two clusters of effectiveness are investigated. The first is related to the processes and operating functions of the CPs: communication, goal setting and decision-making, fundraising and public relations, volunteer coordination and evaluation of the partnership performance, and training community health workers with a primary health care focus. The second cluster examines the effectiveness of involvement and access: involving minorities in CP activities and helping the community emerge as a force on health issues while raising its awareness of health care planning, improving the quality and accessibility of local health services, and enabling health service planning to be more community responsive.

The respondent groups disagree with each other on both aspects of effectiveness:

1. The academics score highest in 80 percent of the questions. This indicates more academic respondents view their CP projects as either effective or extremely effective in their CPs.
2. There is a general trend in the number of stakeholders who feel that aspects of their CPs are either effective or extremely effective. Responses are generally positive but they become negative as the focus of effectiveness moves from decisionmaking and a PHC view of the CPs to aspects of fundraising and the development of public relations or media input. These internal tasks are perceived as more problematic. Responses are more positive regarding CPs as sources for improving the quality and accessibility of local health services, as well as raising public awareness of health issues and planning.

Aside from the clarion for collaboration in direct services, there is a drive for explicit evidence for the effectiveness of health care interventions, and for practice be based on such evidence. While the CP approach is logically appealing, there is little evidence regarding its effectiveness. The literature reveals "coalitions have not been evaluated in an organized and systematic way, and little empirical evidence exists to support their effectiveness" (Butterfoss et al., 1993, p. 315). Limited information exists on what contributes to an effective partnership (Kumpfer & Hopkins, 1993).

Research on the separate impact on individual members, teams, or total coalitions is lacking (Chavis & Wandersman, 1990). Kreuter and colleagues (2000) state, in spite of the substantial investment in collaborative mechanisms, their effectiveness in changing health status in communities needs to be studied. Gillies (1998) reports that the behavioral change effect on the populations involved in partnership health promotion interventions is below 20 percent.

Creating the conditions for working together in collaborative models is challenging (Williamson, 1999). The climate in which a coalition operates may be enhanced when the leadership shares decisionmaking with the general membership (Zuckerman & Kaluzny, 1990), and when no one individual or organization has authority or controls coalition resources. Inequalities of power make it virtually impossible for the less powerful members to speak out (Davies, 2000a). Variation in the stakeholders' authority, weight in partnership decisions, and range of activities is at the heart of partnership interactions (Kegler et al., 1998).

Shared decisionmaking may lead to greater understanding, commitment to the issues confronting a coalition, and input into decisions ranging from advice to control (Wandersman, 1981). Seifer and Maurana (1998) argue that developing a partnership's strategic approach involves asking questions and engaging in a dialogue to help create a vision. The need is to encourage real "conversations"—ones that create a dialogue between people who have yet to understand working together (Zeldin, 1999).

Such dialogue is designed to explore different perspectives, values, and goals (Davies, 2000b) and promotes accountability. Such professionals lose sight of their accountability to communities, the distance between the two parties grows (Richards, 1996). Though democratic processes are valuable, overattention to democracy issues in CPs can be stifling and the time commitment can be prohibitive as most issues require considerable debate (El Ansari 1999c; El Ansari & Phillips, 1998).

Improved teamwork between professionals is strongly recommended in a recent NHS White Paper in the United Kingdom (DOH, 1998). This will require an understanding of interdependence, deliberation, and dialogue. However, some studies conclude problems with collaboration are prevalent (El Ansari 1998d; Larson 1999; Porter, 1995), while others report power differentials as problems (Walby et al., 1994). Inequalities in power can be an undermining factor in partnership efforts as they affect the influence on decisions (Israel et al., 1998).

Partnership administrators and stakeholders must be aware of the barriers to collaborative work. Such barriers include the reduced independence in decisionmaking, insufficient influence in partnership activities, and frustration building to stress and provocation (Kegler et al., 1998; Lasker et al., 1997). Practitioners need to be multiskilled (Carlson & El Ansari, 2000). Partnership work is not 'painless' and requires sufficient time for understanding and operationalizing the concept.

There are a burgeoning number of initiatives involving collaboration (Buse & Walt, 2000a, 2000b). Boherfoss and colleaaagues consider conflict, an inherent characteristic of coalitions, may arise between members of the coalition and its targets, among coalitions' members and other staff, and among coalition partners over issues such as leadership, diverse goals, benefits, contributions, and representation. It is not necessary to choose between power, which leads to conflict and collaboration (Richards, circa 1995). Both are necessary for success and both are needed to achieve educational reform. Although power is critical, sharing of power is necessary in a new organizational structure.

## EDITOR'S NOTE

Though some of the findings show the aims of community education were not achieved, the social barriers confronted are a challenge. The attempt to cross the divides in South Africia produces a significant attempt to integrate theories about partnerships (El Ansari, 1999c). Organizational factors including resources and roles are distant while attitudes are immediate influences on accomplishment and impact. A large number of variables are integrated, but a time line is needed to indicate when distant and closer influences are expected to operate in an effective way.

Innovations within public education can take five years (Mitchell, 1998). In Part I, the evidence supports a life expectancy of three years for partnerships. The timing is critical as is the specific influences, which assists the continuation of partnerships. The evidence from South Africia shows nurses are most likely to be involved in the new community organizations. This is not likely to alter the medical hieriarchy. A broader effort is to join education and social service in an effort to change hierarchies.

The leaders of education could empower poor communities. Rural communities involve the greatest poverty and the largest opportunities for partnerships (Mitchell, 2000a). The training of teachers should be a part of a common effort to come to terms with rural values and the effects of social subordination. Many American CPs, sponsored by the Kellogg Foundation, take place inside rural schools, but with little contact with teachers (Richards, 1996). In Africia or perhaps America, the problems of continuing CPs after the Kellogg grants are gone suggest a greater vision is required. Logically, schools and social agencies are both a part of community education. Each must relinguish some territory for the new vision. The issues raised in Chapter 9 for integrating school districts with DEPC are magnified in South Africa. The problems of conflict resolution are similar.

It is doubtful that these professional groups will relinquish autonomy on their own. Social advocacy organizations are needed as catalysts for change. The Industrial Areas Foundations has proved they can get the Educational Lord, Howard Gardner, to sign a contract to be accountable to their league of schools when they work with him (Mitchell, 1998). Such advocacy groups argue that community members must hold the majority of positions, more than the half required on CP boards because professionals always outtalk laypeople. An active force is required to lead higher status groups to view the world of those they claim to serve as the subordinates see their lives. Only after reversing or merging perspectives will medical and other professionals think community members should be as influential in decisionmaking as they are.

# Afterword for Schools of Education

Most of the authors in this collection suggest different policies or strategies that need to be pursued. While reviewing the experiences of their research work with teachers, Patricia Lauer and her colleagues argue for the diversity of perspectives, which can be a prime consideration for all partnerships. Michele Jacobsen and Brenda Gladstone reveal how perceptive businesspeople and professionals can contribute ideas and partnership advocacy. The work of Deborah Jenkins shows how insightful partners could be organized into interdependent groups rather than individuals sharing perspectives.

The authors, who do not suggest new directions, do outline conditions that most successful partnerships must meet. In her discussion of professional development schools, Rene Campoy shows how the reward systems of founding partners must be altered to encourage cooperation. Melinda Pollack, in her discussion of community involvement by university students suggests that the sponsoring universities must alter their approach for their respective students to develop reciprocal ties. Many of the other contributors to Part II suggest changes in the sponsoring organization for expansion of the services that the writers advocate.

In Part II, the authors argue for a number of changes in organizational structure. Michael Zanibbi shows how a combination of private and nonprofit approaches can create a new form of organization. Promoters that seek contributors for improving the environment can coexist with companies that want to obtain materials or dispose of them. Joseph Hauglie and his associates demonstrate how a new form of training, the virtual school, is developed by a university institute, government, nonprofit organizations, and businesses. Roberta Lamb and Melinda Pollack reveal the latent potentials of remote universities to transform the quality of lives for those in schools and communities. Performing with a symphony can motivate music students while student volunteers are changed by working with activists to help poor communities.

The authors in Part III are opening doors for further study of the new alternatives explored. Lynn Bradshaw shows how two different communities can compliment each other as partners. She draws out the contradiction of partners wanting to retain their autonomy and start competing programs to those offered by the partnership. Michael Barbour shows one small improvement in rural education through the combination of technology and public and private partners. Ann Jones reveals how partnerships support classroom projects by individual teachers and community efforts through relationships to a common environment. Walid El Ansari connects the educational discussion with attempts in medicine to involve the community and heal the wounds of racial discrimination. Teacher education could be similarly involved, although Chapter 1 revealed its prize, professional development schools, to be unrelated.

Part III suggests a range of new approaches if Faculties of Education begin to scout for new opportunities. The same rural sites can be used for the education of medicine, nursing, social work, and education. The opportunity is one in which students can learn to cooperate. Teachers in special education in a few places are part of multiple training in related professions. Special education teachers need to learn to cooperate with regular teachers before they are divided by school barriers (Mitchell, 1990). Rural areas provide many opportunities for close communication and learning of new roles.

Rural areas, as Ann Jones shows in Chapter 11, are full of possibilities for teachers to develop environmental projects. Ecology is an area of broad concern to many professionals. Rural areas allow teachers who know the scene to relate the environment, community history, and service concerns to their individual classes. Teachers and administrators should learn to see different goals before they begin measuring small towns and rural communities against urban schools. Place values are a valuable lesson for professionals in metropolitan worlds.

Though small towns have always been a place where skilled trades are learned, technology is passing them as larger centers advance ahead (Mitchell, 2000a). Web-based instruction only begins to tap the possibilities of technology. Virtual schools, discussed in Chapter 5, and technologically infused education in networks, described in Chapter 3, should be developed by professionals who no longer have to be near central cities. Schools need community development to overcome the rural gap in technology. Community projects can attract professionals in technology if they can provide quality education and medical services in rural places.

Education students have opportunities to develop webs, show teachers and others how technology improves their lives, and act as catalysts or consultants in the new economy. Students can be involved in any of the specific projects discussed in Part I. Education students are capable of working with virtual schools to train welfare mothers, serve in communities, participate in business-schools link, or become participants in arts partnerships. These students should be active contributors rather than guests in schools, as they provide assistance to these projects and communities.

Many of the programs for practicing teachers in Part I provide a different perspective on context or foundational issues. Professional development schools demonstrate the significance of career incentives and conflicts with traditional teachers. Attempts to relate in-service education to innovations reveal the importance of politics and vision in practical activities. Networks of schools show how to avoid the isolation of teachers and schools and reasons why they do not have to reinvent the wheel. A mathematical or philosophical formalization about resource personnel assisting teachers illustrates the relevancy of theory to those who would be practical. Faculties of Education should seize the opportunity to explain ideas as well demonstrate projects and developments across boundaries.

# References

Abdal-Haqq, I. (1996). An information provider's perspective on the professional development movement. *Contemporary Education, 67*(4), 237–239.

Ad Hoc Private Sector Group. (1998). Building better partnerships-statement from the *ad hoc* private sector group at the Jakarta Conference. *Health Promotion International, 13*(3), 191–92.

Allen, S. F. (1997 October). Building harmonious relationships. *Teaching Music, 5*(2), 33–34, 52.

Alberta Science and Research Authority. (1998). *A strategy for information and communications technology in Alberta* [On-line]. Available: http:www.gov.ab .ca/sra/publicdocs/ict/index.html

Alberta Teachers' Association. (1999). *Professional development schools: Research monograph 38.* Edmonton, AB, Canada: Author

Altrichter, H., Posch, P., & Somekh, B. (1993). *Teachers investigate their work.* New York: Routledge.

American Association of Colleges for Teacher Education. (1997). Professional development schools at a glance [On-line]. Available: http://www.aacte .org/glance.html

ANC (African National Congress) Health Department. (1994). A national health plan for South Africa. Johannesburg: Authors.

Babineau, N. (2000, July). Enriching the curriculum—enriching the community: Canadian partnerships for arts education. *Music of the Spheres Conference Proceedings*, 12–28.

Bainer, D. (1997). A comparison of four models of group efforts and their implications for establishing educational partnerships. *Journal of Research in Rural Education, 13*(3), 143–152.

Bainer, D. (1998 October). *Why partnerships endure.* Paper presented at the National Symposium of Partnerships in Education organized by the National Association of Partners in Education, Los Angeles.

Bainer, D., Barron, P., & Cantrell, D. (1996/97). Enhancing science instruction in rural elementary schools through partnering. *Rural Educator, 18*(2), 12–16.

Bainer, D., Barron, P., & Cantrell, D. (1998, Summer). *Scienceing with Watersheds, Environmental Education and Partnerships (SWEEP): Instructor's guide to implementation.* Mansfield, OH: SWEEP Project, Ohio State at Mansfield.

Baker, L. (1994, April). *The politics of collaboration: How an educational partnership works.* Paper presented at the Annual Meeting of the American Educational Research Association, New Orleans, LA.

Barnett, B., Hall, G., Berg, J., & Camarena, M. (1999). A typology of partnerships for promoting innovation. *Journal of School Leadership, 9*(6), 484–510.

Berliner, B. (1997). *What it takes to work together: The promise of educational partnerships.* (Knowledge Brief No. 14). San Francisco, CA: WestEd.

Bloom, M. (1993). *Evaluating business–education collaboration: Values assessment process.* Toronto: Conference Board of Canada.

Blum, J. (2000, May 26). Scores are up in D.C. schools. *Washington Post,* pp. B1, B5.

Bollag, U., Schmidt, H., Fryers, T., & Lawani, J. (1982). Medical education in action: community-based experience and service in Nigeria. *Medical Education, 16,* 282–289.

Bollman, R. (Ed.). (1993). *Rural and small town Canada.* Toronto: Thompson.

Book, C.L. (1996). Professional development schools. In J. Sikula, T. Buttery, & E. Guyton (Eds.), *Handbook of research in teacher education* (2nd ed., pp. 194–210). New York: MacMillan.

Boston, B. O. (1996, August). Report card: A new study identifies successful partnerships in music education. *Symphony, 47*(4), 46–48, 50, 82–86.

Bradshaw, L. (in press). Improving communication across school boundaries. *Delta Kappan Gamma Bulletin.*

Britt, L. (Ed.). (1985/86). *School and business partnerships.* Bloomington, IN: Phi Delta Kappa.

Brousseau, C. (1999, February 6). Harmonious partnership. *Kingston Whig Standard,* Companion section, pp. 1, 3.

Brownlea, A. (1987). Participation: Myths, realities and prognosis. *Social Science and Medicine, 25*(6), 605–614.

Bullough, R., Jr. (1982). Professional schizophrenia: Teacher education in confusion. *Contemporary Education, 53*(4), 207–211.

Bullough, R., Hobbs, S., Kauchak, D., Crow, N., & Stokes, D. (1997). Long-term PDS development in research universities and the clinicalization of teacher education. *Journal of Teacher Education, 48*(2), 85–95.

Buse, K., & Walt, G. (2000a). Global public–private partnerships: Part I—A new development in health? *Bulletin of the World Health Organization, 78*(4), 549–561.

Buse, K., & Walt, G. (2000b). Global public–private partnerships: Part II—What are the health issues for global governance? *Bulletin of the World Health Organization, 78*(5), 699–709.

Butterfoss, F., Goodman, R., & Wandersman, A. (1993). Community coalitions for prevention and health promotion. *Health Education Research: Theory and Practice, 8*(3), 315–330.

Butterfoss, F., Goodman, R., & Wandersman, A. (1996). Community coalitions for prevention and health promotion: Factors predicting satisfaction, participation, and planning. *Health Education Quarterly, 23*(1), 65–79.

Button, K., Ponticell, J., Johnson, M. (1996). Enabling school–university collaborative research: Lessons learned in professional development schools. *Journal of Teacher Education, 47*(1), 16–20.

Calhoun, E., & Glickman, C. (1993, April). *Issues and dilemmas of action research in the league of professional schools.* Paper presented at the annual meeting of the American Educational Research Association, Atlanta, GA.

Canadian Chamber of Commerce (1992). *Focus 2000: Business-education partnerships, your planing guide.* Don Mills, ON: CCH Canadian.

Carlson, C., & El Ansari, W. (2000). Squaring the circle: Developing public health competencies in primary care. *Nursing Times Research, 5*(2), 2–14.

Centre for TeleLearning and Rural Education. (2000, July 10). *Research projects* [On-line]. Available: http://www.tellearn.mun.ca/fresearc.html

Chavis, D., & Wandersman, A. (1990). Sense of community in the urban environment: A catalyst for participation and community development. *American Journal of Community Psychology, 18*(1), 55–81.

Christensen, C. M. (1997). *The innovator's dilemma: When new technologies cause great firms to fail.* Boston: Harvard Business School Press.

Christenson, F., Coopers & Lybrand, L. (1996). *State of North Carolina Smart Start performance audit: Final report.* Raleigh, NC: Joint Legislative Commission on Governmental Operations, North Carolina General Assembly.

Christensen, F., Eldredge, F., Ibom, K., Johnston, M,. & Thomas, M. (1996). Collaboration in support of change. *Theory into Practice, 35*(3), 187–195.

Chalker, D. (Ed.). (1999). *Leadership for rural schools.* Lancaster, PA: Technomic.

Clark, R. (1997). *Professional development schools: Policy and financing.* Washington, DC: American Association of College Teachers in Education.

Clark, C. & Peterson, P. (1986). Teachers' thought processes. In M. Wittrock (Ed.), *Handbook of research on teaching* (3rd. ed., pp. 255–296). New York: Macmillan.

Clifford, P., Friesen, S., & Jacobsen, D. M. (1998, June). An expanded view of literacy: Hypermedia in the middle school. *Proceedings of the ED-MEDIA AND ED-TELECOM 98: World Conference on Educational Multimedia and Hypermedia & World Conference on Educational Telecommunications,* Freiburg, Germany.

Cobb, C., & Quaglia, R. (1994, April). *Moving beyond school–business partnerships and creating relationships.* Paper presented at the annual meeting of the American Educational Research Association, New Orleans, LA.

Cohen, A. & Kible, B. (1993). *The basics of open-systems evaluation: A resource paper.* Chapel Hill, NC: Pacific Institute for Research and Evaluation.

College Board. (2000, January 9). *AP—Subjects* [On-line]. Available: http://www.collegeboard.org/ap/subjects.html

Cordiero, P., & Kolek, M. (1996). Introduction: Connecting school communities through educational partnerships. In P. A. Cordiero (Ed.), *Boundary crossings: Educational partnerships and school leadership* (pp. 1–14). San Francisco: Jossey-Bass.

Corporate Council on Education. (1998). *Employability skills profile: The critical skills of the Canadian workforce.* Toronto: Conference Board of Canada.

Cramphorn, J. (1999). *The role of partnerships in economic regeneration and development: International perspectives.* Luton, England: University of Warwick.

Crow, G. (1998). Implications for leadership in collaborative schools. In D. G. Pounder (Ed.), *Restructuring schools for colloboration: Promises and pitfalls* (pp.135–153). Albany: State University of New York Press.

Crowson, R. L., & Boyd, W. L. (1996). Structures and strategies: Toward an understanding of alternative models for coordinated children's services. In J. G. Cibulka & W. J. Kritek (Eds.), *Coordination among schools, families, and communities* (pp. 137–169). Albany: State University of New York Press.

Cutietta, R. A. (1997). Industry and schools as partners. *Teaching Music,* 5(2), 40–41.

Darling-Hammond, L. (1994). Developing professional development schools: Early lessons, challenge, and promise. In L. Darling-Hammond (Ed.), *Professional development schools* (pp. 1–27). New York: Teachers College Press.

Darling-Hammond, L., & McLaughlin, M. W. (1995). Policies that support professional development in an era of reform. *Phi Delta Kappan,* 76(8), 597–604.

Davies, C. (2000, April 15). Getting heath professionals to work together: There's more to collaboration than simply working side by side *British Medical Journal, 320,* 1021–1022.

Deal, T. E., & Peterson, K. D. (1999). *Shaping school culture: The heart of leadership.* San Francisco: Jossey-Bass.

Department of Health. (1995a). *A policy for the development of a district health system for South Africa.* Pretoria, South Africa: Author.

Department of Health. (1995b). *Restructuring the national health system for university primary health care: Executive summary.* Pretoria, South Africa: Author.

Department of Health. (1996). *Restructuring the national health system for university primary health care: Executive summary.* Pretoria, South Africa: Author.

Department of Health. (1998). *A first class service: Quality in the new NHS.* London: Stationary Office.

Department of National Health and Population Development. (1992). *1991 health trends in South Africa.* Pretoria, South Africa: Author.

Deushle, K. (1982). Community-oriented primary care: Lessons learned in three decades. *Journal of Community Health, 8,* 13–22.

Down East Partnership for Children. (2000). *Five year strategic plan: 2000–2005.* Rocky Mount, NC: Author.

Edwards, H. (1999, February). *The evolution of the Permanent Liason Committee.* Yarmouth, NS: Southwest Regional School Board.

Eisenberg, E. M. (1995). A communication perspective on interorganizational cooperation and inner-city education. In L. C. Rigsby, M. C. Reynolds, & M. C. Wang. (Eds.), *School–community connections: Exploring issues for research and practice* (pp. 101–119). San Francisco: Jossey-Bass.

El Ansari, W. (1994). *Community partnerships in health: Critical lessons learned from a case study of the Hillbrow Primary Health Care Project, Johannesburg, South Africa.* Master's thesis, London School of Hygiene and Tropical Medicine.

El Ansari, W. (1998a). Partnerships in health: The pressing vhallenges. *Public Health Forum,* 2(3), 5.

El Ansari, W. (1998b, Summer). What does it take? Partnerships in health. *Health Action News, 6,* 7.

El Ansari, W. (1998c, June). Partnerships in health: How it's going to work. *Target, 29,* 18.

El Ansari, W. (1998d, November). Tackling health issues at a neighbourhood level—Lessons from South Africa. *Health For All Network News,* 14–15.

El Ansari, W. (1998e, Winter). Partnerships and new ways of learning: A second opinion. *NHS Magazine, 15,* 21.

El Ansari, W. (1999a). *A study of the characteristics, participant perceptions and predictors of effectiveness in community partnerships in health personnel education: The case of south africa.* Unpublished doctoral dissertation, University of Wales College, Newport, UK.

El Ansari, W. (2000). *Health improvement programmes—The future: Partnerships for better health*. Birmingham: The Scarman Trust.

El Ansari, W., & Phillips, C. (1997). Altogether better health personnel education? Findings from three community partnerships in health in South Africa. In J. Conway, R. Fisher, L. Sheridan-Burns, & G. Ryan (Eds.), *Research and development in problem based learning*. (Vol. 4, pp.127–134). Newcastle, Australia: The Australian Problem Based Learning Network.

El Ansari, W., & Phillips, C. (1998, June). Partnerships in health? A case study of an urban community partnership in South Africa. *Proceedings of the Ninth International Congress on Women's Health Issues*, 1–13.

Eng, E., Salmon, M., & Mullan, F. (1992, April). Community empowerment: The critical base for primary health care. *Family and Community Health*, 15: 1–12.

EnterTech Project Reports (1998–1999). *Report on Assessment and Evaluation Strategies for the Learner; Report on Texas Technology Infrastructure; Report on Evaluation Strategies for the Program; Report on Targeted Learner Characteristics; and Report on Knowledge, Skills, and Abilities Required for Entry-Level Jobs in the Technology Industries and the Related Supply and Service Industries*. Unpublished internal reports, EnterTech Project, Austin, TX.

EnterTech Project Report. (1998). *Knowledge, skills and abilities required for entry-level jobs in the technology industries and the related supply and service industries*. Unpublished internal report, IC$^2$ Institute, University of Texas at Austin.

Epstein, J. L., Coates, L., Salinas, K. C., Sanders, M. G., & Simon, B. S. (1997). *School, family, and community partnerships: Your handbook for action*. Thousand Oaks, CA: Corwin Press.

Erdos, J. (2000). *The EnterTech Project: A comprehensive report*. Unpublished internal report, IC$^2$ Institute, University of Texas at Austin.

Fetterman, D. M. (1996). Empowerment evaluation: An introduction to theory and practice. In D. M. Fetterman, S. J. Kaftarian, & A. Wandersman (Eds.), *Empowerment evaluation: Knowledge and tools for self-assessment and accountability* (pp. 3–46). Thousand Oaks, CA: Sage.

Fowler, J. (1991). *A guide for building an alliance for science, mathematics and technology education*. College Park, MD: Triangle Coalition for Science and Technology Education.

Friere, P., & Macedo, D. (1987). *Literacy*. New York: Bergin and Garvey.

Fullan, M. G., & Stiegelbauer, S. (1991). *The new meaning of educational change*. New York: Teachers College Press.

Fuhrman, S. (1999). *The new accountability* (CPRE Policy Briefs, RB-27-January 1999). Philadelphia: Consortium for Policy Research in Education.

Galileo Educational Network Association (2001, Winter). Galileo goes to China. *Galileo Educational Network*, 1.

Giamartino, G., & Wandersman, A. (1983). Organisational climate correlates of viable urban organisations. *American Journal of Community Psychology*, 11(5), 529–541.

Gillies, P. (1998). Effectiveness of alliances and partnerships for health promotion. *Health Promotion International*, 13(2), 9–120.

Gladstone, B. (2000, March). *Galileo Educational Network* [Videotape]. Calgary, AB, Canada: Shaw Communications.

Gladstone, B., & Jacobsen, M. (1999). Educational partnerships in Rocky View School Division, Part 1. *International Electronic Journal of Leadership in Learning*, 3(1) [On-line]. Available: http://www.acs.ucalgary.ca/~iejll/volume3/gladstone.html

Glassick, C., Huber, M., & Maeroff, G. (1997). *Scholarship assessed: Evaluation of the professoriate.* San Francisco: Jossey-Bass.

Glickman, C., Hayes, R., & Hensley, F. (1992). Site-based facilitation of empowered schools: Complexities and issues for staff developers. *Journal of Staff Development, 13*(2), 22–26.

Goodlad, J. (1990). Better teachers for our nation's schools. *Phi Delta Kappan, 72*(3), 184–194.

Gottlieb, N., Brink, S., & Gingiss, P. (1993). Correlates of coalition effectiveness the Smoke Free Class of 2000 Program. *Health Education Research: Theory and Practice, 8*(3), 375–384.

Government of Newfoundland. (1989). *Towards an achieving society.* St. John's, NF: Queen's Printer.

Government of Newfoundland. (1993a). *A curriculum framework for social studies: Navigating the future.* St. John's, NF: Queen's Printer.

Government of Newfoundland. (1993b). *Our children, our future.* St. John's, NF: Queen's Printer.

Government of Newfoundland. (1995). *Directions for change: A consultation paper on the senior high school program.* St. John's, NF: Queen's Printer.

Government of Newfoundland. (2000). *Supporting learning: A report of the Ministerial Panel on Educational Delivery in the Classroom.* St. John's, NF: Queen's Printer.

Gray, B. (1985). Conditions facilitating interorganizational collaboration. *Human Relations, 38*(10), 911–936.

Gray, B. (1989). *Collaborating: Finding common ground for multiparty problems.* San Francisco: Jossey-Bass.

Green, J. P., & Vogan, N. F. (1991). *Music education in Canada: A historical account.* Toronto: University of Toronto Press.

Green, Nathan (1978, May 23). *Evaluation in the matter of complaints by Janice Edith Miller, et al, against Board of Trustee, Digby Regional High School.* Digby, Nova Scotia.

Hamilton, W. (1999). Back from the brink: An administrator's perspective. *Teaching Music, 6*(4), 38–39, 59.

Hargreaves, A. (1994). *Teachers' work and culture in the postmodern age.* New York: Teachers College Press.

Harper, G., & Carver, L. (1999). "Out-of-the-mainstream" youth as partners in collaborative research: exploring the benefits and challenges. *Health Education and Behavior, 26*(2), 250–265.

Haas, T., & Nachtigal, P. (1998). *Place value.* Charleston, WV. Clearinghouse on Rural Education and Small Schools.

Heim, J. (1999, January 11). Top job goes unfilled in many large school districts. *Education Daily, 32*(5), 1, 3.

Heller, K. (1990, Summer). Limitations and barriers to citizen particpation. *The Community Psychologist,* 4–5.

Herzberg, F. (1966). *Work and the nature of man.* New York: John Wiley.

Hildebrandt, E. (1994). A model for Community Involvement In Health (CIH) program development. *Social Science and Medicine, 39*(2), 247–54.

Hofstede, G. (1980). *Culture's consequences: International differences in work-related values.* Beverly Hills, CA: Sage.

Holmes Group. (1986). *Tomorrow's teachers.* East Lansing, MI: Author.

Holmes Group. (1990). *Tomorrow's schools.* East Lansing, MI: Author.

Holmes Group. (1995). *Tomorrow's schools of education.* East Lansing, MI: Author

Hill, L. (2000). What does it take to change minds? Preservice teachers and conceptual change. *Journal of Teacher Education, 51*(1), 50–62.

Hooper-Briar, K., & Lawson, H. A. (1996). *Expanding partnerships for vulnerable children, youth, and families.* Alexandria, VA: Council on Social Work Education.

Hord, S. (1981). *Working together: Cooperation and collaboration.* Austin, TX: Research and Development Center for Teacher Education, University of Texas.

Hord, S. (1986). A synthesis of research on organizational collaboration. *Educational Leadership, 53*(5), 22–26.

Howard-Pitney, B. (1990, Summer). Community development is alive and well in community health promotion. *The Community Psychologist,* 4–5.

Howey, K. R. (1990). Changes in teacher education: Needed leadership and new networks. *Journal of Teacher Education, 41*(1), 3–9.

Huberman, M. (1999). The mind is its own place: The influence of sustained interactivity with practitioners on educational researchers. *Harvard Educational Review, 69*(3) , 289–319.

Huffman-Joley, G. (1996). Professional development schools revisited. *Contemporary Education, 67*(4), 169–170.

Israel, B., Schulz, A., Parker, E. A., & Becker, A. (1998). Review of community based research: Assessing partnership approaches to improve public health. *Annual Review of Public Health, 19,* 173–202.

ITG Information Management. (2000, February 10). *Need and feasibility of developing a fisheries training school in southwest Nova Scotia.* Nova Scotia: Southwest Shore Development Authority.

Jacobsen, M. (1998). A report by the first Galileo Fellow 1997–1998. [On-line]. Available: http://www.acs.ucalgary.ca/~dmjacobs/bpeak/fellow_report.html

Jacobsen, M. & Gladstone, B. (1999). Educational partnerships in Rocky View School Division, Part 2: Galileo Centre at Banded Peak School. *International Electronic Journal of Leadership in Learning, 3*(2) [On-line]. Available: http://www.acs.ucalgary.ca/~iejll/volume3/gladstone2.html

Jacobsen, M., Johnston, S., & Ellis, G. (1998, May). *New approaches to preservice and inservice professional development for integrating technology in teaching and learning.* Paper presented at the Canadian Society for the Study of Education (CSSE), Congress of the Social Sciences and Humanities, University of Ottawa, Ottawa, Ontario.

Jacobsen, M., Stockton, J., & Fritsch, E. (1998, March). *Learned lessons from the Galileo Centre initiative at Banded Peak school.* Presentation at Odyssey '98: A Joint Conference of the Alberta Teachers' Association Learning Resources and Computer Councils, Calgary, Alberta.

John-Steiner, V., Weber, J. R., & Minnis, M. (1998). The challenge of studying collaboration. *American Education Research Journal, 35*(4), 773–783.

Johnson, S. M. (1990). *Teacher at work: Achieving success in our schools.* New York: Basic Books.

Kagan, D. M. (1992). Professional growth among preservice and beginning teachers. *Review of Educational Research, 62*(2), 129–169.

Kale, R. (1995a, May). South Africa's health, new South Africa's doctors: A state of flux. *British Medical Journal, 310,* 1307–10.

Kale, R. (1995b, April). South Africa's health: Impressions of health in the new South Africa: A period of convalescence. *British Medical Journal, 310,* 1119–22.

Kegler, M. C., Steckler, A., McLeroy, K., & Malek, S. H. (1998). Factors that contribute to effective community health promotion coalitions: A study of

10 Project ASSISST coalitions in North Carolina. *Health Education and Behavior, 45*(3), 338–353.

Kisil, M., & Chaves, M. (1994). Linking the university with the community and its health system. *Medical Education Research, 7*, 31–46.

Klein, D., Williams, D., & Witbrodt, J. (1999). The collaboration process in HIV prevention and evaluation in an urban American Indian clinic for women. *Health Education and Behavior, 26*(2), 239–249.

Knapp, M. S. (1995). How shall we study comprehensive, collaborative services for children and families? *Educational Researcher, 24*(4), 6–13.

Knott, J. (1995, March). *Building sustainable partnerships.* Paper presented at the W.K. Kellogg Foundation conference "Building Partnerships: An Agenda for Health Around the World," Miami.

Kreuter, M., & Lenzin, N. (1998). *Are consortia/collaboratives effective in changing health status and health systems? A critical review of the literature.* Atlanta, GA: Health 2000.

Kreuter, M., Lezin, N., & Young, L. (2000). Evaluating Community-Based Collaborative Mechanisms: Implications for Practioners. *Health Promotion Practice, 1*(1), 49–63.

Kumpfer, K. & Hopkins, R. (1993). *Prevention: Current research and trends.* Philadelphia: Psychiatric Clinics of North America. W. B. Saunders.

Larson, E. (1999). The impact of physician–nurse interaction on patient care. *Holistic Nurse, 13*, 38–47.

Lasker, R., & Committee on Medicine and Public Health. (1997). *Medicine and public health: The power of collaboration.* Chicago: Health Administration Press.

Lauer, P. A., Apthorp, H. A., Vangsnes, D. J., Schieve, D., & Van Buhler, R. J. (1999). *McREL collaborative research initiative interim progress report.* Aurora, CO: Mid-continent Research for Education and Learning.

Lawson, L., & Lawson, C. (1998). *Reality of welfare-to-work: Employment opportunities for women affected by welfare time limits in Texas.* Internal report, Center for the Study of Human Resources, Lyndon Baines Johnson School of Public Affairs, University of Texas at Austin.

Learner, N. (2000, March 7). A good school principal is hard to find, study says. *Education Daily 33*(43), 1–2.

Lebrecht, N. (1991). *The maestro myth: Great conductors in pursuit of power.* London: Simon & Schuster.

Lechner, S. (1999, September 17). Common ground: Different backgrounds help GW, Howard University AmeriCorp volunteers effect change. *Hatchet,* D.C. Diary, 4, 6.

Levine, M. (1998). *Designing standards that work for professional development schools.* Washington, DC: National Council for Accreditation of Teacher Education. (ERIC Document Reproduction Service No. 426 052)

Lieberman, A. (1992). School/university collaborations: A view from the inside. *Phi Delta Kappan, 75*(2), 147–156.

Limestone District School Board (LDSB) (2000, August 2). *Focus programs: Choices for secondary students* [On-line]. Available: http://www.limestone.edu. on.ca/ctypgm

Lindsay, G., & Edwards, G. (1988, August/September). Creating effective health coalitions. *Health Education, 19*, 35–6.

Lippert, C. (1999, February). Back from the brink: A teacher's perspective. *Teaching Music, 6*(4), 34–36.

Logan, K. (1997, Winter). Changing roles: Artists and educators. *American String Teacher, 47*(1), 85, 87–88.

Lortie, D.C. (1975). *Schoolteacher: A sociological study.* Chicago: University of Chicago Press.

Mackay, L., Soothill, K., & Webb, C. (1995). Troubled times: The context for interprofessional collaboration. In K. Soothill, L. Mackay, & C. Webb (Eds.), *Interprofessional relations in health care* (pp 5–10). London: Edward Arnold.

MacIntyre, B., Stutz, J., Wallace, B., & Wilson, G. (1999, January 19). *An external evaluation of Galileo Project in Banded Peak School: An evaluation report to RockyView School Division.* Calgary, AB: Rockyview School Division.

Madan, T. (1987). Community involvement in health policy: Socio-structural and dynamic aspects of health beliefs. *Social Science and Medicine, 25*(6), 615–620.

Mawhinney, H. (1996). Institutional effects of strategic efforts at community enrichment. In J. J. & W. Kritek (Eds.), *Coordination among schools, families, and communities* (pp. 223–243). Albany: State University of New York Press.

Meier, D. (1995). *The power of their ideas: Lessons for America from a small school in Harlem.* Boston: Beacon Press.

Melaville, A. I., & Blank, M. J. (1993). *Together we can: A guide for crafting a profamily system of education and human services.* Washington, DC: U.S. Government Printing Office.

Memorial University of Newfoundland, Faculty of Education. (2000, July 8). *Faculty of Education projects and research* [On-line]. Available: http://www .mun.ca/educ/fac_web/proj.html#claren

MENC (Music Educators National Conference). (1996). MENC News: MENC, NY Philharmonic begin collaboration. *Teaching Music, 4*(3), 15.

Mid-continent Research for Education and Learning (McREL). (1999). *McREL's field-based research initiative.* Aurora, CO: Author.

Mid-Continent Research for Education and Learning (McREL) (2000). *Leadership for school improvement.* Aurora, CO: Author.

Mitchell, S. (1990). *Innovation and reform.* York, ON, Canada: Captus.

Mitchell, S. (1996). *Tidal waves of school reform.* Westport, CT: Praeger.

Mitchell, S. (1998). *Reforming educators: Teachers, experts, and advocates.* Westport, CT: Praeger.

Mitchell, S. (2000a). *Rural visions.* Paper presented at the Seventh Annual Conference on Educational Access, University of Arkansas, Pine Bluff.

Mitchell, S. (2000b). *Partnerships in creative activities among schools, artists, and professional organizations.* Lewiston, NY: Edwin Mellen.

Mizrahi, T., & Rosenthal, B. (1992). Managing dynamic tensions in social change coalitions. In *Community organization and social administration: Advances, trends, and emerging principles.* Haworth Press.

Morgan, C., & Murgatroyd, S. (1994). *Total quality management in the public sector.* London: Open University Press.

Morgan, G. (1997). *Images of organization.* Thousand Oaks, CA: Sage.

Mullan, F. (1982). Community-oriented primary care: An agenda for the 80s. *New England Journal of Medicine, 307*(1), 1078–1079.

Myers, D. E. (1996). *Beyond tradition: Partnerships among orchestras, schools, and communities* (NEA Coop. Agreement DCA95-12). Atlanta: Georgia State University.

Myers, D. E. (2000, July). Preparing performing musicians and teachers as collaborators in music education. *Music of the Spheres Conference Proceedings,* 290–302.

Myers, D. E., & Young, M. (1996). *MENC teacher's guide to Live From Lincoln Center, New York Philharmonic: An educational guide to the PBS broadcast, January 15, 1997.* Arlington, VA: Music Educators National Conference.

National Business and Education Center (NBEC). (1999). *Operating principles for business–edcuation partnerships*. Toronto: Conference Board of Canada.

National Progressive Primary Health Care Network. (circa 1994). *Health for the people now!* [Brochure]. Johannesburg, South Africa: Author.

The Network of Community-Oriented Educational Institutions for the Health Sciences (NCOEIHS) (1991). *A short description of its aims and activities*. Maastricht, The Netherlands: Author.

National Institute for Clinical Excellence (NICE). (1999). *A guide to our work*. London: Author.

Nierman, G. E. (1993, Spring). Perspectives of collaboration versus cooperation. *Journal of Music Teacher Education*, 25–28.

North Carolina Child Advocacy Institute (1995). *Children's index: A profile of leading indicators of the health and well-being of North Carolina's children*. Raleigh: North Carolina Child Advocacy Institute.

Nystrand, R. (1991). *Professional development schools: Toward a new relationship for schools and universities, trends and issues*. Washington, DC: Office of Educational Research and Improvement. (ERIC Document Reproduction Service No. 330 690)

*The Ontario Curriculum, Grades 1–8: The Arts, 1998* [On-line]. Available: http://www.edu.gov.on.ca/eng/document/curricul/arts/arts.html

Orchestras Canada. (2000, May). International education models. Orchestras Canada World Conference.

Osguthorpe, R., Harris, R. Harris, M., & Black, S. (Eds.) (1995). *Partner Schools*. San Francisco, CA: Jossey-Bass.

Osguthorpe, R., & Patterson, R. (1998). *Balancing the tensions of change*. Thousand Oaks, CA: Corwin Press.

Palmer, P. (1998). *The courage to teach*. San Francisco: Jossey-Bass.

Panet-Raymond, J. (1992). Partnership: Myth or reality? *Community Development Journal*, 27(2), 156–165.

Pasch, S. H., & Pugach, M. (1990). Collaborative planning for urban professional development schools. *Contemporary Education*, 61(3), 135–143.

Patel, L. (1993). *Children and women in South Africa: A situation analysis*. Johannesburg: Auckland House.

Pfeffer, J., & Sutton, R. (2000). *The knowing doing gap: How smart companies turn knowledge into action*. Boston: Harvard Business School Press.

Popay, J., & Williams, G. (1996). Public health research and lay knowledge. *Social Science and Medicine*, 42(5) 759–768.

Porter, S. (1995). *Nursing's relationship with medicine*. Avershot, UK: Avebury.

Power, D., Stevens, K., Boone, W., & Barry, M. (2000, July 12). Vista School District Digital Intranet: The delivery of advanced placement courses to young adult learners in rural communities. In *Knowledge Society Newsletter* [On-line]. Available: http://www.tellearn.mun.ca/pubs/kssnnews.html

Prestby, J., Wandersman, A., Florin, P., Rich, R., & Chavis, D. (1990). Benefits, costs, incentive management and participation in voluntary organisations: A means to understanding and promoting empowerment. *American Journal of Community Psychology*, 18(1), 117–149.

Price Waterhouse. (1996). *EMC technology forecast for 1996*. New York: Author.

Putnam, R. (1993). *Making democracy work*. Princeton, NJ: Princeton University Press.

Reed, R., & Cedja, B. (1987). *Attributes and preconditions of collaboration between and among schools, institutions of higher education, and state education agencies*. Elmhurst, IL: North Central Regional Laboratory.

Remer, J. (1996). *Beyond enrichment: Building effective arts partnerships with schools and your community.* New York: American Council for the Arts.

Renzaglia, A., Hutchins, M., & Lee, S. (1997). The impact of teacher education on the beliefs, attitudes, and dispositions of preservice special educators. *Teacher Education and Special Education, 20*(4), 360–377.

Rich, R. (1986). Neighborhood-based participation in the planning process: In Taylor, R. (Ed.), *handbook of Community Pscyhology.* New York: Plenum.

Richards, R. (circa 1995). *Building partnerships: The vision and the critical elements.* Bloemfontein, South Africa: MUCPP Management Committee.

Richards, R. (Ed.). (1996). *Building partnerships.* San Francisco: Jossey-Bass.

Richardson, V. (1996). The role of attitudes and beliefs in learning to teach. In J. Sikula (Ed.), *Handbook of research on teacher education* (2nd ed., pp. 102–119). New York: Macmillan.

Richardson-Koebler, V. (1988). Barriers to the effective supervision of student teaching: A field study. *Journal of Teacher Education, 38*(2), 28–34.

Rifkin, S. (1981). The role of the public in the planning, management and evaluation of health activities and programmes, including self-care. *Social Science and Medicine, 15*(1), 377–386.

Rifkin, S. (1986). Health planning and community participation. *World Health Forum, 7,* 156–162.

Rifkin, S. (1987). Primary health care, community participation and the urban poor: A review of the problems and solutions. *Asia-Pacific Journal of Public Health, 1*(2), 57–63.

Rigden, D. W. (1991). *Business/school partnerships: A path to effective restructuring.* New York: Council for Aid to Education.

Rigden, D. W. (1992). *Business and the schools: A guide to effective programs* (2nd ed.). New York: Council for Aid to Education.

Riggs, F. (1987). *Report of the Small Schools Study Project.* St. John's, NF: Queen's Printer.

Rigsby, L., Reynolds, M., & Wang, M. C. (Eds.). (1995). *School–community connections: Exploring issues for research and practice.* San Francisco: Jossey-Bass.

Robertson, H. (1998). *No more teachers, no more books: The commercialization of Canada's schools.* Toronto: McClelland and Stewart.

Rodgers, B. E. (1999). Back from the brink: The community's perspective. *Teaching Music, 6*(4), 40–41, 62.

Rogers, T., Howard-Pitney, B., Fieghery, E., Altman, D., Endres, J., & Roeseler, A. G. (1993). Characteristics and participation perceptions of tobacco control coalitions in California. *Health Education Research: Theory and Practice, 8*(3), 345–357.

Rowe, I. (1989). *School concerts by the TSO, 1925–1957.* Master's thesis, University of Western Ontario.

Sagor, R. (1997). Collaborative action research for educational change. In A. Hargreaves (Ed.), *Rethinking educational change with heart and mind* (pp. 169–191). Alexandria, VA: Association for Supervision and Curriculum Development.

Sandholtz, J., & Merseth, K. (1992). Collaborating teachers in a professional development school: Inducements and contributions. *Journal of Teacher Education, 43*(1), 43(1), 308–317.

Sanford, J., & Mahar, R. (1996). Retrospective of a PDS based urban teacher education program: Its conception, development, and implementation for co-existence with a traditional model. *Contemporary Education, 67*(4), 191–195.

Sarason, S., & Lorentz, E. (1998). *Crossing boundaries: Collaboration, coordination, and the redefinition of resources.* San Francisco: Jossey-Bass.

Scannell, D. (1996). Evaluating professional development schools: The challenge of an imperative. *Contemporary Education, 67*(4), 241–243.

Schmidt, H., Neufeld, V., Zohair, M., & Ogunbode, T. (1991). Network of community-oriented educational institutions for the health sciences. *Academic Medicine, 66*(5), 259–263.

Schoor, L. (1988). *Within our reach.* New York: Doubleday Anchor.

Schverak, A., Coltharp, C., & Cooner, D. (1998). Using content analysis to evaluate the success of a professional development school. *Educational Forum, 62*(2), 172–177.

Seifer, S., & Maurana, C. (1998). Health professions education, civic responsibility and the overall health of communities–campus partnerships. *Journal of Interprofessional Care, 12*(3), 253–257.

Senge, P. (1999). The leadership of profound change: Toward an ecology of leadership. In P. Senge, A. Kleiner, C. Roberts, & R. Sharp (Eds.), *Disturbing the peace: Texas performance review.* Washington, DC: National Alliance of Business.

Shelley, A., & Washburn, S. (2000). Our NCATE report card: A partnership for excellence. *The Educational Forum, 64*(2), 156–164.

Sills, B. A., Barron, P. & Heath, P. (1993, June). School reform through partnerships. In *Report of the Synergy Conference: Industry's role in the reform of mathematics, science and technology education* (pp. 68–71). Leesburg, VA: Triangle Coalition.

Sirotnik, K. (1988). The meaning and conduct of inquiry in school–university partnerships. In K. Sirotnik & J. I. Goodlad (Eds.), *School–university partnerships in action* (pp. 205–225). New York: Teachers College Press.

Sizer, T. (1992). *Horace's school: Redesigning the American high school.* Boston: Mariner Books.

Sizer, T. (1996). *Horace's hope: What works for the American high school.* Boston: Mariner Books.

Sparks, D. (1995). A paradigm shift in staff development. *The Eric Review, 3*(3), 2–4.

Sparks, D. (2000). Partnerships need purpose. *Journal of Staff Development, 21*(2), 3.

Spencer, L. M., & Stonehill, R. M. (1999, October). *Profiles of the regional educational laboratories.* Washington, DC: U.S. Department of Education.

Squires, S. (1996). *Report on workforce readiness.* Austin, TX: SEMATECH Consortium.

Stacey, M. (1994). The power of lay knowledge: A personal view. In J. Popay & G. Williams (Eds.), *Researching the people's health* (pp. 85–98). London: Routledge.

State of Texas Department of Human Services. (1997). *Demographic profile of TANF caretakers.* Austin, TX: State Budget Management Services.

Statham, D. (2000). Guest editorial: Partnership between health and social care. *Health and Social Care in the Community, 8*(2), 87–89.

STEM~Net (2000a, September 4). *Mission goals and objectives* [On-line]. Available: http://www.stemnet.nf.ca/Admin/mission.shtml.

STEM~Net (2000b, December 18). *WebCT course listings* [On-line]. Available: http://www.stemnet.nf.ca:8900/webct/public/show/courses

Stevens, K. (1999). *Vista digital intranet—A model for the organisation of virtual classes. Report presented to Industry Canada, St. John, NF.*

Strawn, J. (1998). *Beyond job search or basic education: Rethinking the role of skills in welfare reform.* Washington, DC: Center for Law and Social Policy.

Tambling, P. (1999). Opera, education and the role of arts organisations. *British Journal of Music Education, 16*(2), 139–156.

Taylor, P. (1996). Supporting community involvement: The organisational challenges. In P. Burton & L. Harrison (Eds.), *Identifying local health needs: New community based approaches.* Bristol: The Policy Press.

Teitel, L. (1996). Getting down to cases. *Contemporary Education, 67*(4), 200–206.

Teitel, L. (1997). Changing teacher education through professional development school partnership: A five-year follow-up study. *Teachers College Record, 99*(2), 311–334.

Teitel, L. (1998). Separations, divorces, and open marriages in professional development partnerships. *Journal of Teacher Education, 49*(2), 85–96.

TeleLearning NCE. (2000, July 8). *Telelearning NCE research themes* [On-line]. Available: http://www.telelearn.ca/g_access/research_projects/noframe _introduction.html

Thiessen, D. (1996). Navigating through uncharted territory: The tensions and promise of PDS partnerships. *Contemporary Education, 67*(4), 191–195.

Tushman, M. L., & Scanlan, T. J. (1981). Boundary spanning individuals: Their role in information transfer and their antecedents. *Academy of Management Journal, 24,* 289–305.

Viljoen, M., & Househam, K. (circa 1995). *A community partnership programme addressing the needs of three partners in a unique way.* South Africa: MUCPP Management Committee.

Vinh, T. (1994, August 30). Twin counties again seek Smart Start. *The Evening Telegram,* p. A1.

Vista School District. (1999a). *A handbook of essential information: Designed for new teachers with the Vista School District.* Clarenville, NF: Author.

Vista School District (1999b, December 26). *About the district—The region/location* [On-line]. Available: http://www.k12.nf.ca/vista/aboutus/regionlocal. html

Vista School District (2000, September 6). *Strategic education plan—Strategies* [On-line]. Available: http://www.k12.nf.ca/vista/aboutus/strategiceducation /section6/index.html

W.K. Kellogg Foundation (WKKF) (1992). *Community Partnerships: Redirecting Health Professions Education Toward Primary Health Care.* Battle Creek, Michigan: W.K.Kellogg Foundation.

Walby, S., Greenwell, J., Mackay, L., & Soothill, K. (1994). *Medicine and nursing: Professions in a changing health service.* London: Sage.

Wandersman, A. (1981). A framework of participation in community organisations. *Journal of Applied Behavioural Science, 17*(1), 27–58.

Watt, A. & Rodmell, S. (1988). Community involvement in health promotion: Progress or panacea? *Health Promotion, 2*(4), 359–67.

Weigold, P. (1999). *Changing arts practice.* Unpublished paper.

Whitt, E. J. (1991). Artful science: A primer on qualitative research methods. *Journal of College Student Development, 32*(5), 406–415.

Wichienwong, W. (1988). *The relationship of administrators' involvement in the evaluation process and evaluation attitudes.* Unpublished doctoral dissertation, Ohio State University, Columbus.

Williams, L., Konrad, J., & Larson, H. (1992). *A guide for planning a volunteer program for science, mathematics and technology education.* College Park, MD: Triangle Coalition for Science and Technology Education.

Winitzky, N., Stoddart, T., & O'Keefe, P. (1992). Great expectations: Emergent professional development schools. *Journal of Teacher Education*, 43(1), 3–18.

Wise, A., & Leibbrand, J. (2000). Standards and teacher quality: Entering the new millennium. *Phi Delta Kappan*, 81(8), 612–621.

Wiseman, D. & Cooner, D. (1996). Discovering the power of collaboration: The impact of a school–university partnership on teaching. In C. D. Schmitz (Ed.), *Teacher education and practice* (pp. 18–28). Austin, TX: Texas Association of Colleges for Teacher Education.

Wolcott, H. (1977). *Teachers vs. technocrats*. Eugene, OR: Center for Educational Policy and Management, University of Oregon.

Wood, D., & Gray, B. (1991). Toward a comprehensive theory of collaboration. *Journal of Applied Behavioral Science*, 27(2), 139–162.

World Bank. (1993). *World development report*. New York: Oxford University Press.

World Health Organization (WHO) and United Nations Children's Fund. (1978). *Primary health care*. Geneva: Author.

World Health Organization (WHO). (1987) *Community-based education of health personnel. Report of a WHO study group*. (WHO Technical Report Series 746). Geneva, Switzerland: Author.

Wright, B. D. (1994). Composition analysis. *Mid-Western Educational Researcher*, 7(2), 29–36, 38.

Wright, B. D. (1996, Summer). Pack to chain to team? *Rasch Measurement Transactions*, 10, 501.

Zakus, J., & Lysack, C. (1998). Revisiting community participation. *Health Policy and Planning*, 13(1), 1–12.

Zalkind, H. (1996). *Down East Partnership for Children (DEPC) organizational development program*. Rocky Mount, NC: Down East Partnership for Children.

Zapka, J., Marrocco, G., Lewis, B., McCusker, J., Sullivan, J., McCarthy, J., & Birch, F. (1992). Interorganisational responses to AIDS: A case study of the Worcester AIDS Consortium. *Health Education Research: Theory and Practice*, 7(1), 31–46.

Zeichner, K., & Gore, J. (1990). Teacher socialization. In W. R. Houston (Ed.), *Handbook of research in teacher education* (pp. 32–48). New York: MacMillan.

Zeldin, T. (1999). How work can be made less frustrating and conversations less boring. *British Medical Journal*, 319, 1633–1635.

Zimmerman, M. (1990). Taking aim on empowerment research: On the distinction between individual and psychological conceptions. *American Journal of Community Psychology*, 18(1), 169–177.

Zimpher, N. L. (1994, November–December). Professional development schools: Ready, fire, aim! *ATE Newsletter*, 28, pp. 4–5.

Zuckerman, H., & Kaluzny, A. (1990). *Managing beyond vertical and horizontal integration: Strategic alliances as an emerging organizational form*. Unpublished manuscript.

Zuckerman, H., Kaluzny, A., & Ricketts, T. (1995). Alliances in health care: What we know, what we think we know, and what we should know. *Health Care Management Review*, 20(1), 54–64.

# Index

# About the Editor and Contributors

SAMUEL MITCHELL is Professor and Coordinator for the Graduate Division of Educational Research, University of Calgary. He is the author of nine books and monographs including two published by Praeger: *Tidal Waves of School Reform* (1996) and *Reforming Educators: Teachers, Experts, and Advocates*. His most recent book is *Partnerships in Creative Activities among Schools, Artists, and Professional Organizations* (Edwin Mellen, 2000).

HELEN S. APTHORP has a doctorate in special education. Her research focuses on individual differences and effective instruction. She is a Senior Researcher at Mid-continent Research and Learning (McREL), a federally supported research center, where she studies teacher and administrator collaboration with school reform.

MICHAEL BARBOUR is Coordinator for the Centre for Advanced Placement Education and a teacher at Discovery Collegiate in Bonavista, Newfoundland. He pursues research on computer-mediated communication and teleteaching or telelearning.

DEATON BEDNAR is the Director of the Learning Center of Excellence for Sapient, Inc., and is the former director of the EnterTech Project at the University of Texas. She has worked for 25 years in workforce development, most recently with the Texas Workforce Commission.

LYNN BRADSHAW is Associate Professor at East Carolina University. She holds a doctorate in educational leadership and a principal's certificate. Her experiences include being a teacher, principal, and central office administrator. Her interest in partnerships developed through contacts with 18 districts and universities.

RENEE CAMPOY is Associate Professor at Murray State University. She participates in a number of university partnerships, including professional development schools in St. Louis, the Different Ways of Knowing project with three universities, and a Math in the Middle curriculum effort in Kentucky.

WALID EL ANSARI trained in clinical medicine and pediatrics before he moved to public health, where he completed a doctorate. He is Senior Lecturer in Public Health and Epidemiology at Oxford Brookes University, in Oxford, U.K., where he leads the Masters Program in Public Health.

JORDAN E. ERDOS is an independent researcher who works on a variety of projects, including biodiversity, genetic resources, rural electrification, and hazardous waste tracking in Brazil, Mexico, and the United States. He holds a master's degree in public policy and Latin America.

BRENDA GLADSTONE is cofounder and General Manager of the Galileo Educational Network. She is a former public school trustee and cofounder of the Calgary Educational Partnerships Foundation and Calgary Family Connections Society. She has written about business partnerships with her co-author Michele Jacobsen.

BRYAN GOODWIN has a master's degree in communications. He is Senior Program Associate at McREL, where his work involves preparing policy briefs and convening meetings with policymakers. He has taught at the school and college levels, and worked as a newspaper reporter.

JOSEPH W. HAUGLIE is a technical instructor for KLA-Tencor Corporation. He was employed previously with the Raytheon Company for workplace literacy instruction, computer-assisted language learning, and adult second language teaching. He holds a doctorate in foreign language education.

MELINDA JACKSON is the EnterTech Project Corordinator and Production Director. She holds a master's degree in instructional technology from the University of Texas at Austin. Her training and work are in electronic performance support systems and digital assistance for individuals with cognitive disabilities.

MICHELE JACOBSEN is an Assistant Professor at the University of Calgary, holds a doctorate in educational technology, and was the first fellow for the Gallagher Foundation. She is involved in electronic publishing and a national evaluation of learning technologies at the University of Alberta.

DEBORAH BAINER JENKINS is Professor at the State University of West Georgia. She was Professor at Ohio State University at Mansfield, where she directed the project, Sciencing With Watershed, Environmental Education and Partnerships (SWEEP). She receives awards for teaching, scholarship, and community service.

ANN JONES is Director of College Prep for Nova Scotia Community College. She was Superintendent of the Southwest Regional Board in Nova Scotia. She was a mathematics teacher, holds two master's degrees, and is a textbook author for McGraw-Hill Ryerson.

ROBERTA LAMB is Associate Professor, School of Music, Queen's University. She holds appointments in the Faculty of Education and the Institute of Women's Studies; she was head of the latter institute from 1991–1993. She is a founder of the Kingston Symphony Education Project.

PATRICIA A. LAUER has a doctorate in experimental and developmental psychology. She is a Senior Researcher at Mid-Continent Research for Education and Learning (McREL), involving learner-centered practices in classrooms, schools, and districts. She teaches in higher education.

MELINDA POLLACK was Coordinator of the George Washington University Neighors Project, where she graduated with a degree in human services and commmunication. She is working for Mercy Housing Southwest in Denver while pursuing a master's degree in public administration.

STEPHANIE B. WILKERSON has a Ph.D in educational evaluation and is a Senior Evaluation Associate at Mid-content Research and Learning (McREL). She specializes in distance learning and education and public outreach and conducts internal evaluations of McREL's projects.

MICHAEL ZANIBBI is Director of Enviroworks. He holds a master's degree in business administration and is completing a second master's degree in education. He is a recipient of two national awards from the prime minister of Canada: the Award for Teaching Excellence and the Teaching Excellence Fellowship.